004.67
2WK.

Digital Jesus

D0493491

Digital Jesus

The Making of a New
Christian Fundamentalist
Community on the Internet

Robert Glenn Howard

NEW YORK UNIVERSITY PRESS
New York and London

NEW YORK UNIVERSITY PRESS
New York and London
www.nyupress.org

© 2011 by New York University

References to Internet websites (URLs) were accurate at the time of writing.
Neither the author nor New York University Press is responsible for URLs
that may have expired or changed since the manuscript was prepared.

Library of Congress Cataloging-in-Publication Data

Howard, Robert Glenn.
Digital Jesus : the making of a new Christian fundamenatlist
community on the Internet / Robert Glenn Howard.
p. cm. — (The new and alternative religions series)
Includes bibliographical references (p.   ) and index.
ISBN 978-0-8147-7308-6 (cl : alk. paper) — ISBN 978-0-8147-7310-9
(pb : alk. paper) — ISBN 978-0-8147-7309-3 (e-book : alk. paper)
1. Internet—Religious aspects—Christianity. 2. Fundamentalism.
3. End of the world. I. Title.
BR99.74.H68   2010
277.3'08202854678—dc22   2010034801

New York University Press books are printed on acid-free paper,
and their binding materials are chosen for strength and durability.
We strive to use environmentally responsible suppliers and materials
to the greatest extent possible in publishing our books.

Manufactured in the United States of America
c   10 9 8 7 6 5 4 3 2 1
p   10 9 8 7 6 5 4 3 2 1

For my mother and father

And though I have the gift of prophecy, and understand all
    mysteries, and all knowledge;
and though I have all faith so that I could remove mountains,
if I have not charity . . .
I am nothing.

—I Corinthians 13:2

Contents

Acknowledgments

I am most indebted to the many respondents who have replied to my emails, engaged my questions, agreed to meet me for interviews, and sometimes even invited me into their homes. This research has been difficult because while I cannot share their beliefs, I have witnessed their compassion first hand. In particular, I would like to thank those who took the time to read and respond to early versions of my research and offer significant corrects, additions, and comments.

For years of advice, engaged discussions, and close friendship, I would like to thank my mentor Daniel Wojcik at the University of Oregon. I would also like to thank Leonard Norman Primiano at Cabrini College for his willingness to mentor from afar. And at the University of Wisconsin, I would like to thank Kristin Eschenfelder for her creative ear for titles; and Erik Hjalmeby for keeping on eye on some of the newest and coolest evangelical media.

I would also like to thank all my colleagues and friends at the University of Wisconsin for their years of support, discussions, and suggestions that helped shape both this work and me. In particular, I would like to thank Rob Asen, Christine Garlough, Jenell Johnson, Jim Leary, Steve Lucas, Marie Stolzenburg, Mike Xenos, and Sue Zaekse. I would also like to thank my teachers and advisors during the first years of this research at the University of Oregon. In particular, I would like to thank Jim Crosswhite, David Frank, John Gage, Anne Laskaya, and Sharon Sherman. I am also indebted to my teachers and friends at UCLA, where I learned to love the study of everyday culture. In particular, I would like to thank Robert A. Georges and Michael Owen Jones.

I am also greatly indebted to the patience and advice of my editor at NYU, Jennifer Hammer. In addition, I would like to thank the series editors for taking on this formidable project, Timothy Miller and Susan J. Palmer. I am also grateful for the support provided by the Wisconsin Alumni Foundation, the Risa Palm Memorial Dissertation Research Award, and to Pamela and George Hamel for their generous support of the research and teaching done in the Department of Communication Arts at the University of Wisconsin.

I would also like to thank my Wisconsin family Kathy, Ned, Mack, and Bob. Also, I would like to thank all my teachers, including Carl A. Cato of Spring Valley Junior High School for a career dedicated to getting seventh and eighth graders to think; and my brother Ken for being one of my first teachers and most committed protectors; my life-long friend James; and my Aunt Sue (though she won't be able to read the final product); and the most important teachers of all, my mother, Pat; and my father, Deane.

Finally, I would like to thank Lily for hearing about this work all these years and yet never uttering a word of her own about it; and my wife, Megan, for being my biggest supporter both when success seemed imminent and when it did not.

Introduction

Vernacular Christian
Fundamentalism on the Internet

Marilyn and Lambert

Late in the summer of 1999 at a fast food restaurant outside Riverside, California, a well-known Christian author and blogger, Marilyn Agee, told me about God's call for her to publish interpretations of biblical prophecy:

> So I'd been typing all day, and I grabbed my Bible by the back of it and I just bounced down across the bed. And I said: "What am I doing all this work for anyway?" The next thing I knew, I'm looking at my Bible—about an inch from my face and Jeremiah 50 verse 2 has a rectangle of light on it. Everything else looks gray. I could have read it if I [had] wanted to, it wasn't that dark, but it looked gray—and this verse had light on it, saying: "Publish and conceal not." (Agee and Edgar 1999)

Marilyn came to believe that God gave her access to divine knowledge.[1] Armed with this certainty, she first published books and then developed a well-known amateur evangelical Web site. At the time, it may have been the most well-known site focused on discussing what its users term the "End Times."

Later that month, I interviewed the builder of another well-known amateur Web site. Lambert Dolphin is a retired Stanford physicist and a man called to Christianity by a different sort of direct experience with God. I had been in email contact with him since 1992, but we met face-to-face for the first time in September 1999. As we spoke about his intense conversion experience thirty-seven years before, Lambert said that it felt like "lights turning on where there'd been a dark house before." He experienced an emotional, immediate, and permanent change. I asked him if this experience gave him special access to divine knowledge. He shook his head, saying no: "In fact, it's probably perfectly acceptable to have equivalent models and use the one that you feel most comfortable with—or the one that fits best to your circumstances" (Dolphin 1999f).

Though both Marilyn and Lambert felt compelled to share their understanding of God with others, they expressed different conceptions of how and what God communicates. Marilyn experienced a clear and resolute call to "publish" biblical studies based on her access to divine truth. Lambert's experience, however, was of an intimate, emotional, and intense sense of "peace," "hope," and "excitement about the future" (Dolphin 1999f). Seeking to share that experience, he began engaging people online by discussing the different "models" that might help them access the same sense of peace.

Even though these two individuals had direct experiences of the same God, their resulting understandings of the divine were fundamentally different. Marilyn locates a single truth in the Bible and then communicates that truth to others. Lambert sees the words of the Bible as malleable. They constitute a resource through which he can guide others toward the same personal sense of tranquility he has been granted. The two of them imagine the Christian god in strikingly different ways.

Given their similar backgrounds, one might expect that Marilyn and Lambert's religious thinking would be largely the same. They have both lived most of their lives in California. They are about the same age. They are both retired. They both came to Christianity through Baptist churches in North America. They both believe in the divine inspiration of the Bible. They both use the Internet daily to engage in amateur Christian evangelism. By 1999, in fact, they were already very much part of the same growing web of online communication.

On hundreds of amateur Web pages, blogs, forums, and other Internet media, everyday members of a new kind of Christian religious movement make links to both their Web sites: Marilyn's *Bible Prophecy Corner* and Lambert's *Lambert's Library*. While Lambert and Marilyn have not corresponded directly, they have shared several correspondents in common. Even as early as 1999, it was clear that Marilyn and Lambert were being connected by thousands of individuals who thought of them as part of the same online web of believers. These individuals made and followed Internet links that subsumed individual differences into something larger. What was the nature of this larger entity? How could it incorporate these two fundamentally different conceptions of the same God? The research resulting in this book began as an attempt to answer these questions. In this attempt, I discovered a new religious movement I have termed "vernacular Christian fundamentalism."

This study begins by exploring the definitive characteristics of the new movement. It is new because it focuses on a particular "End Times" interpretation of biblical prophecy that differentiates it from broader forms of evangelical Christianity. It also constitutes a new *kind* of religious movement because even as its beliefs have diverged from existing institutions, no new central leadership has emerged. Instead, it takes shape as its believers use the Internet to engage in a kind of ritualized deliberation that they believe generates a church that exists only on the Internet. While the dispersed nature of this network-based movement might suggest that it is free from social control, this is not the case. Instead, individual members use the Internet to create a dispersed vernacular authority that enforces a self-sealing ideology.

Chapter 2 documents individuals in the movement as they coped with the shock of the attacks on the World Trade Center and Pentagon building on September 11, 2001. Marilyn Agee publicly posted the rush of email exchanges she had over the course of the day on her Web site. These posts reveal a discursive process so powerful it almost immediately rendered the new facts sensible in terms of the movement's complex prophetic narrative. Tracing the cluster of beliefs associated with the movement from their origins in the nineteenth century, a radical sense of certainty associated with direct experiences of the divine accounts for the powerful social processes that made this assimilation possible.

Chapter 3 goes back in time to document the movement as it first appeared online in a medium called "Usenet newsgroups." When the mainstream Christians that dominated communication in this medium responded with ridicule and hostility to communications about the End Times, individuals in the movement used private email lists to deliberate about their beliefs without facing resistance from outsiders. On these email lists, the cohesive force of the movement relied on the formation of communication enclaves where individuals could most freely engage in their ritual deliberation.

Chapter 4 documents the growing diversity of the virtual ekklesia as it moved onto the Worldwide Web between 1996 and 2000. As the movement adapted, the new medium exacerbated an existing tension between the need to express individual authority and the need to engage others in deliberation. As a wide diversity of individuals experimented with different ways to mediate this tension, Marilyn Agee's *Bible Prophecy Corner* Web site prefigured the most robust deployment of Internet media by individuals in the movement today.

Chapter 5 charts participatory media's rise to dominance in online communication. While differences in the technologies encourage individuals to use them in different ways, today's centrally moderated blogs and forums provide the best environment for individuals in the movement to engage in ritual deliberation. In these media, divergent views can be excluded while, at the same time, adherents can enact complex communication about their belief in the End Times.

Chapter 6 documents the expressions of prejudice that persist in the movement. While well suited for ritual deliberation, moderated participatory media mix with historical tendencies and radical certainty to encourage intolerance for individuals with beliefs or practices that are thought to contradict the movement's basic beliefs. Despite the media's role in facilitating such intolerance, the online deliberation of a new generation of Internet-savvy believers suggests that tolerance may be a trait that users of these media will increasingly demand from their online religious communities in the future.

The conclusion explores the implications of these findings for researchers of contemporary religion and new media technologies. The existence of this new sort of religious movement suggests that individual believers are more responsible for the nature of their religiosity when they are empowered to construct their worldviews from the vast possibilities afforded by Internet communication technologies. Recognizing the increased responsibility afforded by these media, researchers must continue to increase their understanding of the communication practices of everyday religious believers.

Vernacular Christian Fundamentalism

At least since the emergence of mass-produced vernacular Bibles, individual Christians have been confronted with more responsibility for interpreting the Christian message (Howard 2005b). With the rise of secular governments, individual choice has come to be a primary guide for religious expression in the United States, and with new communication and travel technologies, people have enjoyed growing exposure to a vast diversity of religious ideas. Meanwhile, the counterculture movements of the late 1960s and 1970s produced a whole generation of believers more oriented toward non-Western religious and spiritual ideas (Roof 1999).

At the same time, increased immigration into the United States further expanded the diversity of belief. With the widespread adoption of communication technologies during the information age, individuals have been granted even greater control over the ideas they access (Lindlof 2002, 71–72). These technological and cultural changes have cultivated a more voluntaristic attitude toward spiritual involvement. As a result, religious commitment in the United States has grown more individualized and fluid (Ammerman 1997; Clark 2003; Cowan 2005, 195).

With this increased individualization, the authority for religious belief and expression has shifted further and further away from religious institutions. This shift has prompted researchers to consider religion more as it is "lived" and less at the levels of institutional history and theology (McGuire 2008). While the movement I document in this book should be considered "lived religion," it is also specifically "vernacular" because it has grown and spread without forming institutions or relying on centralized leadership for authority.

The term "vernacular" refers to noninstitutional beliefs and practices that exist alongside but apart from institutions. This meaning evolved in reference to languages. All the way up through the Renaissance, "vernacular" referred to any language that was not Latin. This meaning came from its ancient associations first with non-Greek and non-Roman slaves and later with speakers of the varieties of "Vulgar" Latin. These informal and localized forms of Latin eventually evolved into the Romance languages of Western Europe and they were called, as a group, "vernacular" because they existed alongside but apart from the formal institutional language of Latin (Howard 2008a and 2008b).

Though "vernacular" still holds this meaning, its association with the non-institutional gave the term new currency as an analytic category in interpretive anthropology and folklore studies. The term appeared as early as 1960 in an *American Anthropologist* article where researcher Margaret Lantis used it to refer to "the commonplace" (Lantis 1960, 202). While sociologists like Karl Mannheim (1980), Harold Garfinkle (1967), or Peter L. Berger (1990) tend to approach religion by looking at its social structures and (in particular) its social orders, folklorists and anthropologists like Lantis tend to focus more on the expressive human behaviors that create a shared sense of culture. As a result, the expressive and linguistic orientation of the term "vernacular" seems to have given it more traction in anthropology and folklore studies. Applying it to the study of religion specifically, ethnographer Leonard Primiano has described "vernacular religion" as the manifestation of religious beliefs and practices in the everyday lives of individual believers (1995).

Sociologists of religion sometimes refer to this as "popular religion." Historian David D. Hall has pointed out, however, that many researchers use the term "popular religion" to demarcate the difference between official Christianity and pagan elements surviving in popular practice (1997, viii). This suggests an opposition to the official that is not necessarily the case in vernacular Christian fundamentalism. Similarly, folklorists sometimes refer to informally shared beliefs as "folk religion" or "folk belief." However, this terminology suggests a connection to tradition in the sense of an ongoing handing down of beliefs and practices from one generation to the next. This "traditional" characteristic may or may not be present in cases of new or idiosyncratic forms of everyday religion.

Avoiding these connotations, Hall offers the concept of "lived religion." He argues that his "lived religion" perspective focuses on "charting the practices of the laity." This conception does not set these practices in opposition to church leadership or necessarily associate them with any preexisting expressive traditions (1997, vii). Another proponent of the "lived religion" concept, Robert Orsi, notes how Hall's formulation has the potential to overemphasize individual agency because it deemphasizes the power of religious institutions and documents that are not "lived" in the normal sense of the word. Orsi demonstrates the possible extreme of this tendency by referencing Primiano's description of "vernacular religion." As Orsi notes, Primiano seems to emphasize individual agency so completely that the "vernacular" leaves no way to account for the power of religious institutions at all (1997, 20).

Advocating his "vernacular" perspective on religion, Primiano argues that "there is no objective existence of practice which expresses 'official religion.' No one, no special religious elite or member of an institutional hierarchy, neither the Pope in Rome nor the Dalai Lama of Tibet . . . lives an 'officially' religious life" (1995, 46). In Primiano's view, all religion is actually "lived" by individuals and thus even the institutions empowered through them are "vernacular" religious expressions. My redeployment of the term "vernacular" mitigates this difference of views by maintaining Primiano and Hall's specific focus on lived religion but adding a specific theory of "vernacular authority." This authority accounts for both vernacular and institutional power by emphasizing the dialectical definition central to the ancient meanings of the vernacular (Howard 2008b and 2010b).

The Roman Latin noun "verna" specifically referred to slaves who were born and raised in a Roman home. While the term is often associated with this "home-born" meaning, it also carried with it the connotation of a specific kind of power. The verna was a native to Roman culture but was also the offspring of a sublimated non-Roman ethnic or culture group. In Roman society, most slaves were seized during wars, during the suppression of colonial insurrections, or even through outright piracy (Westermann 1984, 101). The majority of these slaves did not read or write Classical Latin or Greek. Since any person born to a slave woman (without regard to the social position of the father) was automatically a slave, female slaves were encouraged to have children to increase the master's slave stock (Bradley 1987, 42–44). These verna could become even more valuable than their mothers when they were trained as native users of the institutional languages and thus able to engage in more technical kinds of work.

Vernacular power, then, came from a dialectical distinction: a verna was made powerful because she or he had native access to Roman institutional language and yet was explicitly defined as something which was separate from Roman institutions. In one of its earliest uses to describe expressive human behavior, the Roman philosopher and politician Cicero suggested that being vernacular was a means to persuasive power because of this unique position. In a work on rhetoric, *Brutus*, he wrote of an "indescribable flavor" that rendered a particular speaker persuasive. This power was "vernacular" because the speaker had learned it outside Roman institutions (1971, 147). Cicero understood the vernacular as alternate to what he and other Roman politicians saw as the institutional elements of persuasive communication available through the formal study of oratory, Roman history, literature, and philosophy (Howard 2008b). The "vernacular" might support or oppose institutional power, but it is specifically and consciously the power of not being institutional. In this sense, it is a dialectical term because it is defined by its opposite.

This dialectical sense of the vernacular maps particularly well onto vernacular Christian fundamentalism because one of the movement's definitive traits is its lack of institutional leadership. In fact, its power to unify people into a church is based on the idea that there is no institutional component to the movement. It is not merely "lived religion," it is a social entity made authoritative by everyday believers' repeated choices to connect. With repetition over time, those choices accumulate to enact a larger shared volition. This aggregate volition is the vernacular authority that gives shape to the online church.

Though this movement is different from the historical movement of Christian fundamentalism in the 1920s, using the term "fundamentalism" helps locate the set of ideas unifying the group both in terms of their historical antecedents and also as a subject of much research (see Marty and Appleby 1995, 6–7; and Harris 1998, 1ff). The movement I have documented is typically not termed "fundamentalism" by its adherents. As I am using it, the term is strictly analytic. This analytic approach to fundamentalism goes at least as far back as the work of biblical scholar James Barr starting in the mid-1960s (Barr 1966 and 1978; Kellstedt and Smidt 1991; Perkin 2000).

For Barr, "fundamentalism" denoted a way of thinking. In historical and discursive terms, Barr's "cognitive" fundamentalism is better understood as "ideological." By ideology, I mean a set of interrelated ideas that function as the symbolic apparatus through which a social group understands its world (Althusser 1984; Eagleton 1991; Howard 2009c and 2009d). In this sense, ideology is a habit of thinking based on shared beliefs. From this perspective, a communication can be seen as participating in fundamentalism whenever specific definitive traits are observed—whether or not the person expressing them is self-identified with a specifically "fundamentalist" group.

Based on ethnographic data collected in the 1990s, researcher of religion Charles B. Strozier constructed the first systematic catalog of the four observable traits that indicate the existence of Christian fundamentalism (1994, 5). In online discourse, I have located a similar set of four core beliefs. They are: a belief in biblical literalism, a belief in the experience of spiritual rebirth, a belief in the need to evangelize, and a belief in the End Times interpretation of biblical prophecy. When these four beliefs are expressed in a noninstitutional communication, that communication participates in vernacular Christian fundamentalism.

The unifying force behind this set of beliefs is an emphasis on a literal interpretative approach to the Bible. This form of interpretation generally assumes that, even in translation, the Bible has a single, simple, and direct meaning. In cases like those presented by the complex symbolic language of the Book of Revelation, this literalism occurs at a secondary level. In the famous passage in Revelation 19:15, for example, where the returned messiah is described as "smiting the nations" with a "sharp sword" coming out of His mouth, a literal interpretation might accept the "sword" to refer to modern weapons of war such as guns, tanks, and so on. How a literal reading would understand the sword as coming out of the mouth instead of held in the hand, however, presents a greater range of possible literal meanings. As a result, the emphasis on a literal interpretation assumes that there is a single and correct meaning even if the language is itself figurative and obscure.

In some cases, a text is even assumed to be literal at a "typological" level. In these cases, texts that make clear and straightforward claims about a specific concrete historical entity are thought to refer not only to that specific case but also to other types, of which that entity is only representative (O'Leary

1994, 55). For example, some references to "the Israelites" are typologically reinterpreted to mean any of those who are chosen by God to be His people. For some evangelicals, this means that contemporary evangelical Christians (as "true" followers of Christ) are typologically referred to as Israelites in the Bible.

While coming to agreement on these sorts of interpretations can be the source of deliberation about many issues, the four distinctive beliefs are thought to be supported by the most obvious meaning of one or more biblical passages and are typically not the basis for deliberation. As a result, individuals deploying this sort of interpretative technique can often simply make an assertion and then quote one or more specific biblical passages that are assumed to prove the assertion, based on a belief in a literal meaning of the Bible. This technique is often referred to by its detractors as "prooftexting."

While a commitment to this kind of interpretation is probably best known as the basis for the rejection of Darwin's theory of evolution, literalist interpreters have applied the technique to other central questions of theology as well. Importantly, it has been used to account for an emphasis on direct experience with the divine popularized by evangelicals like Billy Graham under the name "spiritual rebirth." Inspired by a radical certainty afforded by this intense direct experience, believers locate references to such experiences in interpretations of specific New Testament passages. One passage often used to account for the rebirth experience is Jesus' words to the Pharisee Nicodemus in the Gospel of John: "Verily, verily, I say unto thee, except a man be born again, he cannot see the kingdom of God" (John 3:3). As a result, the first belief (in literalism) supports the second, the need for spiritual rebirth.

Then, in turn, the belief in the necessity of spiritual rebirth drives the third belief: that it is necessary to convert others by inviting them to have their own spiritual rebirth experiences. Even when not evangelizing nonbelievers, Christians emphasize the evangelical component of their belief system by giving testimony of their own spiritual rebirth. By exchanging personal experience narratives about their rebirths as a form of "witnessing," individuals engage in "speaking the truth in love" to each other (Ephesians 4:16). This evangelical witnessing supports the shared understanding of the rebirth experience and links the radical certainty of direct experience with a literal reading of the Bible.

These first three beliefs taken together, however, do not necessarily mark vernacular Christian fundamentalism. Indeed, they could mark any number of more common evangelical ideologies, sects, or movements. Vernacular Christian fundamentalism only emerges when a literal interpretation of the prophetic texts gives rise to online ritualized deliberation based on a belief in the "End Times." This distinctive fourth trait interlocks both with the radical certainty afforded by spiritual rebirth and the need to "witness" their shared literalism by giving everyday adherents a reason to discuss their faith online.

As with the other defining beliefs, the faith in the End Times is located in specific biblical passages. The central biblical idea associated with the phrase the "Kingdom of Heaven" is one often cited as a literal reference to the end of human history. Of the many references throughout the New Testament, the Gospel of Mathew presents a typical one. After Jesus describes at some length the violence and suffering that will mark the End Times period, he states bluntly: "And then shall appear the sign of the Son of man in heaven: and then shall all the tribes of the earth mourn, and they shall see the Son of man coming in the clouds of heaven with power and great glory" (Mathew 24: 29–30). When a literal interpretation of these passages is emphasized, believers assume that Christ will visibly return at some point in human history. When people begin to engage in deliberation about exactly when this return might occur, that activity becomes the distinctive marker of this new religious movement.

While it is clear that these beliefs were being expressed online by the 1990s, the nature of the social entity that the individuals communicating these beliefs comprise challenges our notions of community. These individuals enact a sort of community only so long as they imagine each other as forming a cohesive social group in which they have some stake. At the same time, this sort of online religious community is fundamentally different from "real-world" or geographically based communities. Individuals form it as they express shared ideas instead of when they share physical proximity. As a result, its members are freer to choose with whom they create their community. The radical freedom afforded by network communication technologies makes this new religious movement a new kind of religious movement because it gives form to a "virtual ekklesia."

In this research, I consider vernacular Christian fundamentalism a new religious movement based on religious scholar J. Gordon Melton's definition. It fulfills Melton's definitive traits of a new religious movement. It has emerged "apart from dominant religious culture" as a result of a "significant theological divergence" in its emphasis on the End Times. As a result of this emphasis, its adherents "act in a different manner from the majority" (1999) when they engage in the ritual deliberation that constitutes their online church, their "virtual ekklesia."

The Virtual Ekklesia

Believing that they were acting in a way much like "first-century Christians," one of my respondents told me that he and his wife used the Internet to enact their "ekklesia." Rejecting the need for religious institutions in favor of vernacular authority, he described how "it's absolutely viable for the 'church,' if you understand what I mean by that: the ekklesia; to meet on the Internet" (Jane and John 1999). Ritual deliberation is the primary form this "meeting" takes in vernacular Christian fundamentalism, and that deliberation is an extension of the ancient Christian tradition of *koinonia* or "fellowship." This emphasis on fellowship has proved readily adaptable to the online environment (Howard 2009b).

In Greek (the language of the New Testament), *koinonos* literally means a "partner" or "sharer." In early Christian theology, the Apostle Paul imagined the Christian community as a group of "sharers" of the knowledge that the teachings of Christ were true. Compelling his followers to engage in "sharing" this already shared knowledge with each other, Paul used the Greek word "*koinonia*" (I Corinthians: 10: 16). The members of the early church communicated their shared belief in the teachings of Jesus as they formed new sorts of communities in the midst of diverse Roman cities. Over time, engaging in koinonia came to be a defining mark of membership in the Christian church.

In the online environment today, individuals seldom share the material possessions, resources, or geographical space associated with real-world communities like cities. While this sort of nongeographic fellowship is very different from a typical community, a church based on koinonia readily adapts to an online environment because it emerges in individual acts of communication. When early Christians expressed their shared beliefs, they marked themselves as part of what was, at that time, a newly formed religion. Doing so marked them as different from others in the cosmopolitan cities in which many of them lived because they shared the unique and specific knowledge that the Christian message was true.

The idea that sharing knowledge generates a community is at least as old as the Christian idea of "church" itself. In the Gospel of Mathew, Jesus famously declared: "And I say also unto thee, that thou art Peter, and upon this rock I will build my church; and the gates of hell shall not prevail against it" (16: 18). Here, the word "church" is translated from the Greek word "*ekklesia*." In Classical Greek, ekklesia referred to "an assembly of important persons."

In New Testament Greek, this word came to refer to the congregation associated with a particular synagogue. When the Apostle Paul brought the Christian message to non-Jews, he made it clear that a shared knowledge of Christ's message instead of Jewish heritage was a prerequisite to membership in this new kind of ekklesia (Colossians 1:1–24). Translated literally from the Greek, Paul's role as an "evangelist" was a "sharer of good news." However, this sharing was not just the activity of making new converts to Christianity. It was also the expression of Christ's message among those already converted. Koinonia was the ongoing constitution of the ekklesia through the active sharing of knowledge.

Paul emphasized that shared knowledge marked the members of the Christian community as distinct from nonbelievers when he analogized the community to a "temple of the living God" writing in II Corinthians 6: 14: "Be ye not unequally yoked together with unbelievers: for what fellowship hath righteousness with unrighteousness?" Elsewhere, Paul describes how the individual members of the Christian community must "knit together" the "body of Christ" by "speaking the truth in love" (Ephesians 4: 16). Advocating for unity in the face of an early controversy surrounding the need for non-Jewish Christians to adhere to Jewish law, Paul argued that Christians should foster group cohesion by sharing "the word of Christ" among themselves: "Let the word of Christ dwell in you richly in all wisdom; teaching and admonishing one another" (Colossians 3:15–16).

In a diverse society, individual Christians could understand themselves as members of a distinct community on the basis of their collaborative expression of shared knowledge. The need for community recognition gave rise to the traditions of self-expression referred to as "witnessing" or "giving testimony" in which everyday churchgoers stand before the congregation and declare their personal experiences with the divine (Bruce 1974; Titon 1988). Traditions of testimony and witnessing as forms of fellowship have long been common in Protestantism and evangelical Christianity in particular, but in vernacular Christian fundamentalism these behaviors take on a more central importance because there are no geographically based churches. Instead, the "body of Christ" that is "knit together" by Internet communication creates a "virtual ekklesia."

By "virtual," I refer to the literal meaning of the word as "manifest by effect." While this meaning is similar to that currently associated with "virtual worlds" such as those created by immersive online environments like Second Life, the term comes from the seventeenth-century realization that some plants possessed "virtues" that could only be recognized when ingested as medicines. In this sense, those effects were "virtual" because they were only observable through their effect. Later, the term was brought into physics to refer to subatomic particles that were invisible to microscopy but could be detected by studying the behavior of the particles around them. From there, it moved into computer science to refer to computer memory that was not part of the computer's physical memory.

Building on that common computer jargon to refer to things that were emulated like "virtual RAM," communication theorist Howard Rheingold famously coined the phrase "virtual community" in 1993. At the time, it was not generally accepted that individuals could form geographically separated communities through network communication. Rheingold, however, argued that "virtual communities" were "social aggregations that emerge" through network communication when there is "sufficient human feeling, to form webs of personal relationships" (2000, 5).

For Rheingold, a community can be "virtual" when network communication has the effect of allowing a group of people to sense an emotional stake in a shared social aggregate that has no physical or geographic existence. Applying Rheingold's idea to the study of online religion, communication researcher Heidi Campbell first suggested that when such a virtual community imagines itself as an online congregation, it constitutes a "virtual ecclesia" (2005). While the virtual congregation or, as my respondent termed it above, the "virtual ekklesia," does have the effect of creating a group of people with a stake in sharing their ideology, this sort of community is far more tenuous than one based on a shared physical location.

A virtual community exists only insofar as the community exists in the minds of its members. It is most palpable when individuals are actually communicating online in front of their computers, but it exists "virtually" (it has its effect) so long as individuals imagine that they are members of it. In this sense, the virtual ekklesia is primarily an "imagined community" much as famously described by Benedict Anderson in 1991. Because this community is based on its effect of creating an imagined link between physically separated individuals, repeated episodes of online communication among these individuals become the only means by which the virtual ekklesia can come into being.

However, communication is centrally important in this movement not only because it only exists virtually. It is also important because it has emerged without any modern-day Apostle Paul. In vernacular Christian fundamentalism, individuals use communication technologies to transcend not just geographic locations but also traditional sources of authority in the forms of both specific leaders and institutions. Here, vernacular authority comes from individuals using communication technologies to sacralize their own aggregate social entity by "witnessing" their shared certainty in the truth of their particular interpretation of the Christian message.

As they enact this particular virtual ekklesia, individuals must be marked as insiders who share their special knowledge, while those who do not share this knowledge must be marked as outsiders. There are, however, no physical locations or barriers to separate the believers from the nonbelievers as there might be in a new religious movement that establishes a real-world community. As I have noted, there is also no central leadership to fulfill this role. Instead, a powerful form of social control must emerge from this group's aggregated vernacular authority.

Sociologists of religion have long struggled to understand the different ways social control emerges in new religious movements. In movements that have strongly enforced self-sealing worldviews, researchers have imagined central control being exerted by a leader or leaders, often including pressure to cut ties to nonbelievers and even move into shared living and working spaces. Vernacular Christian fundamentalism complicates this understanding with its virtual ekklesia based only on vernacular authority.

Some researchers have sought to explain the reasons believers would choose to alienate themselves by focusing on extreme cases like that of the People's Temple or Heaven's Gate. These researchers tend to portray believers as mesmerized followers (Davis 2000; Lifton 1989; Schein 1971; Singer 2003). This conception suggests that social control flows down from a specific leader or leaders who command powerful personal charisma (Cialdini 1993; Weber 1978; Lalich 2004, 15). Imagined this way, researchers can attribute any negative outcomes to the movement's leadership (see Lewis 2001; Robbins and Zablocki 2001). This removes both agency and responsibility from the everyday believers.

In vernacular Christian fundamentalism individuals generate powerful social control without any institutions, leadership, or even a shared geographic location. By performing ritual deliberation about the End Times, they choose to follow this specific ideology. In that choosing, they generate the vernacular authority that enforces a self-sealing system of belief that alienates them from the mainstream society in which they live. If we cannot attribute this powerful social control to the manipulative intentions of a charismatic leader, then something about it must appeal to each individual who chooses to participate in enacting the vernacular authority.

Historically, a belief in the impending return of Christ has exhibited a broad popularity across the Christian tradition. Rhetoric scholar Stephen O'Leary has described how these apocalyptic ideas typically function as "symbolic resources that enable societies to define and address the problem of evil" (1994, 6). When evil is associated with mainstream society, however, apocalypticism increases the potential for intolerance and prejudice, because imagining outsiders as agents of an active evil force renders prejudice against them more reasonable.

Historian Richard Hofstadter famously documented a conspiratorial or "paranoid" style in Christian apocalypticism that emerges when individuals describe the world in terms of fundamentally good and fundamentally evil forces (1967, 39). More recently, researcher of religion and folklorist Daniel Wojcik has documented this same dualism in evangelical Christian media that imagines mainstream society as "irreversibly evil" (1997, 140; 2000). In these texts, an adamant belief in the near return of Jesus Christ encourages believers to think of themselves as warriors in a mythic struggle against all who disagree (Howard 2009a).

As Wojcik notes, this kind of thinking breeds the "profound alienation from contemporary society that is central to much apocalyptic thought" (1997, 142). Tracing expressions of this alienation in apocalyptic discourse, researchers of religion Chip Berlet and Matthew Lyons have mapped recurring associations between "aggressive White supremacy, demagogic appeals, demonization, conspiracist scapegoating, anti-Semitism, hatred of the Left, militaristic nationalism, an apocalyptic style, and millennialist themes" (2000, 17).

These prejudices are resilient in contemporary apocalyptic discourse because the dualism and the perceived alienation work together to generate a self-sealing worldview. Analyzing specific examples of this discourse, O'Leary has powerfully demonstrated how End Times biblical interpretation typically deploys an argumentative strategy that "denies the credentials of all authorities who disagree" by arguing that outsiders who dissent are in league with the forces of evil. By presenting anyone with a different view as part of an evil mainstream society, End Times interpretation "transforms their disagreements into further support for the claim by interpreting it as itself a sign of the End" (1994, 170). A feedback loop is completed when the sense that outsiders are evil is validated by a feeling of alienation brought on by considering the overwhelming volume of divergent ideas in mainstream society.

As I have noted, vernacular Christian fundamentalism is characterized by its emergence in network media. The fact that it also exhibits the dualistic and self-sealing qualities typical of Christian apocalyptism suggests that individuals are choosing to use the Internet to foster their own isolation from mainstream discourse. In fact, sociologist of religion Michael Barkun has documented how "those whose worldview is built around conspiracy ideas find in the Internet virtual communities of the like-minded" (2003, 13). This is not what advocates of network communication technology were hoping to find in religious expression as it adjusts to the digital age.

In 2001, sociologist of religion Brenda Brasher voiced the expectation that Internet communication would foster a global tolerance for religious diversity: "The wisdom of Web pages and holy hyperlinks that are the stuff of online religion possess the potential to make a unique contribution to global fellowship in the frequently volatile area of interreligous understanding" (2001b, 6). This attitude is common among Internet communication researchers, and it has emerged from communication theories about the conditions which foster healthy public deliberation.

Some Internet theorists hope that network communication will have a widely positive impact on politics because they feel it harbors the potential for creating more equal dialogue positions between individuals involved in public debates. They argue that individuals in a society who enjoy relatively equal positions are encouraged to tolerate difference because it is through such tolerance that others hear their voices. Referencing Jürgen Habermas's vision of a "public sphere" of open discourse, for example, Internet scholar Zizi Papacharissi has argued that "a virtual space enhances discussion; and a virtual sphere enhances democracy" (Habermas 1974; Papacharissi 2002, 11). Similarly, Yale law professor Jack Balkin has argued that the ability to make links between Web pages discourages fragmentation by encouraging linking to pages with divergent content (Balkin 2004).

In reference to the increased opportunities individuals have to express themselves online, Stanford law professor Lawrence Lessig has lauded a new vigor in communal creative expression he terms "read/write culture" (2008, 28). Well-known communication and media theorist Henry Jenkins has made similar claims in his celebration of "convergence culture" (2006b, 135). Harvard law professor Yochai Benkler is perhaps the most vocal proponent of the idea that the Internet is fostering new kinds of empowerment for everyday people. He has argued for a sweepingly positive assessment of the role of the Internet, describing it as "a mechanism to achieve improvements in human development everywhere" (2008, 2). For Benkler, network communication technologies have fostered a "new folk culture" that encourages "a wider practice of active personal engagement in the telling and retelling of basic cultural themes." For Benkler, this practice "offers new avenues for freedom" (2008, 299–300).

Benkler and others are certainly correct when they argue that the Internet can transfer authority from institutions to individuals. In terms of media production, this is a good thing at least when it allows people to express themselves in ways that were previously only available to the most powerful sectors of society (Howard 2008a). Further, the increased attention to noninstitutional voices associated with these new modes of communication seems to be empowering individuals with new ways to become politically engaged. This increases the possibilities for transformative social change because it opens conduits of influence that can move from the bottom up (Howard 2010a). As Benkler puts it:

> At a more foundational level of collective understanding, the shift from an industrial to a networked information economy increases the extent to which individuals can become active participants in producing their own cultural environment. It opens the possibility of a more critical and reflective culture. (2008, 130)

What, however, of those individuals whose worldviews seem to compel them to use this new freedom not so much to be "critical and reflective" as to locate others with which to form like-minded enclaves of belief?

Benkler acknowledges this problem, noting that it is a "fact that the Internet allows widely dispersed people with extreme views to find each other and talk." He concludes, however, that this phenomenon "is not a failure for the liberal public sphere" (2008, 256). The goal of a liberal public sphere should be to allow people to communicate more or less as equals. Insofar as that condition is aided by the Internet, advocates like Benkler are right to suggest that the resulting empowerment should cause individuals to reject beliefs that alienate them from the mainstream because they stand to benefit by having their voices heard more broadly.

For Benkler, those who fail to reject intolerant beliefs, however, "may present new challenges for the liberal state in constraining extreme action" (2008, 257). While it may be possible to arrest and detain individuals who commit violent acts because of their extreme views, the milder forms of intolerance and prejudice that are associated with some kinds of apocalypticism cannot easily be "constrained" by the "state" without compromising the mainstream value of tolerance itself (see Wessinger 2000b). Instead, these individuals' choices to believe and express their beliefs must be respected as a right even by critics of those beliefs.

This situation tempers the hope of these Internet scholars. The fact that vernacular Christian fundamentalism's dualistic and self-sealing ideology is flourishing online reveals that some Internet users do not place a very high value on the more critical and reflective forms of tolerance an online public sphere provides them. Instead, these individuals seem to place a greater value on the social control they can generate through vernacular authority. For them, network communication enables them to cordon off their beliefs from criticism and enact discourse that portrays any resistance from the outside as proof both of their alienation and their righteousness. In this sense, the Internet is not just compatible with the self-sealing and dualistic ideology associated with apocalypticism, but some Internet users are using network communication technologies to foster it.

Vernacular Webs

When the telegraph first rendered messages into electricity in 1844, the act of sharing ideas was unyoked from the physical movement of people or objects (Carey 1989, 201ff; Fischer 1992). It became possible to replace an individual's physical presence with a "telepresence" (Markham 1998, 17). With the introduction of personal computer technologies in the late 1970s, communication was again transformed because it could be "digitized" into binary numbers (Ceruzzi 2003). As sequences of on-and-off electric pulses or "bits," vastly more and more complex human expressions could be rendered telepresent. Then, persistent webs of telepresent human discourse became possible as computer network technologies were developed into the Internet during the 1980s.

The emergence of vernacular Christian fundamentalism serves as an indication of the profound effects this technologizing of everyday human communication can have. The Internet can elevate individual action to new levels of power by generating distributed vernacular authority. Paolo Apolito, a prominent researcher of technology and religion, has argued that this technological shift toward the everyday and the individual has "marginalized the charismatic, shifting the focus as it does from the 'gift' of [a] direct relationship with heaven to the technical structure of the procedures of vision and contact with the beyond" (2005, 5).

For Apolito, the technologizing of authority has placed distance between the powerful experience of the divine and the humans who seek it. While this may be the case in some ways, it must not be forgotten that these very technological structures are themselves animated by humans. Through digital conduits, repeated individual actions etch channels of shared imagining. Over time, these channels mark an aggregate volition, and this volition is the source of vernacular authority. Even if it is less dramatic than personal contact with the Madonna or space aliens, this authority still moves through these everyday believers to fill their daily lives with the divine.

At the dawn of the twentieth century, one of the first researchers to take a modern approach to the study of religion, Emile Durkheim, famously argued for an almost transcendent understanding of aggregate social action. For Durkheim, "society" can only know itself through ongoing cooperation: "It is by common action that [society] takes consciousness of itself and realizes its position; it is before all else an active cooperation. [. . .] It is action which dominates the religious life, because of the mere fact that it is society which is its source" (1915, 465–66). For Durkheim, cooperative action sacralizes the world because it is only through such action that individual experiences are made sensible beyond the individual self. In this process, the ritual enacting of the social divine renders its presence visible across time by creating, maintaining, and re-creating the shared meanings that link individual humans together.

In this research, I have located individuals communicating the beliefs of vernacular Christian fundamentalism online from the earliest days of the Internet in the 1980s to the surge of participatory media in the early part of the twenty-first century. In so doing, this book documents a vernacular web of expression enacted in the sharing of this ideology. In the thick of this web, Marilyn Agee's site functions as a prominent location for connecting with others who wish to discuss the End Times. While Marilyn is deeply enmeshed in this web, Lambert Dolphin inhabits its edge.

Among the more than seven hundred pages on Lambert's site in 2001, only one page engaged the possibility of a typical End Times scenario. Well known in the community and often referenced as authoritative, this single page functions as the node through which he is drawn into the movement. As individuals move through various links from other End Times sites to his page, his recounting of the prophetic narrative pushes the walls of the virtual ekklesia just a little wider. In these moments, vernacular Christian fundamentalism's web of network locations encompasses both Agee and Dolphin.

While Marilyn and Lambert both inhabit this web, their online expression focuses on very different things. Lambert's site contained a huge variety of theological ideas and teachings in addition to his discussion of the End Times. Marilyn's focused almost exclusively on prophecy. Lambert expressed the idea that maybe different "models" for understanding the divine might work equally well. Marilyn emphasized that any conception of the divine other than her own "is totally false" (Agee and Edgar, 1999). Despite the fundamentally more rigid understanding of the divine that Marilyn holds, these two popular amateur theologians are linked by the beliefs of vernacular Christian fundamentalism.

Lambert hangs on the very edge of this movement only because he does not make his position on literalism clear. He seemed to contradict any strict adherence to a single interpretation of the Bible during my interview with him, and his Web site has information that might suggest almost any evangelical Protestant belief system. Amongst that material, however, he does express his belief in spiritual rebirth, evangelism, and the End Times without any caveat. Since these beliefs are typically found together with the fourth belief definitive of the movement, namely, literalism, individuals recognize his expression of those three traits as supported by the fourth. Reading Lambert's online communication, they assimilate his expression into their movement as their own.

Willingly or not, Lambert's Web page on the End Times participates in vernacular Christian fundamentalism. His case is telling because it demonstrates the interactive relationship between the individual and the social that characterizes this new sort of movement. On the one hand, the individual is disempowered by the social because it exerts control through vernacular authority. It pulls communication into its web wherever it finds support for its core beliefs and it excludes communication that challenges them.

At the same time, the practice of ritual deliberation empowers individuals by tolerating a significant diversity of expression. This tolerance is possible because the four beliefs that define the movement allow individuals to spin and change their interpretations of the prophetic narrative without the constraints imposed by any centralized authority or more complex doctrines. As Lambert's case demonstrates, the vernacular authority generated by individuals spinning out these interpretive possibilities can pull communication into its undulating web even from the extreme fringes.

Long before the emergence of the Worldwide Web, cultural theorist Clifford Geertz imagined humans as "an animal suspended in webs of significance he himself has spun" (Geertz 1973, 5). Today, these webs emerge and extend with the aid of network media. One of these webs continually constructs, maintains, and reconstructs a placeless church based on a shared belief in the imminent approach of Jesus Christ's Second Coming. Not a lifeless structure lifted and turned by the chance of circumstance, this vernacular web is emergent from the aggregate authority of an untold number of individual human choices to engage in ritual deliberation about the End Times.

The implications of this finding are far-reaching.

In the second half of the twentieth century, researchers of religion imagined that U.S. culture was growing more secular (Carter 1991; Ying 1957). Late in the century, however, it became clear that American society was not growing less religious but, instead, that its religiosity was changing (Cowan 2005; Hadden 1987). Today, individuals feel less affiliated with their traditional institutions. They do not necessarily continue to associate with their childhood or family denomination, and they (especially younger believers) increasingly turn to nondenominational and often Internet-based forms of religious community (Pew 2008). Today's media offer individuals more opportunities to construct their own personalized systems of belief than ever before in history, and more people than ever are taking advantage of these opportunities (Ammerman 1997; Cimino and Lattin 1998; Roof 1999).

With the recognition of this broader trend, the virtual ekklesia documented here raises new questions about the nature of religion in an age of network communication. What roles do communication technologies play in these individualistic constructions of religious belief? What dangers are emerging in the heavily mediated and individually constructed religious marketplaces of the digital age? The case of vernacular Christian fundamentalism demonstrates that individual believers can deploy even the most powerful communication media to limit their exposure to the diversity of ideas those media have made available to them. Documenting individuals making this choice without the influence of any central leadership, this research suggests that individual believers empowered by modern technology must be considered responsible for the sorts of religiosity they choose to construct.

The central motive behind these individuals' choice to construct this self-sealing virtual ekklesia may well be a fundamentally human one. As the well-known scholar of communication James W. Carey noted, individuals engage in communication not just to transmit knowledge but also as a means for "the construction and maintenance of an ordered, meaningful cultural world" (1989, 18–19). People do not want to do this alone. They seek to construct their worlds in connection with others. To realize this connection, they seek to share their understanding of the world.

Individuals today are freer to express themselves than at any point in human history. They are freer to gather information from more diverse sources than ever before. They are freer to engage in the wealth of diversity other human beings are expressing. Together, their aggregated volition generates something wholly new in human history. This aggregate action generates a new Christian body, a virtual ekklesia, a digital Jesus. For some, however, this aggregation may be coming at too great a cost.

Today's network communication technologies afford individuals the chance to choose wholly different ways of knowing. In diversity, transformation remains possible. However, the trend toward individually aggregating new information into very tightly focused ideological enclaves like that demonstrated in vernacular Christian fundamentalism suggests that this freedom can also diminish the power of those who have it. As a mechanism that places limits on the consumption and expression of ideas, online communication enclaves like that of vernacular Christian fundamentalism may foreclose some of the new avenues toward the richly meaningful religious life that network communication technologies seem to afford.

9/11 at the *Bible Prophecy Corner:*

Enacting the Virtual Ekklesia

New Events; Same Story

For those in lower Manhattan, at the Pentagon in Washington, D.C., or who had loved ones on one of four commercial air flights on September 11, 2001, the events of that day comprised more than a news story or historical event—they were an intense personal experience. For far more, however, that intense violence was experienced through live television and other news reporting media. At the dawn of a new millennium of global information sharing, this mediated experience was traumatic and transforming. The shocking events of that morning—watching the austere towers collapse into goliath columns of smoke—forced North Americans to adjust their previously held narratives and beliefs about the world. Like having missed an important episode of a geopolitical drama, an unnoticed subplot erupted onto television screens with stark brutality.

This was no less true for the individuals involved in vernacular Christian fundamentalism. By September 2001, the online discourse emerging from this new religious movement had become a huge web of linked Internet sites. At all its nodes, individuals shared the definitive beliefs of their movement. Based on these beliefs, they engaged in the communication that enacted their virtual ekklesia.

For the people involved in the movement at that time, it seemed at first that the prophetic narrative they saw in their literal reading of the Bible made no mention of the 9/11 attacks. Yet, in the immediate aftermath, it was unthinkable that their magnitude would not be marked in the Bible. Instead of perceiving that absence as some kind of possible larger error in their interpretative approach, individuals in this movement redoubled their efforts to locate the attacks in the texts. Engaging in the ritual deliberation that is definitive of the movement, the events were assimilated into the shared understanding of the world that linked these individuals—at least for a few days.

The communication documented on one Web site demonstrates how ritualized deliberation had grown so powerful by 2001 that even unexpected new facts could be quickly rendered sensible by the communal interpretation of biblical prophecy. The specific End Times narrative these individuals shared made this communal agility possible. Theorist of communication and media Walter Fisher has argued that humans think natively not only in *logos*, or logic, but also, and maybe first, in *mythos* or "story" (1985). That is to say, people organize their understandings of the world through interlocking narratives.

With the advent of mass media, people began to have access to the events from which they construct their variant narratives by way of newspaper, magazine, and television news agencies. Since the rise of the public Worldwide Web in 1992, multilateral discussions about these events had become commonplace on a multitude of Web sites, newsgroups, and online forums, as well as in both private and public email lists. As the overall volume of online communication exploded, so too had the online web of vernacular fundamentalism. In the movement, world news events had long provided grist for ritual deliberation. Because of the connections between biblical prophecy and war in the Middle East, the 9/11 attacks both fueled the interest in the End Times and needed to be placed into the prophetic narrative already believed to be the correct literal interpretation of the Bible.

Individuals within Christian vernacular fundamentalism used Marilyn Agee's Web site as a location to perform a communal integration of the September 11 attacks into their End Times narrative. Though none of their short-term predictions based on these events came to pass, their communication ritually enacted their shared ideology. This integration demonstrates how meaning making occurs through vernacular authority. As we have seen, the social aggregate recognizes itself in the myriad everyday expressive acts of ritual deliberation. In the communication hosted on Marilyn Agee's Web site on and shortly after September 11, 2001, the power of this vernacular authority is clear.

September 11, 2001

On September 11, 2001 there was an outpouring of grief, confusion, anger, and shock in the web of online discourse emerging from vernacular Christian fundamentalism. In hundreds of newsgroup postings, email messages, blogs, and forums community members struggled to adjust their understanding of the world to these unexpected events. Because the rebuilding of the Jewish temple in Jerusalem is generally thought to shortly precede the second coming of Christ, conservative Christians have often paid close attention to events in the Middle East. As it quickly became clear that the planes had been hijacked by individuals involved in Middle Eastern politics, individuals in the movement felt compelled to integrate the attacks into their prophetic view of geopolitical conflict, and the events of 9/11 were pulled into the dynamic flow of ritualized deliberation. While no final decision about their significance was made, the challenge to their interpretations that these new facts might have presented was quickly neutralized just the same.

Marilyn's Web site, *Bible Prophecy Corner*, presents a rich and complex example of how the individuals in this movement used ritualized deliberation to enact their ekklesia. As a popular and authoritative figure, Marilyn claimed that God had "led" her in her biblical studies. She placed her own writings in a clear authoritative relationship to the biblical texts she interpreted. Because the movement held the value that the biblical texts are divinely inspired and literally true, Marilyn placed her secondary interpretations of those texts into the realm of divine authority by relating her story of how she came to realize that God wanted her to write books. The desire to communicate her messages based on this authority prompted Marilyn to shift away from publishing books to creating a large Web site dominated by her posts of email exchanges she had with other members in the movement. The ritual deliberation she presents offers excellent examples of how this behavior can be both flexible and support a rigid adherence to the specific set of beliefs that defines the movement.

In 2001, the main section of the *Bible Prophecy Corner* was devoted to what Marilyn terms the "Pro and Con Index" (Agee 1999a). A blog of sorts, Marilyn had been using it to catalog and respond to questions and concerns individuals involved in vernacular fundamentalism had sent to her by email since 1996. In September 2001, the "Index" contained over eight hundred individual entries, many of which were well over five thousand words. Each entry was placed on its own individual Web page. Each contained four to ten "incoming" emails on a particular topic, often from a number of different individuals. In response to the incoming emails, Marilyn wrote "my reply" sections addressing the concerns expressed by her emailers. Often she included whole threads of rebuttals and counterarguments that she had exchanged with her interlocutors.

Marilyn's "Pro and Con" numbered 803 was dated September 12, 2001, and it provides a good opportunity to observe the way in which members of this movement reacted in the hours after the 9/11 events. Because these events were both historic and unexpected, they could have threatened the worldview of vernacular Christian fundamentalism by providing information that should have been but was not accounted for in the Bible. Acting with her community, Marilyn led her fellow believers in ritual deliberation that neutralized this threat.

Nearly five thousand words long, "Pro and Con 803" included thirteen "incoming emails" and four "my replies" which were posted throughout the day on September 11. Marilyn's replies addressed two different broad topics through which she categorized the thirteen communications she received. She posted eleven incoming emails in one group—these were mostly only a line or two and made no specific claims. In an example of this series, one of Marilyn's interlocutors wrote: "WTC-towers collapsing, well that's what i call a sign :)"[1] (Agee 2001b). While the post shows a certain insensitivity to the tragedy, it also correctly anticipated what would dominate the group's response to the events of 9/11. For them, these events were so momentous that they must surely be a sign of the End Times, but where were they in the Bible? Figuring this out was important because locating them in the Bible could function as a marker of the current moment in the prophetic narrative and thus shed light on how soon they might expect the End.

Most of the other emails in this group specifically sought Marilyn's response. One began: "Can you please explain to me how todays bombing is related to the Bible, and the end of time. Could you please give me some Bible verses that I could refer back to. Thank you and God Bless you" (Agee 2001b). By emailing her in this way, the community looked to Marilyn for advice. She responded to them by showing compassion and emphasizing that vengeance was not an appropriate Christian reaction.

In response to more complicated queries, Marilyn began to place the 9/11 events into the specific context of the prophetic narrative. The possibility that the Book of Revelation foretold that asteroids would strike the earth had been an ongoing issue discussed on her Web site in the days before 9/11. She described her views on the issue in the "Pro and Con" from the week before, number 802:

I think God wants as many people as possible to know that there is an asteroid threat. That Rev. 8:8,10 is talking about asteroid impacts could not be known perfectly before the first asteroid was discovered in modern times. Now we can understand it perfectly. Every heavenly body that we have been able to photograph the surface of is pockmarked with craters.

The Earth is not immune, although the Moon may have swept many from our orbital path. Lights that have been sighted on the Moon from time to time may have been asteroid impacts. (Agee 2001a)

On the September 12 "Pro and Con," right after she addressed the unchristian aspect of desiring vengeance, she immediately returned to the topic of asteroids and placed them in relation to 9/11:

The Lord said that vengeance belongs to him. He knows who did what and how to punish them. They don't know what is in store for them for plotting this wickedness. They will get what for without our doing a thing. I'll list below some verses that mention the Lord's vengeance. The asteroid of Rev. 8:8 will fall into the Mediterranean Sea. The star of Rev. 8:10 will destroy Babylon. Rev. 18:21 says, "a mighty angel took up a stone like a great millstone, and cast it into the sea, saying, Thus with violence shall that great city Babylon be thrown down, and shall be found no more at all." (Agee 2001b)

Marilyn's ability to immediately shift from the current tragedy to an ongoing interpretative point shows both her agility of mind and the ability of the End Times narrative to order individuals' understandings of the world. Making this shift, Marilyn relied primarily on two biblical passages. The first was Revelation 8:7. This passage is interpreted by many in the movement to refer to a catastrophic event caused by something coming from the sky. This event comes at a set place in the narrative. However, what exactly comes from the sky offers significant flexibility in interpretation.

Typical of the Book of Revelation, the passage describes a series of catastrophes in highly metaphoric language. Each catastrophe is initiated by the blowing of a trumpet. The First Trumpet is described this way: "The first angel sounded, and there followed hail and fire mingled with blood, and they were cast upon the earth: and the third part of trees was burnt up, and all green grass was burnt up" (8:7). A literal reading of this passage suggests that something "hailed" from the sky that burned a large portion of the earth. During the Cold War, this was typically thought to refer to a nuclear attack (Wojcik 1997, 42). For Marilyn and others in 2001, it was thought to refer to asteroids. Among adherents, the exact nature of the event was flexible. However, its place in the overall narrative was not.

The Book of Revelation describes several more events unfolding after the First Trumpet/asteroid catastrophe. One that has garnered a huge amount of attention in ritual deliberation is called "the Rapture." The Rapture refers to an event or events where the bodies of believing Christians will be literally taken up into Heaven. Though there is disagreement regarding whether there will be one or two such events, Revelation seems to refer to at least one, saying:

> And they of the people and kindreds and tongues and nations shall see their dead bodies three days and an half, and shall not suffer their dead bodies to be put in graves. [. . .] And after three days and an half the Spirit of life from God entered into them, and they stood upon their feet; and great fear fell upon them which saw them. And they heard a great voice from heaven saying unto them, Come up hither. And they ascended up to heaven in a cloud; and their enemies beheld them. (9: 9–12)

Because this Rapture event is described in the prophecy as coming after the "First Trumpet," the narrative order places limits on the interpretation of the text. For a literal narrative to be foretold by the Bible (whatever the First Trumpet turns out to be), it must come before whatever the Rapture event of Revelation 11 actually is. Dealing with these issues in the longest interpretive section of "803 Pro and Con," Marilyn demonstrates how ritual deliberation's ability to generate meaning derives from the flexibility of the End Times narrative. The interpretative exchange took up nearly half the entire Web page. It consisted of an initial email that was sent to Marilyn by a fellow believer identified as "SA," Marilyn's thirteen hundred word reply, a response from the initial emailer consisting of a few sentences, and finally a second reply from Marilyn of over five hundred words. SA initiated the deliberation, writing:

From: SA, Re: The Ark of the Covenant

. . .I was delving into the KJV electronic bible which I have just downloaded and unzipped and the first OT book I went into was the calling of Samuel to serve the Lord. I grabbed my NIV for a second read through since the KJV can be rather oblique at times and reached 1 Sam 4 where the Philistines capture the Ark. I read on till 6:17 and then BAM—realized that here is a connection with Zephaniah 2:4. The Philistines had to send a guilt offering of five gold tumours and five gold rats . . ..and the gold tumours represent Ashdod, Gaza, Ashkelon, Gath and Ekron . . ....and guess where the asteroid strikes!! "Gaza will be abandoned and Ashkelon left in ruins. At MIDDAY Ashdod will be emptied and Ekron uprooted. Woe to you who live by the sea, O Kerethite people . . .."(NIV)

Isn't that a classic—just goes to show—don't mess with the Lord Almighty!!

What would be the significance of 1 Sam 6:1 " When the Ark of the Lord had been in Philistine territory seven months . . ."?

It's just so nice to see how the Lord deals out justice and all the more why we should understand that it is a dreadful thing to fall into the hands of the living God (Heb 10:31)!

I shall continue on and see where the Ark lands up. In Christ and looking up (eighteenth hopefully!!!) Agape (Agee 2001b)

Engaging in a common activity associated with ritual deliberation, Marilyn's interlocutor searched the Bible for references to elements she felt might be connected. She found three: the Ark of the Covenant, destructive natural events, and the number seven. Hoping this pattern might map onto current world events, she described "looking up" in three senses: "looking up" something in the Bible, "looking up" to God in Heaven, and "looking" into the future for patterns that might point to the "(eighteenth hopefully!!!)." Here, the number eighteen referred specifically to September 18, 2001—seven days after 9/11.

For SA, September 18 had taken on special significance because she suspected that the events of 9/11 might be what some adherents called "the Seven Day Warning." This warning was thought to have been given to Noah before the Great Flood depicted in the Old Testament, and some argued that this pattern would be mirrored in the End Times scenario by some "sign" seven days before the First Trumpet. If the September 11 events were a "Seven Day Warning," then the asteroids which Marilyn had been predicting as the First Trumpet should strike the earth seven days after the eleventh: on September 18.

Marilyn followed her emailer's line of thought, and responded with supporting data: "(9–18–01 is Tishri 1, 5761, the Feast of Trumpets, hopefully the Rapture.)" Here, Marilyn translated September 18 to an equivalent date on the Hebrew calendar system that the Old Testament prophets would have used. Based on this dating and in an exchange with a fellow believer, she placed the newly significant date into the context of her ongoing efforts to interpret biblical texts in terms of the Hebrew calendar and modern astronomy.

Earlier that year, Marilyn had publicly declared that the Christian holiday called the Feast of Trumpets (celebrated the same day as the Jewish new year, Rosh Hashanah) in either 2001 or 2002 would mark a significant event in the End Times. In 2001, Rosh Hashanah began at sundown on September 17. This gave Marilyn enough cause to predict that it was "likely" that the First Trumpet would sound on September 18. Referencing her fellow adherents' speculation on the topic, Marilyn responded: "Most suggested that the plane impacts that were instrumental in bringing down the twin towers at the World Trade Center in New York may be a 7-day sign. I think it is very likely. [Because] Sept. 11 is 7 days before the Feast of Trumpets." Her narrative ordering of the Seven Day Warning, the Feast of Trumpets, and September 11, 2001 placed the newly important date into the context of her overall interpretation of biblical narrative. Next, she located evidence in the Bible that supported her new assertion that September 18, 2001 could be the First Trumpet.

> Prophecy casts its shadows before it. Isa. 30:25 says, "there shall be upon every high mountain, and upon every high hill, rivers and streams of waters in the day of the great slaughter, WHEN THE TOWERS FALL." Those words," WHEN THE TOWERS FALL," that have echoed through my head today, tie today's tragedy to the final catastrophe on the Day of God's Wrath. In that day, the UN and UR will be housed in towers in Babylon, Iraq. Those towers will fall. (Agee 2001b)

Here Marilyn made two important moves. First, she claimed that "the words echoed" in her head all day. Because the divine had led her in the study of scripture, it was not an accident that this passage stuck with her. She related her sense of this divine influence to her audience because, from their perspective, this was evidence that she was being led by God in her biblical study. Her second important move was to link a previously unrelated passage from the Bible, Isaiah 30:25, with the newly important events of 9/11 and thus incorporate those events into the prophetic narrative. Her claim that "prophecy casts its shadows before it" was a direct reference to the associative way in which much ritual deliberation about the End Times proceeds.

While she was able to completely ignore the fact that there were four planes and other targets, she was compelled by the biblical passage to which she was led. That passage prompted her to imagine that the September 11 attacks were a warning of two approaching asteroids based on her previous interpretation of Revelation prophesying that God's wrath would rain down on earth in the form of two massive asteroids colliding with Earth. This perception allowed her to stick with her interpretation of approaching asteroids as the First Trumpet and place it within the new September 18 time frame without contradicting the overall shared prophetic narrative or the beliefs that supported it.

In her next lines, she made this interpretation clear by linking the newly incorporated information to a biblical passage she commonly uses as evidence that the First Trumpet will herald asteroids, Zechariah 5:4:

Two planes hitting the World Trade towers picture the two asteroids that will hit Earth on the day the towers fall. Zech. 5:4 tells us what will happen when the curse that orbits over the face of the Earth falls. It says, "I will bring it forth, saith the LORD of hosts, and it shall enter into the house of the thief (False Prophet that steals the church), and into the house of him that sweareth falsely by my name (the Tribulation Pope): and it shall remain in the midst of his house, and shall consume it with the timber thereof and the stones thereof." (Agee 2001b)

As it turned out, no great astronomical events were to occur on September 18, 2001. However, that did not concern Marilyn or her fellow participants in the deliberation. Of her many predictions that the End was near at hand, Marilyn admits that none have yet proved correct. When September 18, 2001 passed without event, the participants in the discussion exhibited little inclination to reconsider their biblical narrative or the beliefs that supported it because the value of this deliberation was not in actually locating any correct interpretation of the Bible.

In "Pro and Con 807," an emailer did chide Marilyn for not dealing with the failed date, saying: "Hey you shouldn't wait so long between post[s] since the 18th has passed, I might think I missed the Rapture. I hoped you had it right. I'm really looking forward to it" (Agee 2001c). Marilyn responded by explaining that she had had some trouble with her husband's medications, had been working on several entries at once, and would get to it soon.

Finally posted ten days later, "Pro and Con 810" was the first containing an engaged discussion of the failed prophetic date. A more typical "Pro and Con" entry than that of September 11, it contained a number of links to news articles about the Middle East, the discussion of a group in Israel working to build the temple in Jerusalem, a question about the length of the Tribulation period, some disagreements about specific calendar dates Marilyn had used, and even a warning about a particular computer virus that had been making the rounds.

Two sections of the page directly engage the failed predictions of seven days before. One was a long section with an email from "Mark," who attempted to adjust the calendar interpretation to push the date for the First Trumpet and the Rapture back a few days. He came up with a concrete new time, September 27, saying:

This is not date setting, but to give your readers hope, and keep them from being discouraged that the rapture has not occurred yet . . . as the last trumpet did NOT sound at the end of Rosh Hashana. We still have 9 days to go. . . . God Bless. (Agee 2001d)

Although Marilyn posted his message, she seemed not to respond to his argument. However, the second emailer who engaged the failed interpretation took a different approach:

10–02 of 2001 will be the 651st day since the winter solstice of 5760. The 651st composite (not prime) number is 790 (10 x 79 Gold). 651 + 790 = 1441 the Jewish day number for 9–11 of 2001. This is a very strong marker for a repeat of the 9–11 attack. YBIC (Agee 2001d)

Here, the emailer offered October 2 as a new significant date. However, this prediction came with the weakened expectation of only a second terrorist attack instead of the catastrophic asteroids. Such an attack, even if it had occurred, would have had no impact of the overall End Times narrative or its indexing in the current events of that time. Because anything less than asteroids rendered the date unrelated to her literal interpretation of the biblical texts, Marilyn replied expressing disappointment:

Ouch. I hope for something better than that, and I don't mean more explosive. I'd say, "What is this world coming to?" but I know all too well what the end of this age will bring. The only funny thing about it is that it is all written down. They could know how it will end, but they don't read it, don't believe it, or don't understand it. I think of Dan. 12:10, "the wicked shall do wickedly: and none of the wicked shall understand; but the wise shall understand." Maranatha! Agape (Agee 2001d)

Evident in this final quote from Marilyn, the failure of September 18 to render any significant events was largely brushed off by the participants in the deliberation. While one individual did it by extending the date and changing the exact contents of the prediction (from asteroids to a terrorist attack), Marilyn shifted focus to the unifying shared faith of her fellow adherents set against the "wickedness" of the mainstream society. Together, the insiders to the group anticipate the End Times with "hope." They look forward to them despite the violence with which they will be attended because these End

Times would mark the final days before the ultimate reunion of human and divine. They hold out this hope for themselves, and they also hold out this hope for each other.

Because the certainty about End Times events was totally unchanged by the failure to predict any significant event, their continued hope points to the function for this communal interpretative deliberation beyond any predictive one. Exhibiting a profound certainty, Marilyn reflected on her literalism: "They could know how it will end, but they don't read it [the Bible]." The audience for Marilyn's statement was, of course, not those who "don't read it." Instead, it was clearly those who *do* read it. For these individuals, the failure of the predictions was a relatively minor concern compared to this communal expression of shared certainty and hope.

In this movement on September 11, 2001, online deliberation functioned to create the opportunity for individuals to express their shared beliefs to each other. By facilitating this communication, it gave them the discursive space to generate their virtual ekklesia. In that communicative action, these adherents could enact the "hope" that their shared faith afforded and which is one of its definitive qualities. This hope was the result of an intense sense of certainty not in their specific predictive interpretations of the prophetic narrative but in the overall truth that Christ will return soon. A driving force in vernacular Christian fundamentalism, the true intensity of this certainty was most clear when I met the members of the movement in person.

A Conversion Attempt

During the 1999 interview I conducted with Marilyn, I experienced her intense certainty face-to-face. After the interview, I sat alone in my car to capture my immediate impressions on the audio recorder. Marilyn and her husband drove away in a new Ford Taurus. Marilyn had attempted to "corner me" outside and "convert me" (Agee and Edgar 1999). At the edge of the parking lot of the restaurant, she moved close to me, and put her hand on my shoulder, smiling. She asked me to "ask Christ into my heart." For Marilyn, any nonbeliever must be exhorted to become a believer.

During our interview, I asked her: "How do people know when they are converted?" She responded:

[The Bible is] the only thing that we have that we know it's all truth . . . Jesus told Nicodemus that you have to be "born again." And so they call it being "born again"; "born again Christian." We're born in the flesh the first time. And then we're born into God's family the second time. And we can't get unborn from that any more than we could the first time.

Then I asked her when she had been born again. She replied:

I can't be sure in my life because I believed what I was told. I was raised in the church, and I believed it from day one—what I was told. But sometime just prior to 1960, I decided I would just turn my life completely over to Christ. Ask him what he wanted me to do. And just . . . be totally sure I was saved . . . and no question about it. And so I prayed then. And I knew then. Then I got the feeling . . . the warmth, the joy, and the happiness that washed over me. (Agee and Edgar 1999)

I asked Marilyn if she had felt this sort of feeling at other times. She smiled and said that sometimes she felt a "rush" when studying the Bible. She said it "feels like my hair is standing up and the hair is standing up on my arms. And I'm warm. It's a manifestation of the Holy Spirit, I suppose." She expanded on the ways that the divine communicated to her. While writing, sometimes the words she typed on the computer would inexplicably appear in all capital letters. I asked her how she knew these communications were from the divine and not some other spirit. She said gravely: "There is no other name given under Heaven by which man can be saved but Jesus Christ" (Agee and Edgar 1999).

While her description of a "warm rush" was typical of the spiritual rebirth experience and belief associated with the movement, Marilyn said that she did not consider any particular experience of the divine necessary to spiritual rebirth. I asked her about visions of the Virgin Mary among Catholics to see if that experience could lead to spiritual rebirth. In response, she stated clearly that "apparitions of the Virgin Mary" have all been "demons." She emphasized that the Bible is the only authority for understanding the divine.

Then I asked her if it was possible that some American Indian traditions could come into contact with Christ—even if it was under another name. She said, no: "The Indians don't worship Him. So theirs is totally false . . . we are surrounded by these wicked angels and they can interfere in all kinds of things like that. They [the American Indians] can have some real things happen, but they are not of God." Then I asked her about the so-called "New Age Movement." She shook her head: "They're so mixed up. I feel sorry for them. Really." She continued:

You gotta take the Bible for what it is says. God knows how to put down what He means. And He don't put it down in . . . He puts down how to be saved plainly. But prophecy, He puts a little here and a little there. And in Isaiah He explains that. It's so that they'll fall back and be taken: the non-believers. (Agee and Edgar 1999)

In a self-sealing line of reasoning, Marilyn contends that God intended for a literal interpretation of the Bible to seem improbable because that is one way that the divine separates the faithful from the nonfaithful. As we shall see, this self-sealing reasoning, militant rejection of other ideas, and the dualistic division of believers from nonbelievers all link Marilyn to the historical movement typically called "fundamentalism." However, the intensity of her belief is itself associated with evangelical Christianity more generally. While they may not be as dramatic as the experiences of more charismatic or institutionally backed religious visionaries, the reality of spiritual rebirth experiences and other personal interactions with the divine is evidenced by the power they exert among the everyday believers in this movement.

Radical Certainty

Among the respondents I interviewed in this movement, the experiences that supported their certainty were generally described as individually sensed contact with the Holy Spirit. When an individual uses personal experience to establish authority, there is little need to engage in deliberation about what he or she knows directly. When that experience is of the divine, the certainty it engenders carries the power of the sacred.

Individuals making assertions based on revelatory experiences claim, by association, some of the authority of the divine itself. Amplifying the authorizing power of claims to direct experience, revelatory claims indicate a more radical certainty than any mundane information, deliberations, or abstract set of reasons could ever instill (see James 1958; and Howard 2005c and 2006c). When this authority is associated with a literal interpretation of the Bible, it indicates the special knowledge that marks these individuals as part of the ekklesia along with the other specific beliefs of vernacular Christian fundamentalism. The idea of a special knowledge gained from a revelatory experience as marking the real members of Christianity is nothing new.

In the Christian tradition, the archetype for such revelatory experience is the New Testament account of the Apostle Paul's confrontation with the Holy Spirit while on the road to Damascus:

And it came to pass, that, as I made my journey, and was come nigh unto Damascus about noon, suddenly there shone from heaven a great light round about me. And I fell unto the ground, and heard a voice saying unto me, "Saul, Saul, why persecutest thou me?" And I answered, "Who art thou, Lord?" And he said unto me, "I am Jesus of Nazareth, whom thou persecutest." And they that were with me saw indeed the light, and were afraid; but they heard not the voice of him that spake to me. And I said, "What shall I do, Lord?" And the Lord said unto me, "Arise, and go into Damascus; and there it shall be told thee of all things which are appointed for thee to do." (Acts 22: 6–10)

Causing Paul to collapse to the ground dumbstruck, this sort of revelation appears as an intense psychic experience that the experiencing individual cannot deny or resist.

Today, revelatory experiences cannot be discounted as delusions or associated exclusively with unstable individuals. Neuroscience recognizes that these experiences manifest in individuals that exhibit no other significant symptoms (Slater and Beard 1963; Bear and Fedio 1977; Persinger 1993). Neurologists have long sought to understand revelatory experiences ranging from an inexplicable "sense of presence" to the full-blown "God-experience." Associated with activity in the temporal lobe of the brain, there seem to be correlations between brain wave patterns and revelatory sensations (Persinger 2001). Further, these brain wave patterns can come to be associated with specific external stimuli, including places and communications (Persinger and Makarec 1992).

The intense physicality of these experiences cannot be denied. For an individual who has experienced such psychic events, questioning the reality of the events is not reasonable. The revelatory experience seems to be a unilateral transference of knowledge from a divine source. It is known to be true because it is felt directly. Elaine Lawless, an ethnographer of religion and folklorist who has worked extensively with North American Pentecostals, describes a revelatory experience sometimes called "tarrying":

Sinners seeking to change their status from sinner to saint and gain membership in the group must do so by first professing their sins in the public context of the church and tarrying at the alt[a]r . . . the kinesic language that accompanies tarrying includes raised arms, waving hands, closed eyes, tears, and the eventual disconnection from one's surroundings that implies a trance state. (Lawless 1988, 50)

Although it is less spectacular than Pentecostal "speaking in tongues," this sort of emotive psychic experience is common among contemporary Protestant groups (Goodman 1972; Kane 1974; and Welch 1998).

Ethnographer Tom Mould has documented somewhat less dramatic forms of revelatory everyday experience among members of the Church of Jesus Christ of the Latter Day Saints (Mould 2009). Wendy Opal Welch, in her research among a wide diversity of suburban Christians in the American Southeast during the late 1990s, has documented numerous examples of individuals telling stories about "getting saved." These rebirth experiences are similar to those of the respondents I have interviewed in vernacular Christian fundamentalism. Generally, Welch found that this experience is characterized by "a sense of relief" (1998, 267). In a Christian context, "accepting God in your heart" or being "born again in Christ" are typical ways of referring to this sort of individual revelation. Among those interviewed, these sorts of revelatory or conversion experiences seem to lead to a simple and unafraid belief. It is a source of radical certainty, and this certainty is evidenced by a profound sense of calm.

While more mainstream forms of evangelical Christianity include an emphasis on conversion and spiritual rebirth, they typically harbor more accepting attitudes toward new ideas and variant interpretations of the Bible. Historically, fundamentalism and a militant attitude became linked with the End Times narrative at a vernacular level. When connected to the other beliefs that define the movement, they were galvanized by evangelical Christianity's general acceptance of the spiritual rebirth experience. While the institution-based fundamentalist movement of the early twentieth century was short-lived, the connections it made to this powerful certainty were readily communicated by the mass media that had emerged at that time. As a result, it was no surprise that Marilyn's strong rejection of alternate beliefs was typical of the respondents I interviewed in this religious movement.

Historical Christian Fundamentalism

Most historians consider Christian "fundamentalism" in the United States distinct from the more conciliatory Protestant "new evangelicalism." While evangelicalism was characterized by openness to contemporary culture, evangelicals who were more conservative saw any concession to secular culture as a sellout to modernism (Balmer and Winner 2002, 81–82). The well-known historian of fundamentalism, George M. Marsden, has suggested that a confrontational intolerance for alternate views was the distinguishing trait of fundamentalism; he calls it "a loose, diverse, and changing federation of co-belligerents united by their fierce opposition to modernist attempts to bring Christianity into line with modern thought" (1980, 4). Most conservative Christian evangelicals today reject the label of fundamentalism because of the negative associations it took on in the 1920s. However, as many historians have noted, the set of ideas that came together as the historical movement of Christian fundamentalism still persists at a vernacular level today.

In the first decades of the 1900s, many middle-class Americans were becoming disillusioned with the modern conception of progress and its technological products. Conservative Christians began to imagine the shocking carnage of World War I in terms of an approaching End Times. During this period, American Protestants were becoming increasingly divided. Conservatives called for a return to the "fundamentals" of Protestant belief. This budding movement was a reaction against a perceived growth of secular influence both inside and outside Protestant institutions. As the movement grew, Protestant leaders became split on the proper Christian understanding of Charles Darwin's theory of evolution. For liberals, the Bible's description of creation in the Book of Genesis was figurative and hence compatible with Darwin's theory. For conservatives who emphasized a literal interpretation of the Bible, Darwin's ideas were replacing a belief in God's divine plan with a belief in random chance and human will.

While liberal Protestant theologians like Walter Rauschenbusch emphasized pluralism and social justice, conservatives like Reuben A. Torrey focused on fending off any turn away from the "fundamentals" of Protestant belief. Starting in 1910, a series of twelve pamphlets edited by Torrey and published by the oil magnate Lyman Stewart called *The Fundamentals* helped popularize the idea of a return to a basic set of Christian principles. That same year, the Presbyterian General Assembly proclaimed the inerrancy of the biblical texts. In that declaration, they agreed on five theological points that represented a basic set of Protestant principles.

For the most conservative Protestants, however, these "Famous Five Points" did not emphasize a literal enough interpretation of the Bible because they did not endorse any prophetic narrative. During the first decades of the twentieth century, the most conservative leaders altered these five points into what they typically called the "five points of fundamentalism" to suit their theological leanings (Marsden 1980, 262). These conservatives exchanged the Presbyterians' fifth point (on the reality of miracles) for a literal reading of the biblical prophecy that anticipated the End Times. As a result, biblical literalism and a belief in prophecy became part of a radicalized platform of a nondenominational fundamentalist movement emerging in the United States at the beginning of the twentieth century (Marsden 1980, 117ff).

As liberal and conservative Protestant leaders began to take sides, Stewart and Torrey continued to publish and freely distribute new issues of *The Fundamentals*. Between 1910 and 1915, they distributed some three million copies. Their conservative message included many aspects of what would come to be called Christian fundamentalism. In fact, Torrey had been the close friend and protégé of an evangelical leader thought by many to be the progenitor of fundamentalism, Dwight L. Moody. Well-known historians of American Protestantism Randall Balmer and Lauren Winner have dubbed Moody "one of the most influential preachers in American history" (Balmer and Winner 2002, 235).

During his long career, Moody garnered huge influence because he pioneered a simple, emotional, and nondenominational theology that appealed to a diverse audience. Deploying a toned-down version of the tent revival style of preaching associated most famously with Charles Finney, he perfected what scholar of religious media Quentin Schultze has termed a "rhetoric of conversion" (see Finney 1868; Schultze 2003, 139ff). With this rhetorical strategy, Moody established the first truly modern evangelical empire. Although he was never officially ordained as a minister of any denomination, he transformed his independent downtown Chicago church into a full-blown Bible training institute. This institute, now the Moody Bible Institute, emphasized a literal interpretation of the Bible, including a prophetic narrative.

In 1857, when Moody moved to Chicago, the city was emerging as a hotbed of urban religious revivals. With powerful eloquence, Moody was soon traveling the country and Great Britain as the most popular public speaker in the evangelical movement. While in Britain, Moody was exposed to the so-called "Keswick teachings" that were gaining a large following there. The Keswick teachings were an adaptation of the Holiness Movement that originated in Methodism. They were strongly evangelical and relied on an emotive conversion experience generally referred to as a "filling with the Spirit of Jesus." Moody himself had had one of these experiences in 1871.

Though Moody was not officially aligned with the Keswick teachings, he incorporated them into his preaching. In so doing, he helped popularize what would come to be called "spiritual rebirth." In 1890, the first of two large conferences of evangelicals was held to explore the direct experience of the "Holy Spirit." The participants in these two conferences included many of Moody's followers, who had already been meeting yearly at the Niagara Bible conferences (see Harris 1998, 24 and 25ff; Moore 1994, 184ff; Marsden 1980, 77ff).

Starting in 1878, a group of Presbyterian preachers had organized the Niagara conferences to form a network of conservative evangelicals who advocated a literal interpretation of biblical prophecy. These preachers were themselves heavily influenced by both Moody and Dispensationalism. Dispensationalism was the prophetic theology of a British preacher named John Nelson Darby. Darby had gained a large following in the United States before his death in 1882. He taught that human history was going through a series of "dispensations" or periods marked by different relationships between humans and God. For Darby, the dispensation during which Christ would return was fast approaching (Boyer 1992, 88–90). When the 1890 conferences on the "Holy Spirit" were organized by and for the same participants as the Niagara conferences, the emphasis on personal experience with the divine could be seen to merge with the Dispensationalist interest in prophecy. As a result, a new nondenominational alliance of conservative evangelicals formed around these central ideas. In 1899, the year of Moody's death, the American theologian C. I. Scofield's immensely popular *Scofield Reference Bible* canonized the powerful combination of a personal experience of the divine and biblical prophecy. That same year, Rueben A. Torrey took Moody's mantle as the evangelical leader of the conservative movement (Boyer 1992, 97–99).

Though Pentecostals largely rejected it, the interest in prophecy continued to grow among other conservative evangelicals influenced by Moody and Torrey (Marsden 1980, 94ff). In 1917, the British government released a document that pledged support for a Jewish homeland in Palestine. Because the reestablishment of a Jewish homeland is overtly mentioned in prophetic texts of the Bible, this document seemed to confirm a literal interpretation. Emboldened by these sentiments, in 1918 the conservative preacher William B. Riley formed the "World's Christian Fundamentals Association" as a coalition of nondenominational conservative leaders committed to political change.

The WCFA aggressively pursued a political campaign to rid the U.S. Protestant institutions of officials who were felt to be too liberal. Attempting to harness the ideas Moody and his followers had popularized, the WCFA advocated for an apocalyptically tinged struggle against modern secular values. Making a doctrinal point, the editor of a Baptist newspaper first coined the term "fundamentalist" to refer to those "ready to do battle royal for the Fundamentals" (quoted in Marsden 1980, 159).

While this battle was raging at a largely institutional level, the well-known Presbyterian politician William Jennings Bryan launched a campaign against the teaching of evolution in schools. Although Bryan may have been more concerned about a link between evolution theory and German nationalism than he was about a literal interpretation of the Book of Genesis, he brought the disputed issues of biblical interpretation into general public discourse.

When John Scopes, a small-town schoolteacher, was charged with breaking a new Tennessee state law against teaching evolution, Bryan was brought in to prosecute him. The popular secular writer and journalist H. L. Mencken sensationalized the 1925 trial and it became a national spectacle. As a referendum on the values of its time, Scopes's defense attorney, Clarence Darrow, put Bryan on the stand and cornered him into denying a "literal" reading of Genesis. Bryan emerged looking inept, and Darrow emerged looking rational and heroic. Though Bryan won the trial in the end, he was publicly ridiculed. The Sunday following his catastrophic testimony, he died from a heart attack in his sleep.

During the Scopes trial, journalists took hold of the term "fundamentalist." Then, with Bryan's bad press and sudden death, the term became associated with the caricature of a hopelessly backward and rural brand of Christianity. Inside Protestant institutions, radical conservatives receded and disappeared. The term "fundamentalism" was largely rejected. However, its ideological components persisted at a vernacular level. Although some conservative evangelicals would take on the name "fundamentalist," these self-identifying fundamentalists remained in the vast minority.

As a result, no particular institution arose to normalize or rename the movement. With the continuation of the ideas but not the name, the historical and ideological definitions of fundamentalism have become too blurred for any simple bright line demarcating just what exactly is or is not fundamentalist. Nonetheless, the conservative evangelical media that had been slowly building their institutions since the early 1800s spread the basic ideas that had emerged around Moody.

As early as the 1830s, large publication houses had produced cheaply printed Bible tracts. In these publications, the Christian message was presented in simple, personal, and sometimes sentimental terms (Nord 1984; Moore 1994; Olasky 1990; Schultze 1988). As the century moved on, Protestant Christian leaders turned to the emerging medium of broadcast radio (Martin 1988). Seeking access to a broader audience, the Moody Bible Institute received its license to radio broadcast in Chicago in 1927. That same year, the Federal Radio Commission (the precursor to the FCC) was founded to monitor the use of public radio bandwidth.

Soon, the FRC began to shut down conservative religious broadcasters because their content was deemed too specific to serve the public good. As a result, conservative preachers and their organizations were forced to purchase their own airtime from broadcasting companies who had already secured control of particular radio frequencies (Schultze 1988; Erickson 1992). As a result of the need to raise money to buy airtime, conservative religious broadcasters became beholden to marketplace economics. They had to locate and please a reliable audience that was willing to fund the broadcasts through donations.

In this commercial environment, the conservative evangelical broadcasters quickly learned how to generate revenues by appealing to wide audiences with exciting emotional and sometimes even inflammatory claims. In the 1930s, controversial radio evangelists like Detroit's Father Charles Coughlin and Aimee Semple McPherson garnered huge audiences. By the 1940s, radio shows like *Religion in the News*, *The Lutheran Hour*, and Charles E. Fuller's *Old Fashioned Revival Hour* had become fixtures. In 1940, Fuller's show aired on 456 stations—60 percent of all the stations in the United States (Schultze 2003, 161).

Coming from the tent revival tradition and heavily influenced by Moody, conservative evangelical broadcasts exhibited a fully developed "rhetoric of conversion" (Schultze 2003, 139ff). This rhetoric was characterized by simple moral messages of personal devotion presented in emotional tones by charismatic preachers. Because evangelistic radio was wedded to a market of consumers, it simply could not overtly challenge that market base with too specific or difficult claims to belief or calls to action (Moore 1994; Schultze 2003). So instead, it depicted powerful scenes of emotional conversion and even faith healing. At the same time, it brought a simple conservative evangelical Christian message to a wide variety of Christians from diverse denominational backgrounds.

After World War II, the rhetoric of conversion was redeployed in the newly popular medium of television. Billy Graham and his close friend and colleague Bill Bright surged into the spotlight. Both were involved with the Fuller Theological Seminary. Bright founded the Campus Crusade for Christ International in 1951 as an organization that specifically sought to evangelize by using personal contact to cause emotional conversions.

Graham was a Baptist minister who began his broadcasting career on the Moody Bible Institute's radio shows in the early 1940s. Growing rapidly in popularity, Graham was able to start his own network radio show in 1950 called *Hour of Decision*. Much like Moody, Graham developed a nondenominational and emotional approach that emphasized personal conversion through a direct experience of the divine. On his broadcasts, Graham specifically "invited" his audiences to "decide" to follow Christ. In the 1980s, his nationally syndicated radio would secure immense popularity, running on some nine hundred stations worldwide.

With Bill Bright in the 1950s, Graham developed the "Four Step" strategy for personal conversions. Later, it came to be well known as the "Four Spiritual Laws" of the Campus Crusade for Christ (Have You Heard . . .? 2001). By the late 1950s, Graham had become famous for exhorting his audiences to "accept Christ as Savior." Typically, this exhortation was the climactic moment just before an "altar call." An altar call is a specific invitation for "sinners" in the audience to come forward and make a personal prayer to ask Jesus for forgiveness of their sins. In 1977, Graham famously codified his technique in the best-selling devotional book *How to Be Born Again*.

Graham added a more intimate and personal touch to the rhetoric of conversion. As mass media brought his voice and face into millions of living rooms worldwide, this style resonated across a variety of denominational boundaries. As a result, the growing mass media audience of Protestant Christian believers became large enough to support an expanding industry of televangelism. As a by-product, this conservative evangelical media spread a coherent set of basic values through its publications and broadcasts. Without relying on any specific Protestant denominational institutions, leaders, or doctrines, this set of ideas became a powerful cluster of vernacular beliefs. It would be a specific subset of these beliefs that allowed the everyday believers of vernacular Christian fundamentalism to locate each other amongst more liberal evangelicals online—and then to forge a conservative virtual ekklesia of their own. For these individuals, the specific prophetic narrative adapted from John Nelson Darby's Dispensationalism and popularized in evangelical mass media came to be identified by the term the "End Times." Central among this media were the books of Hal Lindsey.

In 1970, Lindsey's interpretation of biblical prophecy as foretelling Cold War politics, *The Late Great Planet Earth*, sold 7.5 million copies, becoming the best-selling nonfiction book of the decade (excluding the Bible itself). He articulated a core prophetic narrative and then described various possible scenarios for how geopolitical events might emerge to fulfill it. Following up with a series of similar books, Lindsey's popularity has continued and he has gone on to host his own radio and television shows on the now lucrative evangelical media networks (Erickson 1992).

In the 1990s, the approaching end of the second millennium fueled a renewed interest in the End Times. In 1995, Baptist minister Tim LaHaye published the first in a sixteen-book series called *Left Behind*. This wildly successful series of novels fictionally depicted the End Times narrative, updating it for the post–Cold War era. In 2000, the first book in the series was made into a movie. Later, two more books were made into movies and released on video. In 2001, Tim LaHaye was named the most influential leader in the evangelical movement by Wheaton College. By May 2004 (when the *Left Behind* series was largely complete) LaHaye and his coauthor Jerry Jenkins appeared on the cover of *Newsweek*. The article inside proclaimed that the combined sales of the first twelve books had topped 62 million—excluding "prequels," spin-offs, study editions, companion guides, and children's editions (Frykholm 2004; Hendershot 2004). In 2006, the software company LB Games released *Left Behind: Eternal Forces,* a computer video game based on the series. This immense popularity has made *Left Behind* the single most widespread source for vernacular knowledge of what has come to be called "the End Times."

A Certain Hope

As I have shown, after the collapse of the overtly named "fundamentalist" movement in 1925, mainstream Christian institutions largely rejected the term because it had taken on negative meanings in the wake of the Scopes trial. However, as the well-known historian of American religion Karen Armstrong has noted: "[F]undamentalists had not gone away. Indeed, after the trial their views became more extreme. They felt embittered and nursed a deep grievance against mainstream culture" (2000, 177–78). For these individuals, the group of ideas that Moody and his heirs spread through their evangelical media still persisted. Alongside but apart from any single Protestant institution, the End Times narrative emerged at the vernacular level in combination with the three other distinctive ideological components derived from historical Christian fundamentalism: a literal interpretation of the Bible, a belief in "spiritual rebirth," and an emphasis on evangelism.

By September 11, 2001 this vernacular constellation of beliefs authorized by radical certainty had emerged on the Internet to create the basis for powerful ritualized communication about the shocking terrorist attacks on that day. On Marilyn's *Bible Prophecy Corner*, this communication did not seek any authoritative or final correct location of these events in the text of the Bible. Instead, it was the means by which individuals enacted their virtual ekklesia.

This ekklesia is based on a shared hope that, despite the violence that will accompany it, Christ will return soon. This hope emerged from the radical certainty born of their spiritual rebirth experiences. This certainty underwrote the particular constellation of beliefs that define the movement, and it can be traced back to the historical movement of Christian fundamentalism. Though historical fundamentalism was short-lived at the institutional level, it persisted at a vernacular level because its simple and emotional message was readily adaptable to the mass media of the early twentieth century. In the next chapter, I go back before September 11, 2001 to document how ritual deliberation, the definitive behavior of the movement, proved well suited to some of the earliest forms of Internet media: newsgroup posts and email lists.

3

Networking the Apocalypse

End Times Communication in Newsgroups
and Email Lists, 1992 to 1995

First Contact

I initiated my first Internet-based contact with individuals involved in vernacular Christian fundamentalism on October 30, 1994. I posted an email
message to five Christian Usenet newsgroups. In full, it read:

> Hello. I am looking for anyone interested in discussing the current events
> that are shaping the coming revelation. I am writing a paper for a college
> class on Jack Van Impe and his film Years of the Beast, has anyone seen it?
> Please write me with your comments and views on the second coming.
> Thanks! (Howard 1994)

Starting in 1980, Jack Van Impe and his wife Rexella purchased weekly info-
mercial space from major broadcasters to air a news program-like show called
Jack Van Impe Presents (Erickson 1992, 191). During these broadcasts, Rexella
described various news items from the previous week and Jack placed them in
the context of biblical prophecy. Each broadcast offered a special item for sale
to support the purchase of the airtime. One such special item was the small
budget film depicting a fairly typical End Times scenario: *Years of the Beast*.
Since I was interested in the function of religious media in the everyday lives
of believers, I wanted to find people who had watched the film to participate in
an ethnographic interview. Having encountered trouble locating anyone who
had seen *Jack Van Impe Presents* among my contacts at that time, I decided
to post the above message to the five Christian-oriented Usenet newsgroups.
Somewhat unwittingly, I was swept up into a hidden community of Christians
who were using the Internet to share information about the End Times.

Usenet newsgroups are an early Internet medium. Though now eclipsed by Worldwide Web-based media, they are some of the most multilateral and pluralist Internet communication technologies. Newsgroups are topically defined electronic bulletin boards where individuals can "post" emails. The posted emails are kept on the newsgroup and other people can view and respond to them. Responses to a public post can be either sent to the private email address of the original poster, publicly posted, or both.

When I posted my short message, the public response was small. I received only five replies, and all five were in one newsgroup: "bit.listserv.christia"; all five were also suggestions for evangelical books about the End Times. However, I found no one who had watched *Jack Van Impe Presents* or *Years of the Beast*. After posting several more times, I received only three responses, and all of them voiced hostility. One claimed to have personal knowledge that "Jack Van Impe is an arrogant condescending bastard, while Rexella is just rock dumb" (Stanhope 1994). Another referred to Jack Van Impe, saying: "Great hair on that boy, eh?" (Ediger 1994). The third attacked me more directly by suggesting that my research interest was not worth pursuing:

> You gotta be kidding! jack Van Impe is the worst case of prooftexting the Bible I have ever seen. He can't say a single thing without digging up a *single* verse, taken out of context, to back up his statement. (lab@biostat. mc.duke.edu 1994)

While my posts produced only silence or hostility on the public newsgroups, it was a different story in private. In response to the first post alone, I received fourteen privately emailed replies. These fourteen emails rapidly turned into a series of ongoing email discussions. In a matter of weeks, I had exchanged hundreds of emails about the End Times with more than twenty different individuals. This experience raised an important question. Why was there so much private communication about the topic of the End Times but so little public communication?

One reason was that more liberal Christians did not accept the "prooftexting" style of deliberation that characterizes fundamentalist discourse (Shupe 1997). Because vernacular Christian fundamentalism emphasizes a literal interpretation of the Bible, individuals often refer to Bible passages, as the respondent above put it, "out of context." Many of the more mainline evangelical Christians using the newsgroups in the 1990s were not interested in this sort of deliberation. They did not accept the constitutive belief in biblical literalism, at least when it was applied to the End Times, and they did not accept "prooftexting" as an invitation to ritual deliberation about the End Times.

Individuals who did not accept the premise that a literal interpretation of biblical prophecy predicts the events of human history could not engage in ritual deliberation. If someone understood how the deliberation worked but rejected its premise immediately, they might respond with hostility, as in the above example, because they harbored a fundamentally different religious view. If someone did not even know that this premise was at play, the response might be dismissive because of the seeming absurdity of the topics the deliberation engages. Without accepting the premise of a literal prophecy, those outside the movement had no motive to take up cues to deliberation. Because they typically did not receive appropriate responses to their postings on newsgroups, individuals interested in the End Times turned to private email lists instead.

In private email communication, participants had confidence that their invitations to deliberate about the End Times would be engaged appropriately because they could choose to email only those who they knew were open to deliberation. Having exhibited this interest in the public forum of the newsgroup, individuals were added to private email lists just as I was. If subsequent exchanges revealed that new participants were competent deliberators, they remained on the lists. Many generated their own lists as they responded with their own emails. In this way, small group exchanges formed around topical issues that were premised on the shared interest in the End Times. By locating others based on specific topics for deliberation, individuals created tiny online communities of the like-minded. In so doing, they began to form small communities apart from the Christians on the more broadly inclusive newsgroups.

Birth of a Virtual Ekklesia

In the history of the Internet, the emphasis on enhancing individualism through communication technologies can be traced back at least as far as the influential computer scientist J. C. R. Licklider's 1960 vision of an "Intergalactic Network" (Licklider 1960; Hauben 1996). Licklider conceived of a globally interconnected set of computers through which individuals could quickly access data from any location. Speaking of his as yet only imagined global network, Licklider argued that such a technology could be incredibly liberating for individuals (Licklider 1960). Writing with a colleague, he claimed: "Life will be easier for the on-line individual because the people with whom one interacts most strongly will be selected by commonality of interest" (Licklider and Taylor 1968, 31).

When Licklider and others were hired by the U. S. government to build a communication system that could withstand a nuclear attack, they began to develop a distributed system of network "nodes" where each individual node had all the necessary components to communicate with every other node on the network. In 1969, a version of this technology came online as the ARPAnet (Abbate 1999; Leiner et al. 2000; Segaller 1998). The emergence of the first functioning government network fed an appetite for access to such technologies among an emerging techno-hobbyist counterculture of the 1970s.

Two graduate students at Duke University who were part of this counterculture decided to create a "poor man's ARPANET." In 1979, they formed the Unix Users Network or "Usenet." Their simple network of "newsgroups" was a collection of computers that regularly used telephone landlines to send batches of text to other computers through an informally arranged pattern. Sharing a piece of software called "Netnews," these computers could transmit a dynamic set of messages and organize them on an electronic bulletin board that only resided on the individual computers that were using the modems to call each other. Usenet was conceived of as an egalitarian discussion forum where no single individual had central control (Hauben and Hauben 1997).

Then, in 1981, Usenet's informal array of computers was moved onto the University of California at Berkeley's computer servers. Usenet became accessible from any ARPAnet network location because Berkeley's network was already part of the ARPAnet network. The limitations of using telephone lines overcome, Usenet exploded from 400 sites in 1982 to 11,000 in 1988. Gregory G. Woodbury, a Usenet pioneer, described the idealistic hopes many held for the radical individualism of newsgroup communication in those early years: "News allowed all interested persons to read the discussion, and to (relatively) easily inject a comment and to make sure that all participants saw it" (quoted in Hauben 2001).

From 1988 to 1995, the use of the Internet for personal expression rapidly increased. Because most newsgroup communication is still available in archives, it is reasonably certain that the earliest significant public Internet deliberation about the End Times began in 1992. This communication slowly grew until it supported the creation of the "alt.bible.prophecy" Usenet newsgroup in 1995. This was a watershed moment for vernacular Christian fundamentalism because alt.bible.prophecy was the first public Internet forum devoted to End Times communication, and its creation marks the birth of the movement's virtual ekklesia.

The Internet's emphasis on individualism suited the needs of the budding virtual ekklesia of that time because it gave individuals a virtual location where those with a very specific interest could deliberate. While private email lists had served the same purpose, they were small and did not have a static network location. Without a static location, it was hard for individuals to find each other and the members of any given list were often too transient to form strong links. The formation of the topically specific newsgroup solved these problems.

In 1992, Christian discourse on the Internet was still small in general. Even in the larger Christian newsgroups, messages that touched on fundamentalist ideology only came in short bursts. Searches of archived newsgroup posts show that there were a total of 111 posts referring to the "Endtimes" or the "End Times" from the 1981 inception of Usenet to January 1, 1992. By the end of 1992, however, the total number of posts more than doubled to 380. As overall discourse grew on the Internet, so too did the communication that engaged the ideology of Christian fundamentalism.

Over the course of 1992, there were a total of 269 references to the End Times on Usenet. The vast majority of these posts were met with an audience response that was dismissive or hostile. A typical example of this sort of dismissive exchange is the response to a 1992 post to the "soc.religion.christian" newsgroup. In a post given the subject line "Jesus Returns in 1996?" the poster's use of a question mark seemed to be implying that he was interested in hearing other newsgroup users' views on the idea. However, the post itself was just a numbered list of assertions, and it met with quite a bit of hostility.

In full, it read:

1. The World was created in a seven day period comprised of six days in which God worked and one (the Lord's day) on which he rested.
2. A cycle of seven (the creation week) signifies a cycle taken to completion.
3. Adam was created in 4004 B.C.
4. A day is as a thousand years and a thousand years is as a day.
5. The 2nd coming of Jesus begins a 1000-year (the millennium) reign of God's way on Earth before the final end of the World. BC 4004 Adam's creation; begin symbolic day 1 +6000 Days 1-6; 6000 years of human toil on Earth———AD 1996 THE 2nd COMING; begin day 7 or Lord's day, +1000 The Millennium or 1000 years of God's rule until completion of seven stage cycle.———2996 7000 years; End of the World.

Jesus returns in 1996. Incidentally, some believe that Jesus was born in 4 B.C., that early date, instead of the obvious 0, being attributed to later calendar error. That would put him exactly 4000. (Hamilton 1992)

Of seven responses to this post, none engaged it in a way that encouraged the original poster to respond. Two were ambiguous in tone. One of those was a sales pitch for tapes on biblical interpretation. The other asked for some "archeological evidence," which suggests incredulity toward the claims of the post. The other five responses presented various levels of open resistance. They were all dismissive in the sense that none of them responded with any cues for further deliberation. Most were humorously mocking. One response began: "Gee, this sounds like fun, can I play too?" (S.M. 1992)

A far more cutting response stated:

while on the subject of date-setting for the end times, it is interesting to note that the cover of Michael Jackson's Dangerous LP had a character (Gorbachev?) wearing "1998" as a lapel pin. Now 1998 = 666 * 3 . . . hmmm This also brings back memories of a book which purported to explain 88 reasons why the rapture would occur in '88. This pack of false prophecy was done by a NASA employee posing as a Bible scholar and thereby making a buck or two in all the controversy. (DLEIBOLD@yorkvm1.bitnet 1992)

Two years later, however, End Times discourse on the Internet was exploding. In 1994 alone the overall number of posts referring to the End Times shot up to 1,216. A large part of this public discourse was from individuals simply raising general questions about it. Often, the individuals who populated the newsgroups would gently lead these posters away from "date setting." However, it was still common to find open hostility to End Times discourse. In these cases, more liberal Christians would often harshly chastise individuals for even raising End Times issues.

One typical example of this sort of exchange started with a simple post that asked:

What will Christians do at the end times?
Will it be like the Holocaust?
Will they live as outlaws cut off from food/housing/jobs due to their lack of the mark? (Byron-Brown 1994)

There were four responses to the post. The first seemed to be sympathetic to the poster's interest, but warned against believing in "the Rapture." The second response attacked the first responder's somewhat open stance toward the End Times, saying:

> The "mind your heads, the sky is falling" routine has been preached for two thousand years. Somehow, quite rational people in each generation feel compelled to signs of the end times in their generation. (Clark 1994)

The third response to this post ignored the topic completely by only commenting on the second responder's email signature that contained a pithy Christian saying. The final response, however, attacked the very mention of End Times discourse even more harshly than had the second. Referring to a claim that is commonly raised against conservatives by more liberal Christians, the poster asserted that focusing on the End Times takes away from more important Christian work.

In response to the first question of the original post, "What will Christians do at the end times?" the poster stated:

> Probably wishing they'd spent more time feeding the hungry, housing the home-less, and all that love-thy-neighbor stuff and less time speculating on what the End Times would be like. (Bryan 1994)

These examples exemplify how the mention of the End Times in the general Christian newsgroups resulted in significant public resistance to deliberation about it. When individuals attempted to express this key component of vernacular Christian fundamentalism, they generally faced rejection and ridicule. A virtual ekklesia could not emerge in the existing newsgroups. This was, at least, because the mainstream users of Usenet did not share the definitive beliefs of the movement. They did not accept the literal interpretations associated with the End Times, and they were either unwilling or did not understand how to engage in the communicative norms that those involved in the movement wanted.

In February 1995, however, the "alt.bible.prophecy" newsgroup was formed specifically for individuals interested in End Times discourse. During 1996, the number of Usenet posts referring to the End Times totaled 3,081. Of those, 1,166 or about 38 percent were on the alt.bible.prophecy newsgroup. The other 62 percent were dispersed across 57 different newsgroups where none saw anywhere near the number of End Times posts that appeared on alt.bible.prophecy. Even in its first year of existence, this new more specific newsgroup became the primary location for End Times deliberation. As such, it was the first manifestation of vernacular Christian fundamentalism's virtual ekklesia.

Topical Community Formation

Before the advent of electronic communication, individuals generally formed communities based on geography. They were limited by their physical location because they could only communicate with other people in relatively close proximity (Redfield 1930). Later, individuals sought to create a sense of community through what well-known sociologist Ray Oldenberg has famously termed "great good places." In bars, cafés, coffee shops, churches, and dance halls individuals could easily communicate about ideas they were exposed to in books, newspapers, or broadcast media with other individuals whom they would meet based purely on proximity (1989). In these places, they encountered the real diversity of people and ideas that their physical surroundings offered. They could deliberate about certain general information that they all shared (even if they had not previously met) as a result of exposure to the same mass media sources.

Over time, electronic communication and particularly broadcast radio and television gave individuals access to a larger array of communications. With the large-scale deployment of cable television in the 1970s, the number of mass media outlets for television exploded in the United States. Instead of local newspapers or one of three major television networks, people began to have potentially hundreds of media sources easily available all the time. These media began to change the relationship between community, geography, and the individual. With knowledge sharing that was shorn of its geographical locality, people spent less time at the coffee shop, café, or church and more time listening to their radios and televisions.

For American Protestants, nondenominational religious authorities could be found, increasingly, in evangelical media organizations. For those immersed in this media-dominated environment, messages could be sent from a central source outward, but they could not be sent from all the receiving locations back to the source. In this sense, mass media generated weakly linked "interpretive" communities instead of the geographically contextualized spaces of traditional communities (Jenkins 1992 and 1995). In these interpretive communities, individuals were significantly disempowered because they could only share a unilateral information source. Without everyday people with whom to interact about their shared ideas, they were not afforded the same opportunities to engage in dynamic and ongoing discourse.

With the advent of network technologies, however, the individual was reempowered because new communication technologies made it possible for people to express themselves to each other. When communities of mediated discourse became multilateral in this way, however, they were fundamentally different because they offered individuals the opportunity to engage in communication among multiple users without the aid of mass media institutions or geography. In this sense, these emergent virtual communities had stronger ties than interpretive communities, and many of the designers and enthusiastic early users of network communication portrayed this individual ethos of the "electronic frontier" as revolutionary (Turner 2006, 142). However, the bonds formed by individuals using these technologies were still weaker than those of geographic communities. Often with little or nothing material at stake, people were free to construct their communities based on personal interests alone (Slouka 1995; Downey and Fenton 2003; Sunstein 2001, 8ff; see Putnam 2000).

While mass-mediated discourse placed the power to generate communication in the hands of only a few, the personalization of mass communication made possible by computer networks empowered individuals to limit their own sources of influence. Network-based communication is, in this sense, more individualized than mass-mediated discourse not only because individuals can actually produce the content, but because they consume content based on more individualized choices. For the Christians who used deliberation about the End Times to form a virtual ekklesia, this ability to individualize their media consumption enabled them to exclude those who did not share their ideology. When faced with hostility from other Christians, this new religious movement first chose to use private email lists, then formed the alt.bible.prophecy newsgroup, and later moved on to use newer network technologies to limit the participants in their discourse.

Individuals chose to limit participation based on the exhibition of markers for vernacular fundamentalism through a communicative behavior best described as "topical community formation." Topical community formation occurs when discourse-based communities form around shared topical interests. In the case of vernacular Christian fundamentalism in 1994, this typically occurred when an individual expressed interest in a topic by publicly using a keyword like "End Times," "Antichrist," or "New Roman Empire." Noting this interest, community members invited that person into some sort of more private or topically localized discussion medium. In 1995, individuals could find their way into such forums by choosing to read and post newsgroup messages on the alt.bible.prophecy newsgroup. Later, when the Worldwide Web began its rapid growth in the mid-1990s, people could even more easily locate a topical community by using search engines to find Web pages using the identifying terms of a given topic.

This sort of topical community formation enabled the ritualized deliberation that is the characteristic practice of the movement. Ritual deliberation accounts for the bulk of communication about the End Times online. As we saw on September 11, 2001, this sort of deliberation occurs when individuals involved in the movement discuss the relevance of a specific fact to a larger issue of concern without any expectation of a final solution or resulting action emerging from the discussion. In order for an individual to engage in this sort of deliberation, both sides of the communication must have a certain competence in the discourse surrounding the issue about which they wish to deliberate.

Specific recurring issues offer the opportunity to deliberate about the End Times first because believers agree that the Bible contains a literal prophecy of human history. Second, however, deliberation occurs because they also agree that the exact meaning of that prophecy is difficult or impossible for humans to rightly understand. Communication about such issues often focuses on the nature or the order of specific events as exemplified by the participants in Marilyn Agee's blog regarding the "fit" of the events of September 11, 2001 into the End Times narrative. In the central issue discussed there, the exact nature and timing of the "Rapture" can be deliberated because that "grabbing away" is described in the Bible as coming in close proximity to a violent period of wars called "the Tribulation," but the exact nature of both these events is shrouded in esoteric language.

Regardless of a believer's position on this issue, to engage in ritual deliberation she or he must be familiar with one of the basics of the End Times narrative: that true Christians will join with the returned Jesus Christ at some point near the end of human history. In ritual deliberation, they can actively communicate about very different and often new discursive elements without ever challenging or even directly stating the beliefs that mark their shared ideology.

To engage in ritual deliberation, people do not need to profess their membership in this vernacular movement overtly because they are already displaying it by properly presenting and commenting on the issues that defined the competence necessary to successfully engage in its discourse. As they do so, they create a field of discourse that excludes those not able to deliberate about the End Times. Even in the early 1990s, they actively used network technologies to limit the participation of individuals not already sharing their ideology. They could do this precisely because online communities can be formed "topically" instead of being based on physical proximity.

Displaying End Times Competence

Through topical community formation, participants engaged in discussions surrounding specific issues identified by phrases like "the End Times" or "the Tribulation." By engaging in serious discussions about these terms, the participants displayed End Times competence premised on the belief in a literal but only partially knowable interpretation of biblical prophecy. Displaying the necessary competence then reinforced the behavioral norms in a feedback loop. Discussing the End Times in this discourse meant that individuals could make almost any claim so long as they remained open to rejecting it if it seemed to contradict the definitive beliefs of the movement.

From the common tradition of evangelical ministry, writers and preachers like Hal Lindsey, Pat Robertson, Jack Van Impe, Tim LaHaye, and others perpetuated a well-defined and clear End Times discourse during the late twentieth century, as we have seen (Robbins and Palmer 1997; Strozier and Flynn 1997). By 1992, individuals already influenced by these sorts of non-network media were beginning to go onto the Internet and engage in email discussions about their previously held beliefs, books they had read, and other sources of influence.

At that time, vernacular Christian fundamentalism had already normalized its End Times narrative into a fairly standard set of predicted events primarily based on the influence of Lindsey. This basic set of interpretations functioned as the baseline knowledge for displaying End Times competence (Howard 1997). When I interviewed respondents in 1994, the most common source for their knowledge about the End Times was Lindsey's *The Late Great Planet Earth*. Comparing this book to episodes of the apocalyptic televangelist show *Jack Van Impe Presents* aired over the course of 1994 demonstrates that these two media sources for End Times belief repeatedly expressed the same basic prophetic narrative. This narrative was the baseline knowledge necessary for competence in the discourse.

Analyzing *Jack Van Impe Presents* over a two-month period in 1994, the following list represents the recurring events he and his wife and cohost Rexella referenced as part of the End Times predicted in biblical prophecy. In 1994, Van Impe proposed the following scenario in reference to the United States's ground assault on the Iraqi forces occupying Kuwait at the conclusion of the 1991 Gulf War:

1. Iraq surrenders and negotiates peace;
2. Palestine peace "becomes international in scope";
3. a world leader rises out of revived Roman Empire (the European Union);
4. EU originates and consummates international peace treaty;
5. world coalition of nations is the "New World Order" President Bush spoke of during the Gulf War;
6. Russia breaks away from world organization and attacks Israel at the three-and-a-half-year point of a seven-year peace treaty;
7. the majority of [the] Arab world will align itself against Israel with Russia;
8. England and America ("the English-speaking world") and Saudi Arabia "will raise a voice of opposition" against Russia;
9. "three and a half years of skirmishes climax" in Jerusalem;
10. the "Messiah will come to put an end to it, not wipe out the world, but end the war." (*Jack Van Impe Presents* 1994)

At the time Van Impe located these predictions in the Bible, event number one and, arguably, number two had already occurred. The following eight events were, by implication, on the immediate horizon.

In *The Late Great Planet Earth*, Hal Lindsey presents a similar model. Here, the only substantive differences are the addition of the "secret Rapture" and the post-apocalypse events in numbers twelve through seventeen:

1. rise of New Roman Empire as European Common Market, before 1988;
2. the establishment [of] a world governing body led by Antichrist;
3. Antichrist sides with world government and Israel against Russia;
4. Antichrist dies of head wound, but miraculously recovers;
5. Antichrist is worshipped as a god;
6. 666 tattoo on forehead or palm established as economic mark of European Common Market;
7. rebuilding of Temple in Jerusalem;
8. Arab, other African states, and the Soviet Union attack Israel;
9. Antichrist destroys Soviet Alliance with a nuclear attack;
10. China attacks forces of Antichrist;
11. one third of world destroyed by nuclear weapons;
12. Christ returns to protect faithful, "secret Rapture";
13. mass conversion of Jews;
14. Armageddon;

15. establishment of "atomic material" paradise for a 1,000 years;
16. resurgence of Antichrist put down by Christ;
17. return of "faithful to heaven with Christ." (Lindsey and Carlson 1970)

While Van Impe's model differs in its more contemporary grounding in current events and he excludes the rapture and postapocalypse elements, both schematics focus on the events that surround a great war centered in Jerusalem and incorporating Russia, China, the European Union, the United States, and some African nations. These are represented in Lindsey's numbers one through twelve and Van Impe's numbers three through ten. There are some interesting differences between the two models, but it is clear that the two are not in conflict.

For individuals involved in End Times discourse on the Internet in 1994, Hal Lindsey's work served as the baseline knowledge for End Times competence. In 1995, the publication of the first novel in the *Left Behind* series would rapidly overshadow Hal Lindsey's influence on this discourse, but LaHaye and Lindsey based their publications on a very similar prophetic narrative. From this base, the believers could move out into different camps with a wide variety of theories and incorporate many different ideas.

As individuals suggested different possible correlations between a current news event and a specific prophetic element, those connections became issues that they could deliberate about. However, the deliberation had no hope of concluding because while the deliberators must share the premise that there is a literal interpretation, they must also accept that no human can know that interpretation until the actual Second Coming has begun. This acceptance of the possibility of a literal interpretation while acknowledging the impossibility of attaining it before the End Times have arrived is the basic competence needed to engage in the ritual deliberation that is central to this movement.

Ritual Deliberation

Topics related to the End Times give rise to ritual deliberation, but the larger narrative of a violent Tribulation period followed by Christ's return is flexible, as we have seen; this flexibility is a basic trait that makes the narrative easily adapted to Internet media. As much as Hal Lindsey and Jack Van Impe seem profoundly certain that they are correct in their beliefs about the End Times, those beliefs center on a conviction about the final unknowability of God's divine plan by humans. Because certain truth is only in the biblical texts, any interpretation (no matter how powerfully authorized) is always open to error. Lindsey conveys this idea in his introduction to *The Late Great Planet Earth*, stating: "I am attempting to step aside and let the prophets speak. The readers are given the freedom to accept or reject my conclusions" (Lindsey and Carlson 1970, 6). With this rejection of any final human authority, Lindsey places flexibility at the core of ritual deliberation.

The individuals I found using private email lists to communicate about vernacular Christian fundamentalism in 1994 had already developed the norms of ritual deliberation. As we have seen, this practice allowed them to express their shared ideology while insulating it from those who might call their beliefs into question. Unlike deliberation in its usual sense, this deliberation functioned to create the discursive space of their ekklesia. Here, individuals must be engaged in some kind of actual communication in order to inhabit a given network space. As new people attempt to join the deliberation, the majority can regulate who is allowed to participate and thus inhabit their online discursive spaces. As ritual deliberation emerged on email lists, individuals could rely on topical community formation based on End Times competence to exert social control over their new movement. Here, ritual deliberation effectively performed the regulation of this space without any centralized authority or leadership.

Scholars have long recognized that communities that use traditional ritualized action (like home blessings or groundbreaking ceremonies) can assimilate a specific geographic location into the symbolic space imagined by a community. When religious historian and philosopher Mircea Eliade famously articulated his conception of "ritual construction," he certainly was not looking forward to the purely discursive spaces constructed through network communication. Nonetheless, his idea points us toward the fundamentally ritual function of deliberating about the End Times online.

Religious studies scholar Catherine Bell suggests that rituals exhibit the basic characteristics of "public assembly, the repetition of gestures already considered 'ritual tradition' by a community, and the invocation of divine beings" (1997, 166). Even if we treat online locations as real-world places, online ritual deliberation is not a normal sort of ceremonial "public assembly." More central to all ritual, however, is that individuals must "do something in such as a way that the doing itself gives the acts a special or privileged status" (Bell 1997, 166). Ritual deliberation enjoys precisely this elevated position of "privileged status" because it has no hope of actually ending. It does not seek conclusion, but rather repetitious action. Elevating an everyday activity through repetition is, in fact, a hallmark of ritual.

As ritual theorist Jonathan Smith describes it:

> Ritual is a means of performing the way things ought to be in conscious tension to the way things are. Ritual relies for its power on the fact that it is concerned with quite ordinary activities placed within an extraordinary setting, that what it describes and displays is, in principle, possible for every occurrence of these acts. But it also relies for its power on the perceived fact that, in actuality, such possibilities cannot be realized. (Smith 1987, 109)

Smith develops his idea from the work of the famous anthropologist Claude Lévi-Strauss. Lévi-Strauss describes the power of ritual as emerging from the repetition of "infinite distinctions." While making distinctions is an ordinary behavior in deliberation and elsewhere, ritual distinction ascribes "discriminatory values to the slightest shade of difference. It has no concern for the general, but on the contrary goes into detail about the varieties and sub-varieties in all the taxonomic categories" (1981, 672). Ritual deliberation proceeds in precisely this fashion. It enables individuals to continually locate the minute details of biblical writings in everyday news events. However, it seeks no "general" conclusion. Instead, it ritually constructs the movement's virtual space.

In 1994, new information presented new opportunities to engage in ritual deliberation. Each new bit of data was hashed over for a while to decide on its relative fit to the End Times narrative, but it would never be possible to make any final decision because the initial terms of the discourse assumed that humans could not know for sure when God would initiate the apocalypse. As one respondent put it, "it's just too complex" (Stephen 1994). There were infinite possible facts to be located and discussed and no goal of a final decision. The End was near, but it had not come; only God knew the hour of its coming.

This certain unknowability of God's divine plan is also rooted in a literal understanding of biblical texts. Maybe the most famous passage expressing this idea is from the Gospel of Mathew: "Take ye heed, watch and pray: for ye know not when the time is" (Mathew 24:36). Any facts about the End Times beyond the truth of the Bible and the certain unknowability of that exact truth are strictly in the realm of possibility. This attitude keeps the end of times near, but never too near. As a result of this belief system, the community seems able to deliberate about End Times issues ceaselessly.

As did Marilyn above, individual adherents could even take strong positions and make concrete predictions. When they turned out to be wrong, that only meant that the individual had made an error in interpretation. It did not threaten the truth of a literal reading of the Bible. Following this self-sealing logic, believers imagined that since humans are inherently flawed compared to the divine, such errors only serve to prove the truth of the power of God to know something beyond any typical human reckoning. As a result, ritual deliberation gives everyone in the ekklesia license to speculate as widely as they desire so long as they do not call their own End Times competence into question by contradicting the core beliefs of the ideology.

The issues deployed in this deliberation are flexible because the End Times narrative itself exhibits a profound "modularity," to use Lev Manovich's famous term. This modularity generates the discursive space necessary for ritualized deliberation by creating general frameworks that can then be individualized through the replacement of interchangeable component parts or "mods" (2001). The vague but suggestive biblical texts mixed with the belief in literalism, a lack of institutions, modularity of the narrative, and the chance for individuals to communicate in the multilateral environment of the early Internet resulted in a huge volume of deliberation about "new theories" for interpreting specific elements of the End Times narrative.

In a typical example of how the modularity fueled ritual deliberation, one man covered a wide array of prophetic issues with his probing theories. On one occasion, he emailed a 537-word exposition of Revelation 8:10–11. It serves as a good example of the modular quality of this discourse:

> Here's my new theory on REV 8:10,11, tell me what you think: 10 star, blazing like a torch falls from sky=nuclear melt down (The fissile material burns its way down through the reactor into the ground below) falls on 1/3 of rivers & on springs=fissile core contaminates the ground water and the rivers and streams become radioactive. 11 The name of the star is "Wormwood" (Bitterness)=the Russian Bible uses the Russian word for "wormwood"— "Chernobyl" (now a world famous Russian word). Many people died from the waters which had become bitter=many people have died from the waters which had become radioactive. By uncanny "coincidence" the ground underneath the reactor contains the bones of many massacred Jews from WW2.——————————————
>
> All comments are welcome. (quoted in Howard 1997, 307)

These claims had little or no effect on the validity of the definitive beliefs underlying the narrative. Instead, they presented a very specific interpretation of how Chernobyl might be a sign of the coming End Times which hinges on the translation of "Chernobyl" to the English "wormwood" from Revelation 8: 11. This email also contains examples of typical cues to deliberation in phrases like: "tell me what you think" and "all comments are welcome."

Emphasizing these cues instead of authoritative conclusions in this way, even those who would be in positions to express personal authority were often treated much the same as everyone else in the movement. For example, one respondent suggested that Jack Van Impe was "a good guy. But is he human? Is he capable of error? Can he error by malicious intent? I do not believe he has a mean bone in his body. But, yes, he can be wrong" (quoted in Howard 1997, 307). Though Van Impe was a leading thinker in the movement, his ideas were considered only one possible interpretation of biblical prophecy.

Although Van Impe, Lindsey, LaHaye, and other media evangelists have exerted a large influence through their establishment and dissemination of the core narrative and definitive beliefs of the movement, their statements hold no divine authority. As a result, they can offer no institutionally authoritative interpretations. Instead, they only popularized a narrative structure into which various individuals' mods could be placed. The variability of these mods keeps the deliberation vigorous, and the community specifically values that vigor. One respondent summed up the sentiment quite well when he asked about the European Union as the source for the coming Antichrist: "could this be the dread beast? could this be a compact from the pit of hell? Could all Frenchmen love wine? I see a definite possibility that maybe it might. Pretty noncommittal huh?" (quoted in Howard 1997, 308).

In 1994 and 1995, these individuals spent a huge amount of time searching for facts with which to create and then exchange their personalized End Times mods. In 1994, for example, news reports about the unification of Europe provided a constant source of information for individuals involved in online discourse about the End Times because of the association between the EU and the "New Roman Empire." Because Europe is roughly geographically located where the Roman Empire of biblical times was, the End Times prophetic narrative suggests that references in the Bible to "Rome" are really references to the European Union.

Despite its seemingly not-so-literal quality, this equation between ancient Rome and modern Europe is one of the primary interpretive moves used by those in the movement to make the Book of Revelation relevant in the contemporary world. In 1994 and 1995, the UN, EU, and various economic treaties like GATT or the General Agreement on Tariffs and Trade, were in the news regularly. At the same time, the popularity of conspiracy theories in the 1990s had increased the volume of data available on the subject (Fenster 2008). In addition, the very form of the Internet and its tendencies toward encouraging access to a wide range of new data sources gave everyday Internet users an ever-widening field to mine for new information about the EU, UN, GATT, and so on (Barkun 2003, 13).

In a typical though uncommonly blunt example of this interest in conspiracy theory, one man noted: "it turns out that since about 1933, things have been controlled not by who we imagine to be in control. I am talking about the CFR, Trilateral Commission, the World Bank, the UN, and all that bunch. As you can probably tell, I have read some conspiracy books" (quoted in Howard 1997, 308).

Often respondents displayed their interest in conspiracy theory in references to obscure documents to which they had gained access through an online archive or email exchange. In another typical example, a man noted: "Oh boy, it's really coming! Did you realize that in May a dangerous, historic precedent was set when United States military forces were put under UN command, under a Turkish commander? Are you familiar with State Department Document 7277, a long-standing official US government policy program calling for the transfer of all US military forces to the UN?" (quoted in Howard 1997, 308).

The evidence of access to obscure documents or rumors of such documents often took the form of specific references to governmental sources interspersed with cues to deliberation like "what do you think" and "all comments welcomed." With the access provided by the new Internet technologies, state and federal laws and many proceedings, not to mention other conspiracy theorists, had all become easy targets for probing keyboards.

Another very common issue discussed at that time was the so-called "New Age Movement," or "NAM," as some respondents referred to it. The NAM issue could turn the discussion toward an unsettling intolerance. This issue had long been a focus of many mass media sources for End Times ideas, including Lindsey's *Satan Is Alive and Well on Planet Earth* and Van Impe's *New Age Spirits from the Underworld*. Based on the general End Times narrative, many individuals expressed the belief that the Antichrist would be a political leader who would set him- or herself up as a divine figure and be worshiped as a sort of New Age goddess or god. That was not a debatable issue for those who were conversant with End Times discourse because it is a core part of the narrative. However, the issue could still generate ritual deliberation based on the belief that no one knows for sure who the Antichrist would be.

Because this divinely evil political leader was thought to be coming from the "New Roman Empire," participants in the movement at that time tended to look toward Europe for signs of who, when, and where this leader would turn up. Every End Times narrative describes the persecution of Christians by mainstream society and government because that is central to the Book of Revelation. In the End Times narrative, a European leader gains access to world authority, including that of the United States, through control of the UN. In the final days, Christians must bow down to the political leader/Antichrist during the period of "the Tribulation."

Unfortunately, this scenario can instill a deep sense of fear in End Times deliberation. As Catherine Wessinger has noted, the "stark perspective of 'good versus evil,' 'us versus them,' heightens the possibility that group members will conclude they are being persecuted" (2000a, 271). Fear of the New Age often becomes infused with fear of personal oppression occurring as a result of the New Roman Empire mapped onto the European Union's predicted rise to world domination. For many believers in 1994 and still today, the New Age belief is actually the product of the ancient demonic plan for world domination during the End Times. As one woman described it: "the New Age is a misnomer from the get go. If you look carefully at crystallography, meditation, etc. etc. etc.—they are quite obviously Stolen Pagan beliefs and practices. It should be called OLD AGE STUFF" (quoted in Howard 1997, 310). The linkage between the fears of being persecuted, the Antichrist, and the European Union feeds the generally dualistic worldview in the movement and can take the form of real hostility toward non-Christian ideas about the divine.

The individuals involved in this discourse in 1994 and 1995 clearly saw the New Age as the mechanism that the Antichrist would use to gain earthly divinity. First, the Antichrist would appear as a human prophet or messiah. Then, three and a half years into the Tribulation, Satan would incarnate in the body of the messianic leader. In the Book of Revelation, this leader is said to come to power in Rome. As a result, the updated interpretation was typically that this would be of a leader of the united Europe.

As I shall explore in more detail in chapter 6, some individuals imagined that a "One World Government" would outlaw Christianity and literally persecute Christians. For believers, this meant that New Age belief was not just wrong; it would be one of the mechanisms that would pose very real danger to their physical well-being. When this kind of belief was expressed in terms of outright hostility to non-Christian beliefs, the filtering mechanisms of private email lists or other Internet media resulted in hostile attitudes toward those who might offer counterevidence because alternate voices that might contradict or resist such claims were not present. As individuals moved first onto the Worldwide Web and then participatory media after the dawn of the new millennium, this problem would continue to persist in the movement.

In the newsgroup and private email End Times discourse of the early 1990s, individuals in small and very specific webs of communication adapted and interpreted both the vernacular biblical texts and current news events, recasting them in terms of their shared beliefs. Through their online communication, individuals created, maintained, and re-created an ideology that constantly distilled and reintroduced the same basic narrative. In this way, a diversity of personal interpretation could be tolerated as long as it fit into the overall form that was held to be a literal interpretation of the divine text of the Bible.

The flexibility of this modular discourse is demonstrated in a final example that begins with the following cue to deliberation: "who is The Antichrist? Nobody knows. But there is very strong evidence of a person named Maitreya." Based on information he accessed through a database at a newspaper site in the Netherlands, this individual wrote:

The Netherlands—A motorist picked up a hitchhiker along the motor way. The hitchhiker announced that Christ would return soon, then disappeared. The motorist was so shaken by the experience that he parked his car on the hard shoulder to recover from the shock. He was approached by some traffic policemen to whom he told the story. They replied: "You are the eighth motorist today who has told us this. [March 1991]." (quoted in Howard 1997, 313)

He went on to explain: "You see, Maitreya claims explicitly to be 'a Christ' in the line of Buddha and Jesus, it is no surprise that he is manifesting in the Netherlands" (quoted in Howard 1997, 313).

In this email communication, four distinct and disparate sources are combined with the End Times narrative in a modular fashion. A common contemporary legend reported in a newspaper is interpreted from an End Times perspective and morphed into a prominent non-Christian spiritual figure. The mere availability of newspaper data in the Netherlands made possible by the Internet had transfigured the Vanishing Hitchhiker legend into a demonic false prophet of the New Age—at least for one man in California—who was not really sure about Maitreya being the Antichrist anyway.

This discursive morphing is possible only as a product of the certainty that the "Antichrist" will appear in the first place. The poster cued his audience to wonder who the Antichrist would be, not whether there would be an Antichrist. In fact, his very claim that "nobody knows" who the Antichrist will be presupposed an audience who assumed that there will be, at some point, an Antichrist. At the same time, invoking the shared value that only God knows for sure who the Antichrist will be establishes his competence in End Times deliberation. Because a literal interpretation of the Bible is a definitive belief of the movement, his invitation to deliberate about the "Antichrist" was itself a ritual enactment of membership in the ekklesia.

During this first period of vernacular Christian fundamentalism's emergence on the Internet, from 1981 to 1994 the conservative evangelical Christians discussing the End Times were largely excluded from the Usenet medium because of heavy resistance from the more liberal Christian audience using network communication technologies at that time. As a result, it was not until 1995 that a new newsgroup was formed specifically for End Times discourse. With that technology, conservatives transcended their tiny email list communities to enact a virtual ekklesia based on their shared ideology, and this made possible the discursive norms of topical community formation based on a shared competence in End Times discourse developed in private email lists before 1995.

Enter the Worldwide Web

Though it would continue between individuals who located each other on the Worldwide Web, the establishment of the alt.bible.prophecy newsgroup in 1995 ended the high period of End Times email discourse. Newsgroup discourse, however, was probably never the dominant network medium for vernacular fundamentalism. By the time the numbers of newsgroup users had grown large enough to support a group dedicated to the End Times, a new network medium was growing far faster. The introduction of the first publicly available Worldwide Web browser in 1992 started the mass rush of mainstream North Americans onto the Internet. With the Web, everyday individuals were first offered an easy-to-use graphic interface for network communication. The number of people involved in vernacular fundamentalism online exploded. As it did, individuals went online using Web-based media and Usenet slipped into relative obscurity.

By 1995, the scene for enacting the virtual ekklesia of the movement shifted out of the Usenet and onto the Worldwide Web. However, topical community formation was still quite possible on the Web because keyword search engines like Lycos, Yahoo, and Google gave individuals who already knew the terms associated with the movement the ability to access an obscure but publicly accessible network of linked Web sites including those of Marilyn Agee, Lambert Dolphin, and many others. The Websites of this time were far more static than they are today, and as a result they presented some challenges for those seeking places to engage in ritual deliberation, as we shall see below. Still, the ethos of individualism that allowed users to access a huge volume of data based on their already held interests was embedded in the Worldwide Web.

Claiming to have invented the term "hypertext," the famous computer theorist Theodor Nelson at least helped popularize the idea in the early 1970s. Invoking the image of a "branching informational system" in his small-scale 1974 publication titled *Computer Lib: You Can and Must Understand Computers Now,* Nelson gave voice to the same community of antiestablishment hippy/hackers who had built and used the Usenet. These people saw a linkage between individual information access and populist power (Abbate 1999, 214). For Nelson, using "hypermedia" instead of hierarchical organization links information in more intuitive ways and encourages an egalitarian access that gives the power to everyday individuals instead of powerful actors in institutions (Nelson 1974, DM44[CL85]; Howard 2008a).

In 1990, another counterculturally minded computer engineer named Tim Berners-Lee made the idea of "hypermedia" a reality by developing a functioning hypertext system for the European nuclear agency called CERN. Berners-Lee called his invention "Hypertext Markup Language," or "HTML." Using this simple computer language, individuals could share formatted text, graphics, and other media in a linking web of information. Like Nelson, Berners-Lee wanted to keep HTML very simple so it could be easily learned and deployed by anyone (Turner 2006, 213ff). Then, in 1991, the first HTML browser was given away to the public and Worldwide Web was born (CERN 2000; World Wide Web Consortium 2000).

At that time, Internet users were mostly government and university researchers who had access to ARPAnet. The earliest Web users were computer engineers who built Web pages for institutions on these networks. Seeing them as a means to empower individuals, however, these users also built personal pages. Despite its intended ease of use, two main factors inhibited the initial expansion of the hobbyist or amateur use of the Web to a public beyond these computer engineers. First, although HTML was relatively easy to use, it still required some investment of time for most people to gain even minimal proficiency in its use. As a result, many people just did not take the time to master it. Second, it was illegal to use the Internet for commercial purposes. As a result, there was no money to hire people to build sites or train people as professional site builders beyond that available to researchers under grants.

All that changed in June 1992, when the "Boucher Bill" offered an amendment to the National Science Foundation Act. This amendment changed the meaning of "fair use" for NSF projects, so that the NSF-funded software that made the Internet function (called "TCP/IP") could be put to commercial use (Segaller 1998, 298ff). With the sudden influx of commerce online, the popularity of the Web medium exploded. Commercial interests began to place pressure on the simple but functional capabilities of HTML, and a new kind of Web site began to emerge (Lessig 2002; Rheingold 1992, 2000, and 2001). Commercial sites began to exhibit far more complex HTML coding.

Rapidly, the number of these commercial sites dwarfed the simpler non-commercial Web sites. The Web went from fewer than one hundred Web sites in 1992 to over ten thousand in January 1995. However, the new population of Web users had significantly fewer computer skills than did the early Web community. In 1994, only 11 percent of Worldwide Web users reported having been involved in computer programming for three years or less (GVU 2001a). One year later, in 1995, this number jumped to 35.5 percent. The biggest increase was in those with no high-level computer experience at all; that number leaped up from nearly none to 16.78 percent (GVU 2001b, 2001c, and 2001d). Instead of a network of hobbyists both creating and consuming Web content, the Web that emerged had a few (typically institutional) producers with many everyday consumers for their products.

This split between content producers and consumers created new enclaves of amateur Web content. In the mid-1990s, corporations, government, universities, and other powerful institutions hired teams of computer engineers to create institutional Web sites. Because these institutional Web sites were the product of teams of professional builders, they exhibited more complicated features than hobbyist pages did.

Quickly, strategies evolved for Web designers to make their sites prominent on the relevant webs of linked sites. Soon, it was very easy to find sites built by corporations, schools, and (later) even powerful religious institutions. However, it was not so easy to find the huge web of linked amateur sites. To do that, individuals had to know which key terms to search for. Because only a few evangelical media institutions specifically supported the vernacular ideology of Christian fundamentalism (*Jack Van Impe Ministries* being one of the first and most well-known online), the web of communication emerging from vernacular fundamentalism could only be discovered by a keyword search of "End Times" in a search engine. This web was vernacular in the sense that it was almost exclusively built and maintained by amateur evangelists working in HTML as a hobby.

Because these individuals had little expertise in HTML and often even fewer resources to devote to their Web pages, their sites looked fundamentally different from the rapidly evolving institutional sites that now dominated the attention of online media consumers (Howard 2005d). Because they looked different, institutional sites overshadowed the amateur sites. As a result this vernacular web of sites was pushed into obscurity by the rapidly evolving network. While many computer activists/hackers lamented the failed vision of an egalitarian online network, those who were interested in ritual deliberation about the End Times were well served. This vernacular web of Web sites offered them the chance to build network locations, locate other like-minded individuals, and engage in email or other online media without having to risk significant exposure to people who might offer resistance to their claims. This sort of enclave could thrive in the emerging web of communication because its members engaged in topical community formation.

At the same time, however, the Worldwide Web technology encouraged more individual and authoritative expression than it did the communal deliberative expression that characterized email lists and newsgroups. As a result, these linked Web sites forced people to negotiate between the individual authority encouraged by the medium and the deliberation necessary to constitute the ekklesia. Spurred by the huge interest in the approach of the new millennium during the late 1990s, the explosive growth in Web pages associated with the movement can be considered the period of the "millennial Web." While ultimately Marilyn Agee's "Pro and Con" Web site would prefigure the ways the movement would powerfully deploy the participatory media of a decade later, the millennial Web was characterized by a wide diversity of individuals experimenting with ways to enact their virtual ekklesia in an Internet medium more static than those that had come before.

4

The Millennial Web, 1996 to 2000

The Summer of 1999

After observing the emergence of the virtual ekklesia since 1994, I was able to meet many of my long-term respondents face-to-face during a series of interviews starting in the summer of 1999. At that time, End Times discourse was in full swing on the Worldwide Web. Since 1995, a rush of commercial activity fueled both a wave of new Internet users and the emergence of the "dot.com" economy. This period of rapid economic expansion was an optimistic and exciting time for those involved in building what many were calling the "electronic frontier" (Turner 2006; Warnick 2002, 19–69). In the late summer of 1999, the crash of the technology economy was lurking a year in the future. Just over a year beyond that, the terrorist attacks of 2001 would throw the problems of twenty-first century globalization into sharp relief.

During the summer of 1999, however, the dominant news was the approach of the year 2000. The mainstream news media were in a frenzy of expectation, a sort of "millennial fever" (Brasher 2001a). At the time, most of my respondents deliberating about the End Times no longer considered 2000 a significant date because there had been no acceleration in the appearance of the expected End Times events. Still, I was traveling the country to conduct interviews with as many of them as possible while the mass media kept the new millennium fresh in all our minds. Sometimes meeting for lunch, often stopping at their places of work, and even sharing dinner in their homes, I met their children and their dogs, saw their computers, and got a real sense of each of these otherwise only virtual online personas.

I had already done interviews as far as south Florida, up into North Carolina, and soon I would travel out into the mountain states of the West. In August, however, with the fall closing in, I made the five hundred and fifty-mile drive from where I was living in Oregon to the heart of Silicon Valley. There, in a suburb newly gentrified by the technology economy and not far from Stanford University, I first met my long-time respondents "Cheryl" and "Ernie." I had found their Web site by following a link from another: the *Watcher Website*. I had found the Watcher Website, also built by a Christian couple, when I followed a link to it from Lambert Dolphin's *Lambert's Library*. Cheryl and Ernie were part of the same vernacular web as Lambert and Marilyn.

Of the hundreds of individuals I had met online, I was particularly interested in meeting this couple face-to-face. In email, it seemed like we had connected immediately. When I met them in person, they not only invited me into their home and discussed their most personal religious views, but they insisted on taking me out to dinner afterward. The ease I felt between the three of us was no mystery. They had been Baptists and I was raised in Presbyterianism. All three of us grew up in traditional Protestant families. Like me, they had both struggled with these beliefs as children or young adults. Unlike me, however, both Cheryl and Ernie had experienced intense "spiritual rebirths" that led them to the ideology of Christian fundamentalism.

The implications of this distinct difference between Cheryl, Ernie, and me would be brought home at the end of our interview when I asked them if traditional American Indian rituals had any hope of contacting the divine. In response to this question, they both (without hesitation) affirmed that such rituals certainly did not, and that people who do not accept Christ are doomed to eternal separation from the divine. As with Marilyn's response to the same question, their categorical rejection of the possibility that there are multiple ways to access the sacred suggested a level of certainty I do not have, and that certainty lent their communication a powerful authority.

At the outset of our interview, Ernie chatted about types of computer monitors and the development of the Worldwide Web. He was a computer engineer by profession and quite at home in the world of technological professionals. Afterward, we approached the more difficult topics of Christian belief and faith.

I had set out to interview this particular couple because their Web site was one of the oldest evangelical lay ministries available on the Web at that time. Ernie had been using Internet technologies since the early 1980s. As a computer engineer, he worked for a company that designed and sold quality control equipment used in the manufacture of silicon chips. This job, and the surge of technology production in the 1990s, had brought Cheryl and him a relatively high degree of affluence. In the years just before the technology economy crash, Ernie could afford to take an indefinite leave of absence from his job and spent a year traveling in Asia and Europe with Cheryl. This couple was not worried about the approach of the year 2000. Instead, they enjoyed their affluence with a certainty that whenever the End Times did arrive, they would be welcomed into the Kingdom of Heaven by their savior.

Linked to both Marilyn and Lambert, Cheryl and Ernie's site was pulled into the ekklesia in a way that can be discerned by tracing a path of links between sites starting from theirs in 1999. I selected this path of links from an overall sample of a hundred and twenty Web sites which I located by searching for the term "End Times" in a major search engine and which I periodically archived in 1999, 2000, and 2001. These particular sites demonstrate the wide variety of topics that were being assimilated into the virtual ekklesia at that time. For some people, like Marilyn Agee, discussing the End Times was an all-consuming passion. For others, like Ernie and Cheryl, it was a source of ambivalence. Still, the shared interest in the End Times reached across geography and denominations to expand the movement in the Worldwide Web. However, tracing this path of links and interviewing its Web site builders revealed that this medium was not as well suited for a virtual ekklesia as were the earlier email lists and newsgroups or the participatory media that would come later.

The Worldwide Web of the late 1990s made it easy for people to put their ideas online, but it was harder to engage in deliberation. This was because there were few Web-based mechanisms amateur users could deploy to collect and post public comments from their audiences. It was easy, however, to make links from one's own Web pages to the pages of other individuals. As a result, a new emphasis emerged on building a web of links between the sites of believers.

Looking closely at these Web sites, it became clear to me that those exhibiting more deliberative communication generally had more incoming links from other sites. Those that engaged in more authoritative communication tended to be less linked. In this period, as in the email lists and newsgroups before, the movement valued communication that fostered a sense of community, and these links helped do that. Because individual expression was better suited to the Internet technologies of the year 2000, however, the tendency toward personal authority associated with the movement's emphasis on revelatory experience also became more prevalent.

Strongly authoritative communication does not encourage any response, which inhibits deliberation. Individuals must offer dissenting or at least different views to generate deliberation. When everyone is authorized by personal experiences with the divine, there is little motive to deliberate. Nonetheless, the members of the movement needed to feel engaged with their virtual community in order to gain the sense of fellowship they valued. In more interactive media, this could occur through ritual deliberation. During the early period of the Worldwide Web, however, each site builder had to negotiate this tension in a medium ill-suited to interactive communication. Among a diversity of approaches to the problem, one familiar site in particular demonstrates a form of communication that managed to create a very effective balance.

Despite her own powerful sense of personal authority, Marilyn Agee's *Bible Prophecy Corner* was one of the most well-connected sites in the movement. She demonstrated how personal authority could be managed to generate a sense of fellowship for both her and her audience. Before the rise of new software that would allow the Worldwide Web to easily integrate user-produced content into existing Web pages, Agee created her own sort of proto-blog using simple HTML computer coding. After 2001, the form of Marilyn's Web site suggested it would become the most common sort of site used for ritual deliberation in the movement.

Piercing Beyond the Characters on a Screen

Lucky to have caught them at home, I traveled to Silicon Valley with a simple question for Cheryl and Ernie. Why had they decided to put their amateur "Bible Study" on the Web in 1993? As many respondents who went on the early Worldwide Web reported, they had done it rather innocently and almost accidentally. Once they had put it up, they encountered a powerful sense of koinonia that many of the individuals in the movement reported. In my interviews, Cheryl and Ernie gave the most detailed account of this kind of introduction to the power of online fellowship.

While working in the computer industry in Dallas, Texas, Cheryl and Ernie both felt dissatisfied with their face-to-face church communities. The couple felt that their experiences with institutional evangelical churches were not fully serving their spiritual needs because the church doctrines often simplified difficult questions into "legalistic" answers and failed to connect scripture to their daily lives (Cheryl and Ernie 1999c). In an effort to correct this perceived lack, Ernie and Cheryl began to invite their Christian friends over to their home to read and discuss the Bible over simple dinners. Soon this Saturday night activity became something of a tradition. As Ernie described it: "We had a sense during that time that we had gotten swept into or caught up in something. I had been a Christian at that point for thirteen years and gone to church and had a little bit of a sense of knowing God" (1999c). However, this informal group of friends gave Cheryl and Ernie a renewed sense of spiritual presence.

Through their meetings, they felt they began to "know" God in a far more intimate and fulfilling way. Seldom bringing any particular topic to their meetings, they found that each evening the combination of individuals would, under the guidance of the Holy Spirit, give rise to important insights into biblical verses. Often friends-of-friends or acquaintances traveling through town would unexpectedly show up at these meetings with specific problems or ideas that yielded new insights. After a while, Ernie began to carefully document the informal group discussions. Soon he was writing them up and filing them away, often handing them around to other participants after the meeting and cowriting full discussions of the topics that had emerged.

In 1993, however, after a year or more of these meetings, Ernie's job took the couple to San Jose, California. The Worldwide Web was exploding as a popular medium at that time, and it dawned on him that he could share the Bible studies with his friends both in Texas and California via a Web site.

> When we wrote those studies—given what we have told you—we had in mind that there would be maybe fifteen people who would come; and it was for them. We had absolutely no idea of what I have just told you . . . that they would get spread around later. Ya know; read by thousands of people a day on the Internet. [Laughs] It just seemed kinda funny. The limit of what we were doing was simply to serve the brothers and sisters in Christ that we knew. (1999c)

Other respondents told similar stories. Amateur Web site builders were inspired to take otherwise personal or small-group documents and offer them to friends or acquaintances in a convenient way. After initially placing them on the Web, several respondents, including Ernie, Cheryl, Marilyn, and Lambert, described being pleasantly surprised at a sudden influx of email. Inspired by the correspondence generated by their new Web presence, the spiritual lack they felt in their church institutions abated.

> Ernie: "We find a life and fellowship on the Internet that is embarrassing to admit! Who would have thought? Who would have believed it? [. . . that] the [Holy] Spirit is able to pierce through beyond mere characters floating on a screen." (Cheryl and Ernie 1999b)

Not only did Ernie and Cheryl suddenly start receiving inspiring emails from like-minded Christians, but they were also brought into a rapidly expanding vernacular web of individuals engaged in the movement on the Worldwide Web.

Back in 1994, I found only twenty-two sites that seemed to be interconnected enough to form a coherent group of Christians exhibiting the definitive traits of vernacular Christian fundamentalism. In 1996, I catalogued over one hundred and fifty fundamentalist Christian Web sites. By 1999, I easily located over five hundred sites and left many more undocumented. The sudden surge in the size of this network was clearly a product of the exploding popularity of the Web at that time.

I first found Cheryl and Ernie's site, *Acts 17:11 Bible Studies,* while I was cataloging the links on a site that I already knew well: *Watcher Website* (Watcher 1999a). A mix of biblical literalism, conspiracy theory, and UFO beliefs, this site was one of the most popular on End Times at the time. In the hundred and twenty-site sample, it had incoming links from the most different external Web sites. On a page articulating their basic belief about the impending approach of the second coming of Christ, the site builders placed a long quote from one of Cheryl and Ernie's studies on the End Times with a link to the page (Watcher 1999d). Despite the fact that Cheryl and Ernie's overall site was not focused on End Times discourse, the *Watcher Website* labeled it on their page: "End Time Bible Study Website." This is a telling detail.

By 1996, Web pages were expanding vernacular Christian fundamentalism as individuals located and created links to information that pertained to issues related to the End Times. During this expansion, the impending dawn of the new millennium became one of the most discussed topics. The builders of the *Watcher Website* were caught up in this fervor when they made their Web link to Cheryl and Ernie's site. At that time, following a link on a known site to discover a new site was typically the way people expanded their vernacular web. New sites seemed to appear everyday. As they did, their builders created Web pages of links to sites with shared interests.

By the time I interviewed Cheryl and Ernie in 1999, however, the millennial fervor was already dying down. The predictions and worries about a "Y2K" computer bug that would bring financial and government institutions to a standstill had largely fallen aside. Still, the vernacular web based on the End Times was already well established.

Looking at access logs for Ernie and Cheryl's Web site at that time, it was clear that there were hundreds of individuals looking at their site every day. Further, it was clear that many sites I was familiar with as well as some of the more institutional church-sponsored Web sites had well-worn links to their pages. Cheryl and Ernie's most linked pages were those that dealt with ideas often taken up in the ritual deliberation on the newsgroups and email lists:

a page on New Age "witchcraft," one on the End Times more generally, and one addressing the issue of conspiracy theories.

When I asked Ernie how he felt about the interest in the approaching millennium, he stated simply: "it's part of the Christian message." Even though these were his most popular pages, Ernie no longer paid much attention to people who were focusing on the End Times. He said: "Most eschatological teaching is shameful! Embarrassing. All these ideas distract and bring shame to the cause and name of Christ." Cheryl, at first quiet during this part of the interview, spoke up. She stated that she was still interested in the topic and discussed it with her friends. Cheryl engaged in ritual deliberation both online and off. A brief discussion ensued between them. Then Ernie authoritatively asserted his view of the End Times by expanding on why he considered the topic "shameful":

> We should be like virgins waiting to be consummated with our husbands! So we shouldn't be distracted. If our husband comes and we have our room all coated with charts about when he's gonna come, ya know, I don't think he's gonna say: 'Way to go!'" It's like . . . He would say: "You have no idea what my coming means. It's *not* to see these charts!" [Laughs] (Cheryl and Ernie 1999c)

Despite Ernie's disdain for an overemphasis on locating exactly when the Second Coming will occur in "charts," his engagement of End Times was precisely the reason hundreds of Web surfers, including myself, had located his and Cheryl's site. The link to it from the *Watcher Website* drew their pages into the virtual ekklesia, and the sense of connection that he got from knowing that others were reading his pages seems to be what Ernie valued most from his Web site.

Just one among many, his site exemplifies how many individuals were communicating in more authoritative ways on the Worldwide Web around the year 2000. During this period, the fellowship the movement valued was weakened because the medium encouraged those who, like Ernie, felt they had a powerful individual authority to put up Web pages which offered little opportunity for audiences to respond. Still needing to garner a sense of fellowship, however, people like Ernie sought to foster a sense that others were engaging their ideas. For Ernie, this sense of engagement came in the form of knowing that others were reading his Web pages. Through this weakened form of fellowship, he felt the Holy Spirit could, as he put it, "pierce through beyond mere characters floating on a screen."

While the Worldwide Web was not conducive to ritual deliberation, it did encourage topical community formation because individuals could simply "surf" the Web based on their topical interests. To facilitate this surfing, they used search engines, "Web rings" of connected sites, and the links from the sites they had already found to find new sites engaging the interests of the movement. As these individuals increased the links between their sites, they expanded their ekklesia. As the ekklesia grew, they increased their sense of fellowship by imagining fellow believers reading their Web pages.

While many also seem to have engaged in deliberation with each other through email, the examples below illustrate that many individuals who felt authoritative enough to put up Web pages were less apt at ritual deliberation. On the Worldwide Web of this period, Web site builders seem to have primarily generated their sense of fellowship by producing authoritative communication, placing it on their Web sites, and then linking it to the pages made by other authoritative individuals in the movement.

Starting with the link I followed from the *Watcher Website* to Cheryl and Ernie's page on the End Times, the following sections in this chapter pick a path of links through this authoritative vernacular web. Reconstructed from the hundred and twenty-site sample, it is a real path that any Web surfer could have taken in 1999. Tracing these links demonstrates the diversity of topics this vernacular web encompassed. Combining them with face-to-face interviews reveals the diverse ways individuals tried to negotiate the tension between expressing their personal authority and experiencing a sense of fellowship. Those who negotiated this tension by exhibiting more deliberative communication were more linked to other sites in the movement.

Dean and Susan's Authoritative Vernacular

Going from the *Watcher Website* to Cheryl and Ernie's End Times Web page, individuals could follow an internal link to Cheryl and Ernie's collection of favorite Web sites. On that page there was a link to a site called *CrossSearch*. Appearing online as early as 1996, *CrossSearch* was an outgrowth of Gospel Films, a media-based Christian ministry founded in 1950. Now called Gospel Communications, the organization's primary Web site was this Christian-oriented search engine that seemed to have been modeled on the early *Yahoo.com* style of collecting lists of sites and placing links to them in topically defined directories (Gospel Communications International 1999). Going to the "prophecy" topic, one would have found: *AlphathroughOmega.com*.

Following that link off *CrossSearch*, the individual would have come to a page with a stark default gray background and no graphic images at all. Built by "Dean" and "Susan," this Web site was the result of Dean's direct communication with God. Dean was an employee of Intel and his wife, Susan, was a homemaker. I interviewed them together over breakfast near the Intel headquarters in Hillsboro, Oregon, on October 5, 1999. Although Dean was a skilled computer technician, he was also adept at casting out demons. Dean presents an important case because his personal revelatory experiences yielded the most radical certainty expressed on the sites in the sample set. As a result of this certainty, Dean's online communication was the most authoritative, encouraged the least deliberation, and was the least connected to the rest of this vernacular web.

God had led Dean to present a fairly typical End Times scenario on his Web site. On the front page, he listed many of the issues associated with the End Times narrative: "End Times Studies," "Doctrinal Errors in the Churches," "Open Letter to Satanists and Occultists," and so on. Through the link "End Times Studies," he had a series of pages that outlined a standard End Times narrative chronology.

These pages included descriptions of the "Tribulation period" where Antichrist takes control of the European Union and persecutes Christians during a massive World War III. In addition to using some standard topics, Dean and Susan used the common argumentative style in which a passage from the Bible is presented and then followed by the correct interpretation that Dean had reached through God's direct guidance. On one such page, Dean quoted Revelation 3:10 at the top. Below it, Dean discussed the "Rapture." It is clear that Dean was on the "Post-Tribulation" side of this End Times discussion. However, his take on the Rapture also indicated that he imagined himself engaged in some deliberation about the End Times. Noting his view was different from many End Times interpretations, Dean did not believe that the Rapture would lift the true believers from the chaos of impending apocalypse. Instead, side-by-side with the sinners, these believers would have to weather the plagues of war and other atrocities (Dean 1999b).

Displaying his ability to at least imagine how others might engage his Web page, Dean told me: "Some people point to this verse [Revelation 3:10] as referring to the Rapturing of the church before the Tribulation" (Dean and Susan 1999). However, Dean exhibited a more authoritative kind of communication when he argued that he was certain a pretribulational Rapture was wrong. He felt that he knew that Christians, alongside non-Christians, would have to endure the Tribulation. When Dean acknowledged to me that this view was different from that of most others who studied the End Times, he made it clear that he was not interested in exploring the possibility that he might be wrong because his knowledge was the result of direct experience with God.

His authoritative attitude also manifested itself on his Web site. A good example is when he described the world in stark terms of right and wrong:

This [is] not a game! Either you are for Jesus, or you are against Him. There is no middle ground. As in any war, you must choose sides. Adam sold all of us to Satan in the Garden of Eden through his disobedience. And if there had been any other choice in the matter, Jesus would not have had to pay the hideous price He did on the cross. The choice is yours. If you choose not to accept Jesus as Lord and Master of your life, you have already chosen to make Satan your master. (Dean 1999e)

For Dean, it was quite simple. Either "you are for Jesus" or "you have already chosen to make Satan your master."

On another page, it was clear that Dean and Susan were also interested in the topic of "spiritual warfare" (Dean 1999d). They both had a long relationship with demons. Dean showed me his "Warlock" tattoo as proof he once was "into the occult." In fact, he was so deeply involved that he felt he had become possessed by a demonic spirit. This occurred before Dean and Susan met and while he was in the navy. His personality changed. He became distant and emotionless, and he felt that he had gained minor supernatural powers: mind reading, seeing the future, and partial control of the weather. Because of these powers, he stated that he had quite a reputation aboard ship (Dean and Susan 1999).

One night, having trouble sleeping, Dean went to a part of the living quarters where there was enough light to read. There, he met another sailor.

He saw my tattoo, and he asked me about it. He says: 'Warlock?' He says: 'So you're the guy I've heard so much about!' I looked at him a second and said, "OK." He says: "Well, how do you think you can do the things you do?" I knew the truth but I wasn't gonna tell him. So I said I was using my mind to control a greater outside force. He says: "Well. I'm a Christian." And I knew it. I could feel it. It's . . . it's really weird 'cos people from other religions would come up and try to convert me and I would just laugh at them and walk away. But when there's a true Christian, I could feel it! Without them even saying anything. And he looked at me and he says:

"God's given me the ability to tell when a person's possessed." He looked at me, and something shrank into a cold hard knot in my chest and started moving around like it was trying to hide. And I . . . I just totally flipped out and took off! But it got me thinking about what I was doing, and such like 'at. And that was when God told me. He said: "Now. Decide who you want to follow." And he has since told me if I was to continue to follow Satan, I would be dead. (Dean and Susan 1999)

Both Dean and Susan had been subject to earthly manifestations of demon attacks in the forms commonly found in European and American folk traditions (Ellis 2000; Howard 2009a). This included the direct perceptions of fog, senses of presence, temperature drops, and other sensory phenomena. Their belief in demons was based on these personal experiences. God too, spoke directly to Dean when He said: "Decide who you want to follow." Dean also accepted the direct experience of God acting in the lives of others. This was clear from his acceptance that a fellow sailor had been "given the ability to tell when a person is possessed" by God.

When I talked to them in 1999, Dean and Susan felt that they had become the objects of demonic assault as a result of Dean's turning away from the powers of Satan years before. From this wealth of direct personal experience, they decided to put up a Web site to share their experience and advice with others. As part of this advice, Dean and Susan offered a typical scenario for the End Times on the site. Dean felt his very words, as he wrote them for the Web, were directed by a special personal relationship with God. He was certain that this relationship existed because of his personal experiences of God, angels, and demonic forces. One of the ways God communicated with Dean was through direct personal revelation. Dean recounted this experience on his Web page to further establish his personal authority. He told how, after a night of intense dreaming:

I got down on my knees and gave my life back to Him. And when I did, it felt as if 10,000 tons fell away from my spirit as Jesus Christ cleansed me of my sins and restored me again as a son of the Kingdom. And I'm not ashamed to admit that at 23 years of age I cried, I felt so happy to be released from bondage. (Dean 1999e)

Dean presents an excellent example of an individual heavily relying on personal experience in his appeals to authority both in person and online. Dean was on the further extreme among the hundred and twenty-site sample. For him, there seemed to be no desire to hear back from anyone at all. Instead, the evidence that validated and organized his beliefs seemed completely reliant on his direct experiences of spiritual forces. As a result, Dean's sense of fellowship was limited to his expression of authority to others instead of the interactive communication of deliberation. This rendered the Worldwide Web particularly good for the role he imagined himself playing in the movement.

His desired goals were also reflected in the authoritative form his online expression took. Dean and Susan were not interested in making flashy Web pages, nor did they engage in online discussion. Instead, Dean felt it was his duty to put up the pages and allow others to benefit from the experiences he had gained as a result of his direct interaction with spirits and God. Dean did not engage his audience directly. Because of the certainty he and Susan's experiences yielded, he felt very little need to cultivate deliberation. The Worldwide Web gave Dean the means to express his certainty to others without having to confront any responses at all—or any resistance to his authority such responses might offer. For these reasons, Dean's site represents the extreme of authoritative communication I found in the sample.

Lambert's Deliberative Vernacular

On Dean's entire site, there were only two external links. One was to *Amazon. com* so that some of his recommended books could be purchased. The other was to *eQuip.com*, the Web site of a North Carolina radio evangelist (Christian Research Institute 1999). Primarily a means to sell books and tapes, this evangelist's commercial site had no external links at all. If, however, a Web surfer backed up from Dean's site to *CrossSearch.com*, she or he could find one of the most well-known amateur Christian Web sites at that time: *Peggie's Place*. A self-identifying born-again Christian who was a member of the Assemblies of God in Missouri, Peggie had an extensive collection of links to like-minded Web pages (Peggie 1999). Among these, there was a link to a page on Lambert Dolphin's site about the names of God in the Old and New Testaments (Dolphin 1999e).

On the opposite end of the spectrum from Dean, Lambert's site presents an extreme example of deliberative communication engaged by individuals involved in the movement. Based on its links from other End Times-oriented Web sites as well as the statements of interviewees, his site was extraordinarily well-known (Dolphin 1999c). In the hundred and twenty amateur sites I archived and tracked, Dolphin had the most incoming links overall and the second-greatest number of links from different external sites: forty-nine overall links from twelve different Web sites.

I had been in email contact with Lambert since 1994, but his site was a little bit older than that. I finally managed to interview him face-to-face in early September 1999. At that time, his was one of the largest independent Christian sites on the Web: 69.9 megabytes[1] for some 1,449 files. Although this site was well-known in the community, as I noted above, his actual beliefs place him on the fringes of the movement. In fact, of all the respondents I interviewed, Lambert is the only one to concede that it might be possible for non-Christian spiritual practices to access the divine.

His popularity was certainly due in part to his site being large and having been around for so long. It was also because of his resume—which he placed on his site. It included a long list of credits accumulated from a career of sound and light wave research at Stanford University. Lambert was a retired physicist, and this fact gave power to his online authority (Dolphin 1999a).

The bulk of his material was in a section of the site entitled "Lambert Dolphin's Library." He told me why he first put up the site, in words that echoed the experience of Ernie and Cheryl.

> I started just filing things on my Web site . . . and it became handy to find things there and that motivated me to write a little bit more deliberately for the Web site specifically. So the email comes in and finds what I have to say interesting and worthwhile or it generates comments so I think it is worthwhile. (Dolphin 1999f)

Instead of focusing on the transmission of knowledge, as did Dean and Susan, Lambert considered his Web site "worthwhile" because it "generates comments." The "library" included materials and articles he had collected and developed for use in his lectures, Bible study groups, and Sunday school programs.

Some of the most popular of these materials were eschatological. There were over forty End Times-oriented links to articles and other materials he had written and created for the library. One of these links led to his "time-line" from 1997 (Dolphin 1999d). It presented a fairly standard series of events for the End Times. However, the only date Lambert placed on his time-line of Biblical events was "1997," representing "the present" or the last time he had updated the graph.

Unlike other End Times time-lines Lambert's offered his audience no predictive value, because his understanding of the End Times could offer no date setting nor concrete evidence of who the Antichrist would be, and so forth. In 1999 Lambert reworked his 1997 timeline, making it far more colorful. Although the events listed on the chart were exactly the same as those in the 1997 chart, the central date had been changed to 1999. Lambert demonstrated a deliberative attitude about the exact dates of his End Times scenario when he had no problem updating the chart with a new date. In fact, Lambert had left both charts on his Web site for his audience to compare. Lambert presents the most extreme example of deliberative communication in this sample of sites. Like his fellow adherents, however, he had a deeply experiential basis for his belief in the Christian message.

As we have seen, Lambert, Dean, and Susan had all had similar conversion experiences that included a strong sensation of euphoric joy brought on by prayer and sometimes lasting for days or weeks afterward. For Lambert, this experience played a central role in his spiritual belief system. Lambert described his "rebirth" experience in the following terms: "There was this feeling of being washed, and clean, and guilt going away, and this sense of peace of mind about the future, and hope, and then this new excitement" (Dolphin 1999f). This experience was not like Dean's direct aural or visual contact with the divine. Nor did it offer Lambert any final or direct knowledge from God of anything more than His grace itself.

Instead, Lambert imagined the replicability of experimental trials: "And then I can go compare notes with other people who have had an experience like mine, and does their experience seem similar—and then I asked, 'Is this the real thing?'" When I asked him if he was able to "scientifically" verify his experience, he responded: "Is it verifiable? Not scientifically verifiable, but it is experientially verifiable" (Dolphin 1999f).

Although Lambert had a profound conversion experience, that was in and of itself not the only evidence he relied on to locate the correct knowledge of his religious beliefs. Instead, Lambert went a step further. Having had an experience that led him to Christianity, he engaged other believers to verify his individual judgment that he had experienced rebirth. While there was no questioning the reality of the experience for Lambert, he did take his interpretation of that experience to others in order to validate it as an authentic Christian rebirth.

The comparison of Dean and Susan with Lambert offers the extremes of deliberative and authoritative expression in this virtual ekklesia. Dean and Susan showed very little need for deliberation about their spiritual knowledge because they relied solely on the authority of direct experience. Lambert, though he had a direct experience of the divine, felt he still needed to engage with a community to establish the correct interpretation of that experience. Online, Lambert found value through the ongoing email correspondence his Web site generated, and this correspondence functioned to "experientially verify" his personal revelation of the truth of the Christian message.

While these three very different individuals or couples exemplify the extremes of the authoritative and deliberative communication possible during the period of the millennial Web, most of those involved in vernacular Christian fundamentalism at this time tended toward the center of this continuum. Though typically far more authoritative than deliberative, each case exhibited some level of both. Testifying to their spiritual rebirth, they exhibited a radical certainty. Then, however, they typically offered cues to deliberation in a variety of ways. These cues made it possible for them to imagine, if not actually interact with, an audience with whom they could share their revelatory certainty and thus enact the ekkelsia.

One such case could be found by following a link on Lambert's pages to an amateur ministry Web site called *The Open Scroll* (Christian Research Ministries . . . 1999). From its links, one could go to *The Eyedoctor's Site*. This was the homepage of an ophthalmologist in Florida who (though brought up in Catholicism) had posted an extensive argument on his Web site that the Antichrist would arrive on earth by 1997. He based his interpretation on the Hebrew calendar and the 1994 collision of the Shoemaker-Levy comet with the planet Jupiter (The Eyedoctor's . . . 1999). From *The Eyedoctor's Site* list of links, one could find the site of "Tim" who, at the time of our interview, was an optometrist in Olympia, Washington, and a long-time correspondent with the builder of *The Eyedoctor's Site*.

Tim's "Scientific Truths"

I met Tim at his downtown office on September 19, 1999. At the time, he was very busy running his own business as the primary physician, but he agreed to go for lunch at a nearby restaurant. Although our discussion ended up making him late for his after-lunch appointments, it proved interesting and fruitful for both of us. While Tim engaged in some online deliberation, I came to realize that this contact only served as a means to an end—that end being what he termed "research." Tim mediated the tension between authority and deliberation primarily by engaging others as information sources that could support ideas he had already largely formed.

Online, Tim sought to locate what he termed "scientifically" certain "truths." Having located such truths, he then adjusted them to fit his specific take on vernacular Christian fundamentalism. Adding this data to his Web site, Tim then presented his claims with an air of authority. His practice of doing online research provided just enough of a deliberative attitude for him to engage others in the virtual ekklesia. However, he maintained a sense that his scientific interpretations were better than those of the individuals with whom he interacted.

Tim was raised in a Seventh Day Adventist home. Although he always considered himself a Christian, he was not particularly focused on his faith until he experienced a spiritual rebirth during his college years. Feeling that the Seventh Day Adventists were too "legalistic," Tim "really got to know God by reading the simple English [Bible] and saying, 'A-Hah!'" The focus on the specific rules and doctrines of the Adventists seemed, for Tim, to obscure the actual experience of God. After his spiritual rebirth, he felt that he finally really understood his relationship with God. As he put it: "I am saved by faith; by my relationship with Him. That he loved me so much that he would die for me" (Tim 1999c).

This very active personal relationship with the divine was the motivating factor in his spiritual life. Seeking his "A-Hah!" experiences, he had spent considerable amounts of his free time researching aspects of Christianity that he felt were not adequately covered by institutional religion or "pastors" and "churches," as he put it. In so doing, Tim developed a distinctive way of interacting with the ekklesia that allowed him to imagine himself as authoritative while still garnering a sense of fellowship.

Like Lambert above, Tim imagined a scientific approach to knowledge. Also like Lambert, he had a rebirth experience. Stemming from that rebirth experience, he developed a sense of certainty. Unlike Lambert, however, Tim developed a unique and idiosyncratic logic of knowledge. He expressed that logic in its most general terms, saying:

A few things are associated with it [the experience of rebirth] definitely because God created feelings and it's a good feeling. But to me it's more of the *logic*. And that's the "A-Hah!": the logic and the wonder of it and the. . . . Yeah it's a blending of both: the feeling and the logic. That's what's neat about it. And it's not like this ecstatic speaking-in-tongues thing that I think is a counterfeit. (Tim 1999c)

Although Tim here expressed the belief that "speaking-in-tongues" as well as other common Christian forms of divine experience can be evidence of Satan acting to lead humans astray, he was not totally closed to the possibility of revelatory experiences as sources of divine knowledge. In fact, he noted that his wife commonly had revelatory experiences in the forms of predictive dreams that they had both come to believe were "gifts" from God.

Tim saw his own "A-Hah!" experiences as a lesser, but equally potent, form of revelatory experience. Tim explained:

> The thing that God has revealed to me in my studies I feel has *almost* been that [a revelation like his wife's dreams]. But it's more been like He has opened it up through the Bible and through science to me rather than . . . this actual dream like my wife gets. (Tim 1999c)

Tim believed that God revealed correct knowledge to him through his active pursuit of biblical studies. These studies led him to build his Web site: *Spirit Shower*. He put up the Web site in response to the sudden realization that the very stars were God's way of communicating His intentions to humans. Because of Tim's reliance on mathematical relationships between astronomical events and calendar dates, he presented an authoritative attitude that emerged from his particular blending of Christianity and astronomy. As he noted:

> The main frustration I had was finding the beginning and ending of those dates [referred to in biblical prophecies]. And so I was searching the Web and I don't know what it was, but all of a sudden it clicked when I started seeing astronomy. And I was starting seeing how signs and seasons are the signals. And it really just all started coming together for me. (Tim 1999c)

Tim said to himself: "Well, yeah! That's what God originally set up: the stars and the earth and day and night and everything with the planets." From Tim's perspective, God created the stars so that the dates of biblical prophecy could be calculated: "That's all it does. Those would be the signals He would give us to begin and end these three and a half years [referred to in the Book of Revelation as marking the beginning of the Tribulation period]." And this recognition was Tim's primary moment of divinely led knowledge. He recalled it, saying:

> It was just like a light. It was one of those "A-Hah!" type of things when I started seeing that, and thought: "Oh this is how the beginning of these things starts." So then I started studying the solar eclipses, the lunar eclipses, the conjunctions of Mars and Jupiter, and I . . . and I studied 'em in reference to time cycles. (Tim 1999c)

After several years of study, Tim hoped that, through his Web site, he might share his knowledge with other people and, as a result, he might find new sources of information. Tim remembered:

> It was amazing to see how when I started studying these things they started lining up with the three and a half years! So I started studying all this stuff, and man aloud! . . . till I got thinking, "Well I gotta share some of this stuff, and see if anybody else is studying this ya know." (Tim 1999c)

In 1999, the Web site was modest in size at only .76 megabytes and 48 files. However, it was rich with original texts and graphics that Tim had composed. He explored various topics relating to biblical prophecy on the site. He included numerous time-lines he created based on his studies.

Some of Tim's Web pages used a style typical of literal prophetic interpretation where a passage from the Bible is quoted and then placed into a contemporary context. His page on the temple in Jerusalem, for example, included seven blocked off quotations from the Bible that contained what he saw as key information about the rebuilding of the temple just before the End Times. His own explication of those passages required only five short text blocks. Out of an overall 1,233 words on that page, only 368 were Tim's own. The vast majority were direct quotations from the New Testament.

The temple Web page functioned as the defining theme for Tim's overall work on the Web site. The page stated:

> As we shall see in the following studies this language has reference to the spiritual message of the stars, not worshiping them like the Athenians, but knowing how they signal the appointments with God and revealing how God wants to habitate in human body sanctuaries to make them brides for the Bridegroom who will come for her in the starry heavens. (Tim 1999a)

The idea of the "temple" had two main functions for Tim, which exemplify the complex ways in which he negotiated between his authoritative certainty and his desire to engage others as sources of new ideas. First, the stars act as unequivocal "signals" in that they mark, in their very physical manifestation, the "appointments with God" that will be the major "dispensations" or divine epochs as well as key historical events which will lead up to the Second Coming.

In addition to signaling divine appointments, however, the stars teach the spiritual doctrine of the "Bridegroom." As the page explained, "God wants to habitate in human body sanctuaries." That is, the Holy Spirit enters the individual at the moment of spiritual rebirth in order to act in that person's life. Tim's belief was that those who are saved actually harbor the Holy Spirit in their bodies. For him, this spiritual doctrine was written above in the stars. In fact, unlike many others in the movement, Tim was not at all interested in the rebuilding of the actual temple in Jerusalem. Instead, the literal meaning of the rebuilt temple is, in the Bible, a purely "spiritual" concept. For Tim, the temple-Bride concept typologically refers to the relationship between the believer and Christ. This belief about the temple, and modern Israel in general, had significance only in this spiritual way.

Discussing his approach to Christian teaching during our interview, Tim described participating in online discussions about the specifics of his biblical interpretation and astronomical dating. He acknowledged that his, and everybody else's, ideas about prophecy were really just "divine speculation"— his term for a sort of ritual deliberation.

> A lot of people will be arguing about whether—say for instance the seals— whether they were in the past or in the future. Or they'll argue exactly what could be . . . or get into detailed stuff. But we aren't gonna know until things really happen anyway. So all we can do is just kinda speculate. What I call divine speculation. Put it out there and see what happens. (Tim 1999c)

Tim had engaged a number of well-known individuals involved in the virtual ekklesia I was documenting. In fact, he said he was fond of Lambert Dolphin's Web site. At the mention of Lambert, Tim noted that he, like Lambert, enjoyed discussing the specifics of Christianity online: "I think it's good to look at their ideas." However, Tim limited the validity of online discussion when he added: "[And] put them together [various people's ideas], but I like to put together science and the Bible in the most . . . in the best way possible to verify what's going on. And I like Lambert Dolphin's site because he does look at science" (Tim 1999c).

During our interview, Tim always came back to "science" as a powerful authorizing source for his "divine speculation." While Tim exhibited significant certainty based on his revelatory experiences, he was most interested in the aspects of his belief system that were rooted in science as he understood it. He located evidence for his scientific sense of knowledge in his research into astronomy.

Tim had been working on his complex astronomical interpretation of biblical prophecy long before he put it up on the Worldwide Web. When he chose to put it up, he did so out of a hope that people would see and respond to his ideas. However, Tim's sense of what sort of response he hoped for was limited by his emphasis on the evidence of science. He did not expect to gain any significantly new or different knowledge from his online interaction with other people. Instead, he hoped to gain access to more scientific data to support or expand the ideas he already held as certain.

In fact, because Tim felt that God would "lead" people to his Web site, any information that he gathered from people who contacted him online was already, at least partially, divinely authorized. Tim explained:

> I just put it [the Web site] on there because I saw how people were using the Web for their studies, and I wanted to put it on there to see if anybody would give me any ideas about anything or to see if it would bless other people. And I don't advertise it at all. I figure God will direct people to it. To me it's just a way that I feel directed [by God] to do. Put it out there for people to see, and for God to . . . to use as He would. (Tim 1999c)

Although Tim's site was nowhere near the size of Lambert's or many others' and it was not widely linked to other sites in the sample, Tim did have some interaction with his audience. He recalled his exchange with the eye doctor in Florida: "He's a Catholic. Which I think is interesting because it's interesting for me to see that a Catholic would look at some of my viewpoints and see more stuff than a lot of these other people do" (Tim 1999c).

Tim engaged others in the ekklesia while searching out information that would support his claims. In this way, Tim's certainty was complicated by his seeming desire to locate and engage new data sources, but he mediated this complexity with a desire to locate "scientific truths" that were placed there by God to help Christians understand the End Times narrative. For Tim, online interaction with others served the purpose of locating such facts. As a result, he could engage others online without compromising his authority.

Jack's "Accountability"

Less interested in making connections than in doing online "research," Tim's site was more authoritative than deliberative. Predictably, it had only five links. One link he did trade was with the ophthalmologist in Florida. From *The Eyedoctor's Site*, a Web surfer could follow a link back to *The Open Scroll*. Among the many links there, individuals could go back to Lambert's site, and then from Lambert's site follow the link back to the large Christian search engine *CrossSearch*. Browsing the links to prophetic interpretations on *CrossSearch*, a Web surfer might have chosen to follow the only known link to the most obscure site in the hundred and twenty-sample set: *Symbols Unveiled*. If Tim presented a complex case of the tension between authority and deliberation from squarely within the movement, Jack, the builder of *Symbols Unveiled*, offers an example of a believer who used the Web in a way that rendered him a more marginal participant.

For Jack, the Web functioned strictly as an opportunity for his own unidirectional communication. In this sense, Jack represents the individual least involved in the fellowship associated with the movement and thus the least connected to the virtual ekklesia. Jack's motivation for building his Web site was primarily to sell a book version of his interpretation of the prophetic narrative, and this was the reason he was linked to the virtual ekklesia.

However, Jack also acknowledged the need for fellowship to, as he put it, "give some account" of his beliefs to others. This belief created the typical tension between authoritative and deliberative communication. However, the way Jack mediated this tension garnered him very little if any attention in the movement because he focused his deliberation on the value of deliberating about the End Times itself. Based on how well his book was selling, how well-known his site was, and its lack of links, this approach left him very weakly connected to the ekklesia.

I interviewed Jack on August 27, 1999 near his home in Redding, California. Jack was "saved" in 1969, and this experience led him to write the book *Symbols Unveiled: Revealing the Symbols in the Book of Revelation* (1996). While Jack felt that his book was the result of his direct "leading" by God, he had a hard time publishing the work. At the time of our interview, Jack had self-published it. I purchased a copy from him when we met. Originally Jack had hoped that he would be able to sell his book through mail order from the Web site he had set up. However, he quickly realized that this was not realistic. Although he had some success selling small quantities of the volume through Christian-oriented distributors, he said that, as of August 1999, he had sold only one copy through the Internet site.

The site itself was starkly uninteresting. Consisting of only 148 kilobytes of data for some thirteen files, only seven files were actual text written by Jack for the Web site. All the pages were in two colors: pastel green contrasting with a strong violet. These colors were the same as those used for the front cover of his book. The front page of the Web site contained a few graphic images and several links to endorsements of his book, a description of the book, and a copy of its first chapter. In 2000, Jack added a link to a commercial bookseller's Web site so his book could be easily ordered.

He put up the Web site sometime shortly after his book came out in 1996. At that time, he engaged in only a small amount of email discourse surrounding the Web site. The initial motivating factor for Jack's beliefs as well as inspiration for the writing of his books was, as it was for all my respondents, a rebirth experience—as Jack described it, a "Paul experience." Jack recalled:

> I basically had a Paul experience . . . where God was taking me out, aside, and taught me the Word and things on my own. And what I did with that then was, I would bounce that off of other people so that I knew that I wasn't way out in left field some place. And that's part of the accountability [. . .]. You examine each others' doctrine and you have to be accountable. (Russell 1999b)

Jack exhibited a trait very similar to the deliberative sort of attitude displayed by Lambert above. He described his intense experience, which he felt it was necessary to "bounce" off other people in order to verify its meaning. He felt that engaging with a community about his experience functioned to solidify his understanding based on a sort of "accountability." However, this communal accountability was tempered by a focus on the specific words in the Bible:

> You have to be able to go to the Word and say, "This is why I believe this." And give some account of that. Whether people agree with you or not is secondary, but you do have to have some kind of a reason. You can't just pick stuff out of the air and say, "Oh, I believe this." (Russell 1999b)

Here Jack modified his claim about the "accountability" of the community when he noted that gaining agreement from his community members is "secondary." While this is certainly a more deliberative attitude than found in Dean above, it is not as much as Lambert or even Tim. Although his interpretations must make sense to his community, their agreement or disagreement had no authority. Instead, it was "the Word" that Jack's revelatory experience authorized.

As should now be expected of individuals in the movement, Jack's rebirth experience was intense and undeniable. He recalled it with his typical understatement:

> Well . . . I think in my salvation experience I had a real feeling. Just kinda short and sweet. I was at work one night. A fella asked me if I was saved. I said, "I dunno know. I think so." He said, "Would you like to know?" I said,

" Yes." And so we just prayed The Sinner's Prayer and I went to bed. And I woke up the next morning, and I knew that God was real and that He had saved me . . . and to the point I wanted to get up on the roof of the firehouse and shout it out. So I had an experience there. As far as knowing that the Holy Spirit was leading my life, I think that came a little later and I grew into that. Mainly because of ignorance. I didn't know about the Holy Spirit. I mean I knew there was a Holy Spirit, but I didn't know what its function was and I didn't know how He related in this situation. (Russell 1999b)

As Jack began to learn after his "Sinner's Prayer" experience, the Holy Spirit acted in his life to "lead" him to a correct understanding of the world. This included a correct understanding of the Bible. Because Jack felt that his life in general and his call to write in particular were the results of direct guidance from the Holy Spirit, this guidance was the most basic level of authority for Jack. At this level, God acted in Jack's life to lead him to correct understandings. His community's input was, as he says, "only secondary."

It was this sort of quiet divine leadership that guided Jack in the writing of his book. He explained: "Basically I just studied the Word and He just gave me a way of kinda walking me around in the Word. . . . And that's what happened to Paul." While Jack's experience of divine leadership seemed, from his own descriptions of it, less dramatic than that exemplified by the biblical account of Saul's conversion to Paul, it points out the important way in which Jack was understating his reliance on certainty. For Jack, divine leadership in his life was a simple fact of experience. That rebirth experience, even if "slow" by his own account, led Jack to reorganize his life around a Christian worldview as well as to devote immense amounts of time to study and writing (Russell 1999b).

Jack's certainty in his own individual interpretations of prophecy yielded a powerfully authoritative attitude, and this led to Jack's unique way of mediating the tension between that authority and the need to place some value on fellowship. For Jack, ritual deliberation about the End Times was not useful; instead, he attempted to engage others in the movement by opening himself to deliberation about the role of deliberation itself. Based on his authoritative communication style, however, the general lack of engagement he found with others in the movement was predictable.

Jack specifically called Hal Lindsey and others with similar interpretations of Revelation "futurists." He noted that he himself was not a futurist, but a "spiritualist." From Jack's perspective, it was possible to interpret the Book of Revelation as a predictive document in the way that Hal Lindsey and other such "futurists" did. However, Jack felt it was more fruitfully interpreted in a "spiritual" way.

For Jack, to engage with the Book of Revelation as a predictive document was a misdirection of energy. Jack explained:

> Hal Lindsey's view and most of his futuristic view is geared toward the physical well-being of people. The spiritualistic view basically goes to the other side. These are the things that are happening in the spirit and some of those things have a bearing on the natural man and some of them really don't, as far as concerns go. And I make that statement in *Symbols Unveiled* and my understanding of the Book of Revelation is that there is no fear and anxiety for those that are believers. (Russell 1999b)

Because Jack's interpretation of Revelation did not focus on the predictive possibilities of the text, he effectively rendered it useless for the vast majority of those interested in ritual deliberation. He acknowledged that, in the Book of Revelation, "God's given [humans] a clear picture of how things are gonna come to a climax." However, it was unhealthy to focus on that aspect of the book because the things that the book revealed "for the most part bring anxiety and fear to people's hearts." Such fear was, in Jack's view, not the goal of a spiritual life (Russell 1999b).

This interpretive strategy both in the book and in our face-to-face interview allowed Jack to disengage from the vast majority of End Times discourse. For Jack, however, that did not mean that Hal Lindsey or other End Times deliberators were wrong in their predictions. Instead, it just meant that Jack was refusing to engage in that kind of speculation. Typical of those in the movement, Jack acknowledged that deliberation could not really access correct knowledge because it was beyond humans. He took it a step further, however, by arguing that ritual deliberation focusing on the End Times missed the real point of the Book of Revelation. As a result of his overt turn against deliberation about the End Times, Jack remained a marginal member of the virtual ekklesia.

At the same time, Jack expressed a specific value for fellowship. By trying to render his oppositional interpretation reasonable to others in the movement, he acknowledged those who do engage in more normative ritual deliberation. In fact, he integrated his desire to deliberate with others into the specific take on the Christian belief system in his sense of "accountability" to the community. Too weak a solution to the tension between his authority and his desire for fellowship, however, other individuals in the movement largely ignored Jack's Web site.

Even though Tim and Jack both exhibited significantly authoritative communication, they also presented very different attempts at enacting fellowship in the virtual ekklesia. While Tim's beliefs seemed to support a complex but basically authoritative attitude that led him to see people at least as the sources for potential information, Jack's certainty only allowed him to try to sell a book online that argued that ritual deliberation was useless to a community whose only existence was through such deliberation.

In both cases, their use of the Web expressed their personal authority in ways that attempted to open them to online fellowship. While Tim had some success in that he did interact with others in the movement, Jack really only engaged the virtual ekklesia by putting up an advertisement for his book. While Tim did interact with others, he only did so in order to further "research" that would yield facts supporting his own authority. As a result, neither of them emerged as very well-known figures in the ekklesia. In the sampled Web sites, there were only two links to Tim's site and there was only one to Jack's. These were the two least connected sites in the sample.

Peter's "Hate Mail"

Jack and Tim presented two cases whose mediation of the tension between authority and deliberation resulted in weak connections to the rest of the virtual ekklesia. The next example presents a case where the respondent attempted, with great persistence, to engage an online audience. However, the authoritative communication he used was so extreme that it caused him to encounter significant levels of resistance even from individuals with whom he largely agreed. This person attempted to enact online fellowship by mediating the tension between authoritative and deliberative communication with a particularly aggressive personal authority.

Those who followed the only link given on Jack's *Symbols Unveiled* Web site, would find themselves on the home page for a home church organization Jack was affiliated with, called *The Worship Center*. With only three external links (one of which went back to *Symbols Unveiled*), this site was not much more connected than was *Symbols Unveiled*. One link off *The Worship Center* did lead, however, to the home page for a Christian-oriented cafe called "One Accord Coffee House." The coffeehouse had a page of links to "Partners and Friends." On that page, one could go to an amateur Christian ministry for youth called *The Shed*. From a list of resources on that site, one could go back to *CrossSearch*. Using *CrossSearch* to look at more sites about biblical prophecy, the Web surfer could visit the large and well-known End

Times site call *TribNews*. By fully exploring *TribNews*, one would have come across a link to the amateur site called *"Peter Smith's" Ministries*.

I interviewed Peter in Beaverton, Oregon, on August 11, 1999. He was an insurance salesperson who engaged in a large volume of online communication in his spare time. At the time of our interview, his Web site was moderately sized at 110 megabytes for 118 files. A simple but professional-looking site, Peter included sections on his own "testimony" where he described his spiritual rebirth. On his page about "Salvation," he described what he felt it meant to be saved and, at the end, he invited the sinner to ask for God's forgiveness in a Sinner's Prayer. On the "Apologetics" page, he described what his studies and writings were about within the context of traditional Christian writings.

In the "Prophecy" section of that page, he laid out a typical End Times narrative. On the "Social Issues" page, he railed against the practice of abortion by relating it to Adolph Hitler's National-Socialists' attempt at genocide. In a section he called "Inspirational Stories," he wrote "stories to warm the heart and feed the soul." In the "Cults" section, he specifically attacked New Age believers and Mormons by asserting that their beliefs were "counterfeits" of Christianity created by Satan to lead humans astray. Finally, he had a page of links, a "guest-book," and his email address with an invitation for the Web surfer to send him "questions, comments, or prayer requests" because (as Peter put it on the page) he "would love to hear from you!" (Peter 1999b).

With his invitation for people to email him with responses to his Web site, Peter was giving his audience an overt cue to engage him in deliberation. When I asked Peter about why he put up his site, he described how he hoped it would encourage people to email him. He went on to tell me about how he built his Web site as a result of his experiences with an email discussion list hosted by the *TribNews Network* or TNN.

Peter went on to describe how he disagreed with the ideas he felt were dominating the discussions there. Despite this, Peter hired TNN to host a Web site of his own. Because he did not have the time to both write up his Bible studies and learn HTML programming well enough, he felt he could not create the professional look he found in other sites. Peter recalled: "I was searching the Web one day, and I had a Web site that I designed myself and being a novice at Web site design it was . . . it didn't have all the bells and whistles that some of these cooler sites did" (Peter 1999d).

Getting in touch with the Web site builder of *TribNews*, Peter sent in his simple Web pages and the TNN staff turned them into what Peter felt was a professional-looking site. He was happy with the work and put his site entirely into a subdirectory on the TNN server.

Peter explained:

> I don't have a lot of time to do it myself. It takes time to write, so I just give it to him. So that's how I got with the *TribNews Network*, and like I said . . . I subscribe to what they call their "chat email." Which I totally disagree with everything on that one, but that's because they're post-Tribulation views. (Peter 1999d)

When I asked Peter about his experiences with the TNN email list, he expressed his concern that "argument doesn't pay." Peter described a recent exchange saying that he tried to get his points heard, but "We [pre-Tribulation believers] get ganged up on! So it doesn't pay to argue." Instead, he felt that the email list participants told him that the focus of the email list was "post-trib. And this is why. And you shouldn't be arguing back and forth if you are all pre-millennialists" (Peter 1999d). In September 1999, at least partially as a result of a lack of deliberation on the list, the moderators at TNN had actually shut down the email list completely, stating that it "has not developed as we at TNN had hoped" (Editor 1999).

The site may have emphasized a post-Tribulation view, but it was still solidly part of the ekklesia. On a newer version of TNN's Web site, it clearly states: "We hold to eschatological views consistent with historical pre-millennialism, and we do not hold to amillennial, post-millennial, or preterist eschatology" (*TribNews Network* 2008). This detail suggests that even though he attempted to engage with others in ekklesia, Peter did so by seeking out a point of contention that others did not. Looking more closely at his Web site as well as his descriptions of the online exchanges he was having, it is clear that Peter used more aggressively authoritative language than his fellow believers valued in their ritual deliberation.

Peter told me that the primary goal of his online communication about the End Times was to "help" the many individuals he found online who were "in error." Peter said:

> The reason I do it is not to attack them. It is because I have a love for them, and I want them to see that they are heading down . . . that they are being deceived by Satan. And they are gonna end up in the wrong way. Their eternal salvation is at stake! And I think they need to get back on track. And Satan wants to take as many people from Christ as he can. (Peter 1999d)

Peter was involved in a personal war against Satan, and perceived that, as a result, he received quite a bit of what he called "hate mail." As he described it: "I have been getting some email activity . . . hate mail. I call it hate mail because they're calling me a bigot and anti-Christian and all this" (Peter 1999d). In addition to hate mail, Peter sometimes received positive feedback. The power of this supportive email suggests that, even for Peter, fellowship within the ekklesia was a significant motivating factor in his online communication about the End Times. He described how he sometimes caught himself wondering "why bother?" writing and posting his ideas, but God was leading him to write by leading people to send him a positive response. He reported that when he was most down:

All of a sudden, I get a positive email from somebody. Who has been blessed by the Web page. And I know that the Lord had something to do with it. That he wants me to keep writing. And he will lead people as it need-be to my Web site. (Peter 1999d)

With this infusion of positive responses, Peter was able to keep up the effort to "reply to every email" he got. However, most of the emails he received were negative because he was seeking out and emailing the builders and users with whom he disagreed. When I interviewed him, he was specifically interested in Web sites he felt were involved with the "cult problem." As he explained it, "Cults are everywhere. From the huge and socially acceptable Mormons to more obscure theological heresies. Jesus warns us in the last days false Christs and false prophets would arise to deceive many" (Peter 1999a). On his Web site, Peter had a page about the Church of the Latter Day Saints (LDS) specifically.

On this page, it became immediately apparent that Peter felt LDS writings and doctrines were not valid. He first quoted a passage from the Book of Mormon. Then he quoted a passage from the Bible and compared them in a brief exposition. At the top of the page, he noted: "Each Mormon quotation is marked: <LDS>. Each Bible quotation is marked: THE TRUTH: Items in [brackets] are commentary." Clearly, the "LDS" passages were not "THE TRUTH," but the Bible passages were.

When I asked him about this Web page, Peter described the tactics he used to combat the teachings of the Church of the Latter Day Saints. After locating an LDS Web site, Peter would email its builder or builders:

I point out the errors of their teaching. And ask some specific questions to explain this: "If you are Christian, and you say that you believe in the Bible then why does the Book of Mormon say this?" Or "Why does Joe Smith say this?" Or "Why do you guys believe this, when the Bible says this?" And they don't. And once they get my email I never hear back from them. (Peter 1999d)

I asked him why he thought he didn't generally hear back from the Web site builders.

I don't attack them. I ask them questions: "I want you to take a look at your theology. Take a look at what the Bible says. And answer my question." And I just want 'em to think. And if I can get them to think, maybe the Holy Spirit or some other Christian can harvest that seed to where they'll get saved. (Peter 1999d)

Here, Peter expressed his belief that his audience would be pushed by the Holy Spirit "or some other Christian" to move away from their error and "get saved." Peter had confidence that the Holy Spirit (once Its "seed has been planted") would help the Mormons reject their doctrines. Emboldened by the certainty afforded him by his spiritual rebirth experience, Peter engaged in aggressively authoritative online communication to combat the beliefs of those outside the ekklesia. However, he took this same aggressive attitude toward those in the ekklesia with whom he disagreed. As he put it: "I feel I have a *duty* to point out where you're going astray from what the Bible says. And that's what I do" (Peter 1999d).

I asked Peter how he could be so certain when others had "gone astray." He told me that he knew because he had had the direct experience of grace in spiritual rebirth. At the time of his experience, Peter had hit rock bottom. He was "completely broken." He said: "I was contemplating suicide. I was just depressed. Nothing was going right." But then, "after I said that Sinner's Prayer and got saved, I was on a euphoria for about six weeks where I didn't sleep! I could not sleep! I was on like a high *for six weeks!*" At the climax of this six-week experience, Peter's grace was confirmed during a church service. He explained:

I was in a church service the week after I got saved, and they were singing a praise song. And all of a sudden, I felt this . . . my knees started buckling. I started crying for no reason. Everybody around me knew what was going on, but I had no idea. I was being baptized in the Holy Spirit. And . . . it was just an amazing experience and I cannot explain to somebody who's never gone through it. It's just when God touches your life. (Peter 1999d)

Peter approached his online communication with the assumption that the Holy Spirit would act in his audiences' lives much as He had acted in Peter's. Peter could not explain, or argue about, the experience of "God touching your life." Instead, he knew it happened because he had personally experienced it. As Peter described it: "Let me give you an example of Faith. Have you ever seen the wind? But you know the effects of the wind!" He continued:

It's the same thing with my faith in God. I have never seen him personally. I've seen his works. I've seen people's lives change. I've seen people healed from terminal cancer. In my own life, I was . . . I was just one S.O.B. In my younger days, I was like the Apostle Paul [. . .] I was very bigoted in my opinions. (Peter 1999d)

There is, in Peter's case, a profound irony. From his perspective, he was "bigoted" before his conversion experience. So when people responded to his unsolicited emails questioning their interpretation of the Bible, he was confused about why they called him "a bigot." What he termed "hate mail" was clearly the response of individuals who were reacting to his overwhelming sense of personal authority.

During our interview, he specifically offered an example of how he attempted to initiate deliberation with others in the ekklesia. In this case, he used such authoritative communication that it resulted in significantly hostile responses from his fellow believers. He described how a woman posted an interpretation of one of her own dreams on a Christian email list in which she believed that God was leading her to see that the United States would be attacked with nuclear weapons on September 11, 1999. Peter told me that he responded to her, saying: "'When September 11 comes around, I am gonna be the first one to email you and call you a false prophet'" (Peter 1999d).

Despite the aggressive and insulting nature of calling another Christian in the ekklesia a "false prophet," Peter confessed that he could not see why this email seemed to be "getting people all bent outta shape" (Peter 1999d). His complete assurance that the Holy Spirit could bring people a rebirth experience much like the one he had had himself was a significant contributing factor to his insensitivity. While he seemed truly compassionate in his intentions, the authoritative attitude he took from this experience presents maybe the least subtle strategy for mediating the tension between authoritative and deliberative communication. Simply certain he was correct, Peter engaged in ritual deliberation by informing others in the ekklesia that they were "going astray."

Tim and Jack also exhibited authoritative communication. Peter's case was different, however, because he sought out and participated in a great deal of ritual deliberation. He did not seem to be very satisfied with his results. His attempt at mediation between authority and deliberation largely failed because he expressed his authority far too aggressively. As a result, his attempts at deliberation seem to have elicited a generally hostile response.

The next case is very different, and it is one with which we are already familiar. As we have seen, Marilyn Agee had a powerfully authoritative attitude. However, that certainty was mitigated by a clever use of the Worldwide Web medium. As a result, she gathered a significant audience and—unlike Peter, Tim, or Jack—became a well-known figure in the ekklesia.

Marilyn's Authoritative Deliberation

From a page of links on Peter's site, one could have followed a link back to *TribNews*. From there, one could find a link to the *Watcher Website*. Deep within that site, there was a page that specifically considered whether the Rapture might occur before, during, or at the end of the Tribulation period. From that page, one could have followed a link to one of the most popular sites in the community. With eighteen incoming links from twelve different Web sites, Marilyn's *Bible Prophecy Corner* was the third-most connected site in the sample, behind only the *Watcher Website* and *Lambert's Library*.

Entering *Bible Prophecy Corner* from the *Watcher Website*, one would have traced a full circle from Ernie and Cheryl's site discussed earlier in this chapter. More than just an amateur Web site builder, Marilyn was a well-known figure because of the success of her three books. At the time of our interview in 1999, she reported selling some 90,000 copies altogether of the three texts. In the most recent of those books, she had predicted that the bodily Rapture would occur on Pentecost in 1998 (Agee 1997, 122ff). Disagreeing with Marilyn's prediction of the Rapture, the *Watcher Website* page refuted her claims and then made a link to a page on Marilyn's site where she made this prediction.

By the time I interviewed Marilyn, there had already been a lot of talk about the failure of her published prediction for 1998, both on her own Web site as well as on other Web sites and discussion boards. At our interview, she acknowledged that she had been mistaken, and she told me her new prediction was that the Tribulation would begin a year or two in the future on Pentecost 2000 or 2001 (Agee and Edgar 1999). Her failed 1998 prediction did not appear to concern or trouble her.

When I bought her three books during our interview, she noted the reasons for her incorrect prediction in the first page of one of the books by writing, "I now think the Rapture will probably be on Pentecost, 2000. In Luke 13:6–9, Jesus only looks in the first two years. He comes and speaks in the third year" (Agee 1999c). Despite her mistake, Marilyn still spoke with an authoritative voice. While she acknowledged she had made a mistake, it was the mistake of an expert. As we saw, Marilyn perceived herself as an expert because God had commanded her to write by giving her a vision of a biblical passage which instructed her to publish and share her knowledge.

Deeply enmeshed in the vernacular web that made up the virtual ekklesia, Marilyn's site garnered a large audience because she had developed an effective way to mediate the tension between her own authority and the sense of fellowship necessary to enact the ekklesia. The other sites discussed so far all seem to have failed to garner wide audiences. Jack, for example, had sold only a single copy of his book online, and his site had almost no known links to it. Similarly, Tim had some discussions with people he met online, but he was not well known in the community and had very few links to his site. In the most extreme example, Dean built a Web site specifically to help out other people who might have been having problems with demons. Writing from experiences with such demons, Dean demonstrated his certainty most prominently of all those in the hundred and twenty-site sample. However, he seemed to have garnered almost no online audience at all. The only known link to Dean's site was through a large Christian search engine. Though very authoritative, Marilyn was different.

Discussing with me how she knew her interpretations were correct even with a growing track record of errors, Marilyn stated that she had spent seven years reading "everything man had written about the Bible," but was disappointed with their lack of understanding:

> I wanted to know the hard things. So I just opened my Bible, and put my hands on it, and I said, 'Lord you'll have to show me.' The next seven years I learned so fast I could hardly keep up with it. (Agee and Edgar 1999)

Marilyn's claims to authority were based on her personal experience of studying under the unseen guidance of the Holy Spirit and thus on her perception of a divine infusion of understanding. On her biographical page, she stated that she was "a Baptist believer who has been studying the Bible as deep as I can go for over 38 years." This "depth" came by way of being "led by God" in her studies (Agee 1999b). In this divinely led study, Marilyn proceeded with authority, much like Jack, Tim, and Dean. Unlike them, however, Marilyn's Web site had been a community fixture since 1996. It was helped by broader media publicity afforded by the success of her books. There was also, however, a qualitative difference between Marilyn's Web pages and the other largely authoritative sites. Unlike the others, Marilyn's authoritative attitude was mitigated by her masterful display of ritual deliberation.

The bulk of her Web site was in a distinctly deliberative form that prefigured the participatory features of later blogs. The main section of the *Bible Prophecy Corner*, some 13 megabytes in size, was devoted to the "Pro and Con Index" where the deliberation about the September 11 attacks was enacted, as described above. The main part of this site was a handmade blog with over four hundred individual dated pages that documented a lively email-based dialogue between her and her audience in the community (Agee 1999a).

Each chronologically organized page contained an email exchange. She built these pages in simple HTML code without the aid of the more powerful software that would make participatory media the primary location for ritual deliberation in the coming years. As we have seen, on each page she would first quote an incoming email. These incoming emails typically had a question or complaint about something she had already said or written. Displaying an apparent openness to deliberation, Marilyn would then email back and forth with the individual. Once she felt the discussion was complete, she posted what appeared to be the entire exchange for her audience to read.

Putting these exchanges on her Web site, Marilyn presented ritual deliberation in the distinctly noninteractive medium of the early Worldwide Web. In our interview and in her biographical statement on the site, however, she established significant authority by claiming to have a personal relationship with the divine. In fact, all her discourse, starting with her first publication, was inspired by that divine direction, quoted in full above: "And this verse had light on it, saying: 'Publish and conceal not'" (Agee and Edgar 1999).

On the one hand, Marilyn's blog demonstrated that she understood how ritual deliberation was expected to proceed in the ekklesia. On the other, she expressed a clearly authoritative attitude about her literal biblical interpretations. Fortunately, my interviews with other members of the ekklesia turned up evidence that revealed how Marilyn was mediating this tension on her Web site. Based on that interview evidence, I concluded that Marilyn's blog was not as deliberative as it appeared. Instead, it seems that Marilyn was willing to talk only as long as she felt that the discussion was forwarding her already held beliefs. When she was confronted with what she considered to be excessive resistance from her audience, she seems to have cut off the discussion.

In my interviews, I managed to document at least one case in which she did just this: cut off a discussion and simply refuse to engage those who questioned her. In this case, she later posted the exchange on her Web site in a way that made it appear as if the deliberation had ended in agreement when, in fact, it had not. In this sense, Marilyn mediated the tension between authority and deliberation by displaying a deliberative attitude, while maintaining strict control over the deliberation that she hosted on her site.

The Truncated Deliberation of "Pro and Con 223"

The truncated deliberation occurred between Marilyn and the builders of the *Watcher Website*. The builders of this site referred to themselves by the collective pseudonym "the Watcher." In the fall of 1999, I would interview them face-to-face, but (by that time) I had already learned that they were actually a middle-class married couple in Helena, Montana, named "Jane" and "John." According to them, Marilyn simply refused to respond to all further communications from them after they expressed disagreement with her. Even though they all shared the beliefs of vernacular Christian fundamentalism and despite her popular representations of ritual deliberation on her Web site, resistance to her interpretation of a very specific biblical detail revealed just how tightly Marilyn clung to her personal authority.

On October 17, 1999, I drove to Helena and interviewed the Watcher couple. Since 1993, they had built and maintained one of the most distinctive and well-known End Times Web sites in the ekklesia. They had been featured on the television show *Strange Universe*, a cable network documentary, and even had longtime ABC news anchor Ted Koppel comment negatively on their beliefs during the aftermath of the 1997 suicides of the religious group "Heaven's Gate."

Jane and John's site was one of the two most-connected sites in the sample set. It had twenty-nine incoming links, second only to Lambert Dolphin. Those links came from fourteen different external sites, even more than *Lambert's Library*. A significant presence in the web, those incoming links included several from familiar sites like *Bible Prophecy Corner*, *Lambert's Library*, *TribNews*, *The Eyedoctor's Site*, and *CrossSearch*. In addition to its popularity and extensive connections, Jane and John's site proved particularly interesting because the couple had a long-term email relationship with

Marilyn Agee. More telling than the relationship itself was the story of how it soured.

Jane and John had both had typical spiritual rebirth experiences and felt certain about the truth of a literal interpretation of the Christian message. Those beliefs placed them squarely within vernacular Christian fundamentalism. Less common, but not unheard of in the movement, they also expressed a strong belief that extraterrestrial beings pilot some UFOs. In fact, they shared an interest in extraterrestrial intelligence before they experienced spiritual rebirth and became Christians. At the time of their spiritual rebirths, John was a lapsed Catholic and Jane was practicing a form of contemporary paganism Jane termed "Wicca." After their conversions, they took a literal approach to interpreting the Bible. Engaging with others in the movement online, they realized that many sharing its core tenets felt that a literal interpretation of the Bible excluded the possibility that UFOs were piloted by non–earthly beings.

In the typical literal reading of the Bible, the creation story in Genesis does not mention intelligent life other than humans. As a result, vernacular Christian fundamentalism's interpretation of the Bible generally rejects the possibility of extraterrestrial intelligence. John told me, however, that he and Jane wanted to share their conviction with other Christians that these two beliefs were quite compatible. To that end, they decided to build a Web site. As John described it:

> The reason we put the Web site up was because we wanted to combat this cognitive dissonance that's set up by the fact that UFOs exist *and* there's a Gospel. Then we wanted to point out that the Bible does clearly define what's exactly happening and what will happen and outlines what UFOs are. Then there's this idea that there's actually monuments on another planet—and that blows most peoples' minds! (Jane and John 1999)

By 1999, this effort resulted in 4 megabytes of text and images about monuments on Mars, UFO technology, government conspiracy, the television show *The X Files*, and much more. When I interviewed Jane and John, I mentioned a page I had found on their Web site where they specifically refuted Agee's assertion that the Rapture would occur in two distinct phases, a form of "mid-Tribulation" Rapture belief. They told me that a few years prior, Marilyn had emailed Jane after she had surfed onto the *Watcher Website*. Soon Jane, John, and Marilyn were engaging in ritual deliberation about the End Times through email. However, the deliberation stalled over an interpretation of the second chapter of Second Thessalonians. For many in the movement, these passages seem to state that at least some Christians would live to see the Antichrist in power (Watcher 1999b).

From Jane and John's perspective, this meant that there would be no pre-Tribulation Rapture. Marilyn, however, disagreed. She argued that there would be a two-phased Rapture. As we have seen on email lists and will see in blogs, participants in the movement are typically able to discuss a diversity of possibilities and theories about when and how the Rapture would occur. Most often, this discussion continues to function as ritual without ever endangering the participants' ability to enact the virtual ekklesia. In the ritual deliberation between Jane, John, and Marilyn, however, this ability to act together was lost.

On Marilyn's "Pro and Con Index" Web page number "223," she posted a document of over 4,500 words containing email exchanges she had with Jane and John discussing the issue of Rapture. As presented on Agee's page, Marilyn, Jane, and John's communications seemed to be ritual deliberation—much as we have seen on email lists. They extensively quoted biblical passages in support of their arguments, and they referred to other possible literal interpretations without making a final definitive conclusion. The bulk of the discussion was about the relationship between what Marilyn called "inspired" calendar dating systems and the typical calendar system used in the secular world. Marilyn chose to end the representation of their deliberation on the Web page with what appears to be the tentative resolution that there would probably be a two-staged Rapture on Pentecost 1999.

On the page, Marilyn detailed how she came to a 1999 date for the first stage of the Rapture. Her 1998 prediction having failed by the time of this post, she explained why she now hoped 1999 would be the year:

> This is 14 years (7 good and 7 bad) from the signing of the Oslo Accords on Sept. 13, 1993 (1993 + 14 = 2007). Our year 1993 + 7 = 2000. The ratification of the Oslo Accords in Jerusalem three days later on the Jewish Tishri 1, 5753 + 7 = Tishri 1, 5760 (our Sept. 11, 1999). I think the Rapture should take place within these 7 good years. In Egypt, Joseph took up a fifth of the grain in the 7 good years. We are wheat, so it fits us well. Our time is getting short. I am hoping for next Pentecost. (Agee 1999d)

Marilyn's final lines, "I am hoping for next Pentecost," is an example of deliberative communication because the word "hope" suggested that Marilyn was not certain. Expressing this lack of certainty was a cue to the audience that Marilyn was open to altering the date. If she was open to altering the date, she should have been open to the input of other theories from her audience. If she was open to input, then deliberation about the possibilities of the date could have continued. According to the story Jane and John tell, however, this deliberative style of communication did not actually mark a deliberative attitude in Marilyn, and this attitude caused their deliberation to cease.

Talking about their email exchanges with Marilyn, Jane said:

> We just tried so hard to say, "Marilyn, what does this passage in scripture mean then? How can you interpret it any other way, because it's in black and white, the Greek means this." And she won't look at it because it hurts too bad. It's a very painful thing to think. (Jane and John 1999)

Jane believed that Marilyn's theory about the "two-staged" Rapture was a result of Marilyn's intense desire to avoid the Tribulation period herself. Jane postulated that "it's very painful" for Marilyn to imagine that she too, as well as all other true Christians, would have to endure the pains of persecution that the Tribulation period would bring (Jane and John 1999). Jane cued her own openness to deliberation by indicating her readiness to reconsider Marilyn's two-Rapture assertion by asking, "what does this passage mean then?" For Jane, if an alternate meaning could be found that did not contradict the literal meaning of the passage as she read it, then Marilyn's theory would remain a possibility.

Marilyn, however, refused to continue the discussion and their deliberation ended. In fact, Marilyn refused to respond to Jane or John's emails. While Marilyn posted the email deliberation as a "Pro and Con Index" entry, she presented it as a deliberation with a typically open-ended ending. For Marilyn, that ending seemed to point to her correct literal interpretation. The fact that Jane and John were not convinced was simply ignored—as were the subsequent emails Jane and John sent to Marilyn on the topic.

Having carefully examined all the "Pro and Con Index" entries in 1999, I did not find a single clear example of Marilyn acknowledging an adjustment of her position based on deliberations she conducted online. This suggests that her exchange with Jane and John was not idiosyncratic. In my interview with her, an authoritative attitude became even clearer when she stated that Satan inspired apparitions of the Virgin Mary, American Indian traditions, and New Age beliefs.

At the same time, however, she showed a clear understanding of how ritual deliberation should proceed by presenting what appeared to be deliberative communication on static Web pages in the "Pro and Con Index." In "Pro and Con 223," for example, she used words and phrases like "I am hoping for next Pentecost" and "probably" to cue her own uncertainty. She also used cues to indicate that she was open to new ideas about her interpretations. In "Pro and Con 223," she represented herself inviting further discussion in an email: "I would be glad to discuss the reasons for the chronology and calendar in future E-mail or phone calls." Even the "Pro and Con" form itself implied that she was open to discussing ideas and exploring them in concert with others.

However, she seems only to have adjusted her claims when faced with the undeniable fact that she was not bodily taken into Heaven. This occurred in 1998, 1999, 2000, and 2001. Repeatedly wrong in the face of this physical reality, she still asserted a sort of divinely inspired authority. In that sense, her authoritative attitude remained intact and strong. While far more authoritative than Lambert, Jane, or John, she remained extremely popular in the ekklesia. Her site was nearly as connected as those other two top sites in the sample set. One reason for this was that, at least in public, she strongly encouraged people to email her. This is clear from the sheer number of "Pro and Con" pages she was able to produce. By the end of 2001, she had a total of 853 "Pro and Con" pages.

Marilyn's ability to create the appearance of deliberation in static Web pages is much like the moderated "blog" or online forums that surged to popularity in 2001. The moderated blogs and forums are particularly well adapted to ritual deliberation because they allow individuals to respond to each other while at the same time allowing the moderator or creator of the blog to reduce or eliminate ideas that would introduce too much diversity into the deliberative exchange. Marilyn's ability to be very authoritative while still offering the appearance of ritual deliberation gave her site a high profile in the movement. In this way it demonstrated the value placed on ritual deliberation as well as the need to balance that deliberation with the authoritative control that can keep dissent in check.

As a location of what appeared to be ritual deliberation, Marilyn's site was highly connected despite her own authoritative attitude. In fact, her site was one of the first to present ritual deliberation on the Worldwide Web itself. The "Pro and Con Index" gave Marilyn a Web-based space to represent deliberation much like what might have occurred on the Usenet or on email lists in the early 1990s. Marilyn's clever site design, the media exposure she had as an author, and her longevity in the virtual ekklesia all combined to make Marilyn's site the third most connected site in the sample.

Jane and John's Virtual "Ekklesia"

Although Marilyn's deliberative display contributed to the huge popularity of her site and she was very well connected to the vernacular web emerging from the End Times, Jane and John's site was slightly more connected. While John eventually published a book on their beliefs, by 2000 John and Jane had, unlike Marilyn, gained their popularity in the virtual ekklesia almost exclusively through email and their Web site. Another major difference between Marilyn and them was that though they claimed to be "born again," they did not believe, as did Marilyn, that their specific interpretations were divinely led. Instead, they were constantly forming, updating, and altering their literal understanding of the Bible. For Jane and John, a powerful playfulness mediated the tension between the authoritative nature of their certainty and the fellowship necessary for the virtual ekklesia.

Unlike any other in the sample set, their Web site was a pastiche of seemingly incongruous claims. With juxtaposed images of the Egyptian Sphinx, Martian craters, and cartoon characters from the television show *The Simpsons*, a playful and often humorous tone made their site appear to be an experiment with many different kinds of ideas. As a result, their online communication seemed more deliberative than authoritative.

This is not to say that Jane and John did not also have their own sense of radical certainty or that they did not exhibit any authoritative communication at all. Milder than Marilyn on both counts, John and Jane rejected claims to authority based on exceptional revelatory experiences that included direct aural or visual experiences of God. Specifically, they did not believe that Marilyn's highlighted passage directing her to publish was a true revelatory experience. John called it "mildly neurotic." This assessment was not surprising because John was a practicing psychologist. He had a more surprising response, however, when I asked what they thought about Dean's dramatic experiences with demons. Both Jane and John agreed that such beliefs are dangerously rooted in "superstition" and such beliefs were not benign. Instead, Jane and John stated they were a demonic tactic to lead humans away from Christ (Jane and John 1999).

Speaking of Dean's experience of possession and getting rid of demons, John stated:

He's tricked! It serves a huge point because all it is, is a red herring. The forces that they're playing with are all the same. Their [the demons'] agenda is only one: to get man away from the truth. So. If you can get them to think, ya know—to play good cop/bad cop that's *super* effective. (Jane and John 1999)

Jane and John limited the validity of direct experience of the deity to conversion experiences similar to that which they themselves had had. This belief had to do with their literal interpretation of the word "angel" as Hebrew for "messenger." For Jane and John, the individual experience of the divine is limited to an experience of the angelic messenger that they identified with the Holy Spirit.

They believed that God no longer spoke directly to humans. As a result, they thought that any such visionary experiences were the result of satanic misinformation. John discounted Agee's experience as merely benign because it was only "mildly" delusional. As a Christian, he viewed Dean's experiences as potentially demonic and dangerous because the intensity of his experience led him to mistake demonic misinformation for real spiritual truths. For Jane and John, the only valid experience of the deity was the entering of the Holy Spirit into one's consciousness in the experience of spiritual rebirth.

They also believed in the imminent approach of the End Times, made arguments based on literal interpretations of the Bible, and specifically built a Web page designed to engage in the evangelism associated with vernacular Christian fundamentalism. With their emphasis on spiritual rebirth, Jane and John's beliefs clearly marked them as participants in this virtual ekklesia. However, they did not use claims to revelatory experience to position their own interpretations as authoritative. In fact, they rejected such authority in others. They were more interested in enacting the virtual ekklesia through ritual deliberation than they were in asserting their own authority.

Jane and John displayed deliberative communication in a more sustained way than had Marilyn, and, in the example above, their commitment to enacting ritual deliberation seems to have outlasted hers. They wanted to keep exchanging emails even after she had closed the case on their discussion. In the end, Marilyn's need to express the knowledge she had gained from her divinely led studies trumped any desire to discuss the Bible with Jane and John. In this sense, her desire for authority trumped her desire to enact the ekklesia.

Jane and John, on the other hand, limited their personal knowledge of the divine to a very particular kind of experience. For them, grace was known and attained in a moment of personal certainty. On the validity of their spiritual rebirths, it seemed that debate was not possible. By rejecting claims to special access to the divine like those of Marilyn, however, they also limited the authority that any single individual could claim based on being "led" by the Holy Spirit. Combining this emphasis on the true unknowability of God's divine plan with their commitment to the core beliefs of vernacular Christian fundamentalism, the couple could discuss biblical prophecy seemingly endlessly through email with their fellow believers. This commitment to ritual deliberation carried over into the style of their Web site.

Their site exhibited a very different sort of communication. Though they had no blog-like participatory features, they did have a wide range of interesting and suggestive, instead of authoritative, information on their pages. Despite their site's lack of actual ritual deliberation, it drew a large audience. Based on interview data, they engaged in a lot of private email communication with individuals who were reading their site.

As they recounted during their interview, Jane and John wanted to continually exchange, engage, and reassess their own beliefs about the End Times with others in the virtual ekklesia. As John put it, their understanding of the divine was "dynamic." The sort of communication they most strongly rejected was that which functioned to shut down discussion by asserting a special personal authority, which was just the sort of authority Marilyn claimed. If Marilyn was most interested in communicating her authority to others online, then Jane and John struggled to keep deliberation going with Marilyn because they had come to consciously realize that their virtual ekklesia must be enacted through online fellowship.

In fact, I quoted John's explanation of the virtual ekkelesia at the outset of this research. It was from him that I learned of ritual deliberation's central role as fellowship in the movement. As he put it: "any time people are together—two or more are gathered in His name: there you are! You're the ekklesia!" Rejecting the need for institutional religion, John stated clearly that Jane and his communication online functioned as a virtual ekklesia:

> There is no real reason you have to show up at a denomination or every Sunday show up at this certain location in the city or else you're a reprobate. And I think it's absolutely viable for the "church," if you understand what I mean by that: the ekklesia; to meet on the Internet. And I have seen it happen a lot. And that's pretty much where we hold our church. (Jane and John 1999)

Jane and John needed to give cues to deliberation so that their audience could easily engage them in discussions, because creating the virtual ekklesia through fellowship was their conscious motive for communication about the End Times online. Their humor, pastiche of disparate ideas, and, in particular, their willingness to email with Marilyn longer than Marilyn was willing to email with them, all demonstrate their deliberative attitude. This attitude led them to mediate the tension between personal authority and deliberation by rejecting the possibility that anyone (including themselves) could have greater access to divine authority than anybody else in the movement.

Marilyn's high-profile positioning in the ekklesia was something that eluded people like Dean, Jack, and Tim at least partially because they gave few cues to ritual deliberation. However, like them (and unlike Jane, John, or Lambert), when Marilyn was faced with Jane and John's insistent rejection of her personal authority, her ability to communicate seemed to cease at least in part because she was simply not interested in engaging in ritual deliberation when her ideas were treated as equal to those of others. This fact, however, did not divide Marilyn, Jane, and John from the movement in which they all participated. Despite these differences, their shared certainty functioned to unite them in the movement—if not as friends.

Digital Jesus, 2000

While the Watcher couple was saddened at the loss of the friend they felt they had in Marilyn, they both told me specifically that "Marilyn is saved." That is, even if they thought she was dogmatic and wrong, she was a true Christian and she would be saved in the end. About that, Jane and John had no doubt. They had no doubt because they all shared the certainty characteristic of those in their ekklesia. They knew they shared this certainty because, without it, they would not have been able to deliberate about the End Times with her at all.

They had found each other through topical community formation based on their interest in the End Times. Though their differences caused them to stop discussing the topic directly with one another, they were still united in the web of communication that gives life to the movement through the links between their sites. Even after Marilyn had broken off their deliberation, John and Jane felt that they were all part of the same virtual ekklesia because they shared the beliefs of vernacular Christian fundamentalism.

While they might disagree on the exact literal meaning of the prophetic biblical texts, the belief that those texts contained literal truth was beyond question. Spiritual rebirth supported this belief and then supported the remaining beliefs that defined their otherwise diffuse, diverse, and individualistic new religious movement. Because of the centrality of these beliefs, the fact that Marilyn was saved was never brought into question. Because she used the terms "born again," she, Jane, and John could enact their virtual ekklesia in ritual deliberation about the End Times—despite disagreements.

As we have seen, at the end of 1999 institutional mass media was fascinated by the sensationalized possibility of the Y2K computer bug and a general anticipation of the calendar change from 1999 to 2000. As the clock struck midnight across North America on December 31, 1999, more individuals than ever before in the history of human consciousness stopped to take note of those moments.

Of course, nothing much happened.

The members of this virtual ekklesia had already realized that this particular moment in time would not be the Second Coming. Their understanding of the divine narrative of human history had too many loose ends yet to be fulfilled in 2000 and beyond. However, they had forged a vernacular web of interconnected sites that unified a wide diversity of ideas even while it amplified a fundamental tension in their movement. In this web, they explored different ways to mediate the tension between the individual authority associated with revelatory divine experiences and the need to engage in deliberative communication. In the end, Marilyn Agee's site seemed to anticipate the solution we shall now see playing out in the powerful forms of participatory media where the movement primarily exists today.

The new millennium dawned on a changing Internet. The newsgroups and email lists lingered, but overall the Internet had been transformed from a realm of computer specialists and researchers into a vast marketplace frequented by individuals of every sort. From ready access to obscure information to the wildly multiplying sources for mail-order products, the average North American was now wedded to Internet communication. Finally a truly everyday medium, the ease and intuitive nature of the Web created a massive boom in Internet use.

At the same time, Web-based computer language technologies were rapidly becoming much more powerful. Soon amateur Web site builders could expand their sites to include more interactive media like comments sections and forums. The shift from the older forms of HTML to these new and more powerful Internet computer languages also made it far easier for Web site users to place more personal content online. After 2002, the Worldwide Web began to dissolve into a new array of media characterized by the possibilities for interactive communication.

Today, these powerful forms dominate everyday Internet use. In so doing, they encourage individuals to both consume and produce far more vernacular communication than ever before. Particularly well suited for ritual deliberation, these media produce Web pages that exhibit characteristics much like those of Marilyn's "Pro and Con Index." Marilyn's construction of the "Index" allowed her to host ritual deliberation while retaining direct control of how those email-based exchanges appeared on her site. In similar ways, the participatory Web sites that best foster ritual deliberation enable authoritative individuals to quietly manage the communication processes on their sites in ways that exclude those who might express opposition to the ideology of vernacular Christian fundamentalism.

This deployment of participatory media emerges from two alternate impulses already suggested by the movement's use of the Internet. On the one hand, placing individual expression online is typically free and requires little computer expertise. Because online expression requires very little commitment of resources in terms of time or money, the average Internet user has no pressing need to satisfy the expectations of a broad audience. Since they do not need an audience to support advertising or donations to pay to build their Web sites, people can simply assert their opinions authoritatively without adjusting their claims to any who disagree.

At the same time, the vast amount of online expression available for individuals to consume encourages them to explore divergent voices. Opening to the expression of others, individuals attempt to aggregate that expression into a unified understanding of the world in which they live. For those with their own participatory media sites, they can authoritatively express that aggregated understanding back at the network locations they control. In this way, participatory media enact a feedback loop of content consumption and individual expression that is much like what Marilyn's "Pro and Con Index" displayed. With participatory media, however, individuals can go beyond displaying like-minded deliberation. In these media, they can create communication enclaves for their ritual deliberation safe from those outside the ekklesia.

For the individuals enacting the virtual ekklesia of vernacular Christian fundamentalism, participatory media help resolve the tension between authority and deliberation by enabling them to collect, link, and repost content they gather from divergent and even hostile sources while at the same time excluding any communication that does not support their shared ideology. As it turns out, the features of participatory media proved far better suited to ritual deliberation than any of the popular Internet media that had come before.

5

The End Times in Participatory Media

Rapture Ready *and Beyond*

Aggregating the Virtual Church

In the year 2000 the technology economy collapsed, ending a period of seemingly unfettered financial growth in North America. Then, in 2001, Middle Eastern militants dramatically attacked targets in the United States, transforming the American psyche and prompting protracted and bloody international conflicts in Afghanistan and Iraq. Through the tumultuous years that followed, Marilyn Agee continued to produce her Web pages for the "Pro and Con Index." In 2002, she had 912 entries. In 2010, she had over 1,500. Over those years, fears emerged about new terrorist plots, weakened global economic conditions, massive deadly pandemics, natural disasters associated with the growing recognition of climate change, and the planetary positions predicted by the Mayan dating system for the year 2012. Through it all, Marilyn's site offered her fellow believers a network location to witness the ritual deliberation that enacts their virtual ekklesia.

Over the course of the first decade of the new millennium, the virtual ekklesia emerging from vernacular Christian fundamentalism continued to expand and change with the changing media technologies. In particular, the development of increasingly powerful network-based software created different ways for individuals to place their personal content online. Associated with the rise to prominence of the term "blog," "participatory media" has come to dominate the Worldwide Web. Participatory media are typically Web sites that contain features allowing the "coproduction" of content. Coproduction occurs when both a Web site builder or builders and the Web site's general audience contribute to the content on the site. Using none of the automated interactive features associated with coproduction, Marilyn had anticipated the suitability of participatory media for ritual deliberation by mixing her own voice with those of her audience for over twelve years.

Since at least 1996, Marilyn had used the Internet as a way to make her and her fellow believers feel more connected. She also recognized, however, that divergent or hostile voices can drown out the expression of the shared beliefs that enact the virtual ekklesia. To reduce this possibility, her "Pro and Con Index" displayed deliberations in which she tightly controlled the appearance of dissent. As became evident in her relationship with Jane and John, Marilyn was the ultimate arbiter of these public displays. She filtered out dissenting voices by reproducing her email-based ritual deliberation on each "Pro and Con" Web page in an edited form. In so doing, Marilyn seems to have anticipated the delicate balance between authoritative control and deliberative participation that is now very easy for nontechnical users to attain by adding a forum, comments sections, or similar participatory features to their Web sites.

In 2002, Marilyn updated her Worldwide Web presence by purchasing her own domain name: "bibleprophecycorner.com." Leaving a duplicate site at her old location, she moved the main version of her pages onto the server of a Christian software company in Oklahoma. Creating a top-level page simply entitled "Prophecy Corner," Marilyn included several links to other End Times-oriented Christian sites. In June of that year, Marilyn created a whole new page of links to other sites, including online Bibles, the "U.S. Naval Observatory Lunar Eclipse Computer," a host of online calendar dating tools, and fifty-four sites of other individuals participating in vernacular Christian fundamentalism (Agee 2002a).

One of those links was to a site called *Rapture Ready*. This site demonstrates how participatory media encourage a combination of topical community formation and individual expression that mediates the tension between authority and deliberation. In so doing, the site also exemplifies how these media can create the closed enclaves of online discussion that vigorously foster ritual deliberation. A central feature of such enclaves is their ability to gather information collected from other media, both vernacular and institutional, and aggregate it together in terms that give it specific ideological meaning. In the case of *Rapture Ready*, the guiding ideology is that of vernacular Christian fundamentalism.

Rapture Ready first began as *The Rapture Index* in 1995 (Strandberg 1999a). In 1997, Todd Strandberg, its builder, renamed the site but continued to feature the "Rapture Index." This "Index" is a number based on news events that Todd culls from a wide range of media outlets. Sorting all the news reports he finds into forty-five "categories" ranging from "False Christs," "The Occult," and "Satanism" to "Liberalism," "The Antichrist," and "Earthquakes," Todd generates a number he characterizes as "a Dow Jones Industrial Average of end time activity."

Asserting that the index is not meant to be predictive, Todd describes it as a "prophetic speedometer": the "higher the number, the faster we're moving towards the occurrence of pre-tribulation rapture." In March 2008, the index was at 169. Its record low was 57 on December 12, 1993. Its record high was 182 on September 24, 2001 (Strandberg 2008b). Each of these index numbers represents Todd's assertion about how much anticipation for the Rapture (how "rapture ready") he and his fellow believers should feel.

Todd, and many people like him, build and use Web sites that are tightly focused on topics they believe are important. Participatory media facilitate this kind of communication because they elicit more individual expression. They have made it easier for people to create their own "blogs," other Web sites, and to comment on forums. Then, in turn, the diverse expression of these individuals combined with the information they gather from institutional news media can be aggregated onto other topically focused Web sites. This availability of expression encourages individuals to bring a huge diversity of ideas together on Web sites with very specific interests and users (Sunstein 2007, 138). In a distilled form, this is just what Todd's Rapture Index does. It aggregates instances of news events from both vernacular and institutional media into a specific number, the "Index."

This aggregation is not a mere mechanism of communication technologies. Instead, the cultural forces inherent in the media Todd experiences through the Internet shape it. Interacting with human history and culture, Todd acts out of his own volition when he aggregates information. As a result, his aggregations are not reflections of that external information. Instead, they are assertive inflections of his own understanding of the media world he inhabits. Participating in vernacular Christian fundamentalism, Todd's Index asserts his acceptance of that ideology. As others read his Web site and agree—if not with the specifics, then with the validity of his anticipation of the End Times—they contribute to another kind of aggregation: the aggregate of individuals who enact this virtual ekklesia. This occurs as the media elicits more individual expression about the End Times either on those individuals' own Web sites or on the coproduced sections of other sites.

Among individuals deploying participatory media in this movement, two alternate impulses emerge in association with eliciting and aggregating discourse, and these impulses point back to the familiar tension between authority and deliberation. On the one hand, the ability to easily communicate to a large audience encourages individualistic expression (Howard 2005a). Such expression tends to include more authoritative claims. On the other hand, the availability of so many different people with whom to form a community encourages the aggregation of diverse new content. Individuals who choose to engage new or divergent content would seem to be interested in more deliberative modes of communication.

The virtual ekklesia that emerges from these alternate impulses integrates both individual and communal communication in a way that facilitates the ritual deliberation that gives it existence. Individuals need to express themselves so that they can recognize and feel justified in their shared beliefs. For this, they need a receptive audience. At the same time, they need broad public access to their expressions so that fellow believers can find each other and engage in deliberation. One potential impediment to this deliberation has repeatedly confronted the movement. The broad public is not End Times-competent and, in fact, has shown a tendency to be hostile toward those discussing the End Times.

Faced with the potential hostile comments of outsiders, those network locations that find a balance between eliciting individual expression and curtailing dissent become the most popular locations for enacting ritual deliberation. In the participatory media that came to comprise the virtual ekklesia after 2001, that balance, much like Marilyn's site, includes the display of open deliberation that is authoritatively managed by a central moderator. Carefully balancing these two modes of communication, the most successful locations for ritual deliberation create communication enclaves where new or divergent ideas can be rapidly assimilated into the already shared ideology of vernacular Christian fundamentalism.

Among the different forms of participatory media, more authoritative communication and a weakened form of ritual deliberation dominate the video blog, while examples from Web-based forums tend toward a stronger form of ritual deliberation. In between these extremes, the text-based blog has become by far the most common use of participatory media in the movement. On text-based blogs, Web pages that combined authoritative moderation with strong deliberative cues proved to be the most conducive to ritual deliberation. After 2001, these text-based blogs became the primary locations from where participants in the movement enacted their virtual ekklesia.

The Rise of Participatory Media

Heralded as marking a new era of "participatory culture," the number of Web pages considered "blogs" exploded in the first decade of the new millennium (Jenkins et al. 2006a). In July 2002, 3 percent of Internet users reported having their own blog. By November 2005, that number had jumped to 10 percent. At that time, 27 percent read other people's blogs and 19 percent of teenage Internet users maintained their own blogs (Pew 2005; Lenhart and Madden 2005). Since then, it has been estimated that 70,000 new blogs and about 700,000 new posts to existing blogs are appearing every day (Technorati Data 2006).

This explosion has fueled and been fueled by a growing diversity of media forms. Famously termed "Web 2.0" by computer media CEO Tim O'Reilly, these forms were made possible by innovations on the original HTML computer language that Tim Burners-Lee created in 1992 (O'Reilly 2005). With the surge in popularity of a software application called "Blogger," HTML and its follow-ons began to be replaced by more robust languages. Unlike HTML, these new languages used the Internet itself as a platform. In so doing, software applications using these languages made it easier for Web users to add, change, and personalize the content on Web sites they otherwise had no control over.

Typically free, these software applications offer their use in exchange for the integration of commercial advertising on the various personal pages created by the Web users with the software. Because these applications function by allowing the individual to simply fill in content on predefined Web page templates, the specific design of the software heavily influences the kinds and forms of content individuals put online (Howard 2005d, 323). While these participatory media are in a constant state of change, their diverse forms are often referred to by the blanket term "blog."

Emerging out of what is considered the first digital genre on the Worldwide Web, "Web logs" were part of the content that was considered characteristic of personal "home pages." In the early days of the Worldwide Web, "home page" was a technical term that denoted the "root" or "index" file on a Web site: the default file accessed by a HTML browser when no file is specified. Typically, this page was considered the "entry" or "front page" of a Web site. All Web sites had home pages in this sense. Because many of the original "home pages" were also the personal network "homes" of computer-savvy hobbyists, it came to be expected that home pages would have certain features (Dillon and Gushrowski 2000; Asteroff 2001). One feature was the "log" of Web sites that the home page builder collected. Often, the builder would write comments about each site she or he found and documented in her or his log.

Over time, the "Web log" emerged out of this practice of documenting personal lists of favorite, or hated, Web sites (Blood 2000; Jerz 2003; Turnbull 2002). In 1999, several companies released software designed to automate Web site creation in an effort to harness the growing popularity of so-called "Web logs." The most successful of these ventures was the "Blogger" software of *Blogger.com*. Because of the specific features that it popularized, "Blogger" shaped the expectations of many "blog" users and helped define the features of the emerging medium (Blood 2004; Herring et al. 2004). Instead of emphasizing simple "logs" of links, however, Blogger emphasized features that encouraged more direct coproduction of Web page content. Primary among these features were the reverse-dated entries of a single writer. Secondarily, Blogger included a "Comments" section after each entry. These comments sections allowed audience members to post responses to the blogger's entries.

With *Blogger.com*, the sheer number of individuals able to create "blogs" rendered the previous conception of "Web logs" obsolete. As well-known blogger and scholar of communication, Rebecca Blood, has described it: "With the overwhelming adoption of Blogger . . . the blog-style Weblog was born" (Blood 2004, 53). Reverse-dated personal entries with comments sections underneath dominated this style, and the term Web log gave way to "blog" (Miller and Shepard 2004). By 2003, as many as four million blogs were hosted on these sites, becoming the easiest way for users to post their own personal content online (Henning 2003).

Today, the forms of participatory Web sites loosely referred to as "blogs" are expanding the genre to include a wider and wider range of network applications and media. These media encourage both authoritative and deliberative communication. Because it is typically free to post text, graphic, or video content, individuals often use these media to make personal statements. This encourages more authoritative communication. At the same time, comments sections have come to be expected and are most often incorporated into the individual posting medium. This encourages more deliberative communication.

To document the virtual ekklesia in these media, I located a sample of participatory Web pages by searching the terms "End Time," "End Times," "Endtime," and "Endtimes," in two common search engines on June 28, 2007. During 2008 and 2009 I tracked the Web sites captured in that search. The initial results of the search indicated that four primary forms of Web page were associated with participatory media. All four of these media can be considered "participatory" because their content is coproduced. Coproduction occurs on at least two levels. At the first level, the emphasis is on individual expression. Because the commercial software is free and easy to use, it elicits individual expression. Because few resources need to be committed to the expression by the individual, very specific, idiosyncratic, and personal content can be placed online as long as it does not violate the policies of the company offering the online service. At a second level of coproduction, the emphasis shifts from the individual to the community.

This shift is facilitated by the inclusion of areas on these sites for audience comments. At first, "comments sections," "walls," or "bulletin boards" allowed only text postings. Now, they allow audience members to post text, graphic, sound, and video content in a wide range of formats. Often, these "posts" are actually links to content that is housed on another site. In this way, individuals can "post" the video or graphic content they have uploaded to a site dedicated to that purpose on someone else's text-based blog. Because of this increased integration and ease of posting, it has become easier for individuals to aggregate information from a variety of sources and then express it on topically focused blogs.

As a result of these features, participatory media encourage communication that is more focused on the aggregation of information and less on the expression of ideas about that information. When a Web site emphasizes this aggregation, it is characterized by more authoritative communication—not unlike the static Web sites documented in the last chapter. On the other hand, Web sites that have more extensive comments sections foster more deliberative communication and can host stronger ritual deliberation. Blogs focused on information aggregation do not need to have mechanisms for audience members to comment. Without audience members publicly commenting, the blogger has complete authority over the content she or he aggregates onto the blog.

To most strongly encourage ritual deliberation in the Web environment, however, Web site builders can deploy participatory media to allow user input, while at the same time excluding those who do not display adequate competence in End Times deliberation. At the network locations where moderation effectively balances deliberative and authoritative communication, ritual deliberation flourishes more richly than it has in any other medium.

The sample set of Web pages in this chapter demonstrate how well suited moderated participatory media are to ritual deliberation. The two search engines used to create the sample were *Google Blog Search* and *Technorati. com*. *Technorati* traces "112.8 million blogs and over 250 million pieces of tagged social media" (Technorati 2008). These search engines locate this data using "Web feeds" in the two most common formats: RSS (Really Simple Syndication) and Atom. Most participatory media use these mechanisms to automatically broadcast information about additions, changes, or updates to the specific blog or other participatory media site.

Collecting these feeds, the search engines rank their search results based on the inclusion of the key words searched for, or "relevance," how often the overall site is updated, and how many other individuals are linking to or reading the blog. The two search engines generate different results because they calculate these factors differently. For the sample set, I combined the top one hundred hits from each of the two search engines and created a collection of two hundred specific Web pages. While most of these pages were part of personal text-based or video "blogs," some are more properly imagined as "forum" entries or social networking "profiles."

Online media generally termed "social networking tools" like *Friendster*, *MySpace*, or *Facebook* combine blogging, file sharing, and social functions to help individuals locate and make connections with other people who share their interests. These generally participatory sites offer easy-to-use personal content hosting services for text, graphic, and video files. They emphasize presenting individuals' real-life identities by describing their personal interests. Users can make connections based on references made to the End Times in these descriptions, and thus use the media for topical community formation. Based on such connections, individuals can initiate ritual deliberation through email, chat services, or in posts to forums and comments sections.

Socially Networking Prophets

The least common kind of medium appearing in the sample were the "profile pages" of social networking sites like *MySpace* and *Facebook*. By seeking to present more of the complex whole of individual personalities instead of providing places to discuss specific topics, these sites tend not to facilitate as much ritual deliberation. However, some individuals involved in the movement deployed these sites to draw like-minded people to view content they had aggregated onto their profile pages.

Profile pages contain personal information including text, graphic, and video content. Based on a variety of software tools, users are able to search for, view, and link to each other's profiles based on shared interests. Profile information typically includes schools attended, work places, geographical location, hobbies, political views, religious affiliations, favorite music, television shows, movies, and similar items. Typically, each individual's profile contains a list of links to other people who have agreed to become their "friend." When "friending" others, links between the friends' profiles are automatically generated by the software. Once friends, individuals can post comments to the profiles of their friends. Many users regularly post new information to their profiles as well as comment on those of their friends. Some even maintain text or video blogs on their social network profiles.

Among individuals using social networking sites to locate others interested in the End Times, two basic deployments of the medium emerge. In the first, they use these sites to engage in the whole range of activities and features the medium offers. In the second, they primarily deploy their profiles to make authoritative claims about the End Times. For people using social networking sites to connect with lots of other people based on a wide variety of traits and interests, the End Times is just one of the interests expressed on their profiles. For such people, vernacular Christian fundamentalism is typically not central in their lives. In this sense, they are typically only peripheral to the movement.

A good example of this first deployment of the medium is the *MySpace* profile of a sixty-one-year-old man in Fort Collins, Colorado, named "Paul." Discussing the question, "How are the recent sex scandals in the church affecting you?" he suggested that they may indicate the approach of the End Times. Without further comment, he cited Jude 1: 18: "How that they told you there should be mockers in the last time, who should walk after their own ungodly lusts." The rest of his *MySpace* usage touched on the many other topics of interest that emerged around his real-life identity (Paul 2007).

In another example from *MySpace*, a thirty-six-year-old man named "Kenneth" who lives in Arkansas, noted in the first of his six blog entries that Christ as described in the Book of Revelation "could knock your socks off" (Kenneth 2007). Like many *MySpace* users, Kenneth read others' blogs and commented on them. One of these comments noted, "The end times are near . . . come quickly Lord Jesus!!!! May we all take this to heart." This comment came in response to another blogger named "Rhonda" with the *MySpace* profile name "His Messenger." People like Kenneth and Paul remain on the periphery of the movement. However, His Messenger exemplifies the second sort of user. These individuals primarily deploy their profiles as an online location to post their personal claims about the End Times. For them, social networking sites provide another outlet for their expression of belief in vernacular Christian fundamentalism. The communication among those in this second group tends to be more authoritative.

Rhonda (or "His Messenger") was linked to Kenneth as a "friend" and provides a good example of the more authoritative use of social networking (Kenneth 2007). Rhonda described having intense "seer states" during which "the Lord speaks" through her as "His Messenger." A forty-nine-year-old partially disabled grandmother living in Indiana, Rhonda stated that her primary reason for using the Internet was that "I do not have many people in my life at this time." She went on to describe using *MySpace* to contact other people and engage in a range of activities including emailing, messaging, performing "Theophostic healing," and praying. Finding significant fulfillment from her online communication, she has had emails from people as far away as Saudi Arabia, Africa, and China.

For Rhonda—and for others in the movement, as we have seen—the Internet functioned as a virtual ekklesia that she explicitly associated with early Christians. She saw her online fellowship activities functioning much "as it was in the beginning—[in the] Book of Acts." While she claimed a central interest in fellowship, her online communication was highly authoritative. This authority came from her belief that she was a prophet and that God spoke through her while she was in a trance state. Through visions and trances, Rhonda believed that God "positioned" her "for the end time battle" in which there "[were] many principalities [or demonic forces]" she was constantly "warring" against (Rhonda 2008c).

Rhonda first put up a Web site to publicize her visions in 1996. Using the free hosting service *Geocities* at the time, she decided to start a *MySpace* page in 2006. She posted a note on the *Geocities* site, saying:

> Something New the Lord is Having Me try for Him is "My Space" There are a lot of things I have yet to figure out (like how to correct the site and take off worldly features like "Zodiac Sign" . . . etc). This is brand new for me so bear with me . . . but if you have a prayer need or question and are looking for me online, you could try this location! (Rhonda 2006a)

In the months after she started using *MySpace*, Rhonda shifted her online activity primarily to that medium. She began hosting a blog on *MySpace* and began posting her prophetic messages there. Describing her attraction to *MySpace* in a final post on *Geocities*, she wrote:

Information is current/up-to-date on the MySpace site and I encourage all to get an account and "come and see" for that is where my team and I fellowship with one another most (because there is opportunity for interaction) whereas this site is "stationary" and does not afford the opportunity to receive incoming messages in real time. (Rhonda 2007)

From 2006 on, Rhonda began posting to her *MySpace* blog every other day.

Rhonda's profile page on *MySpace* was highly modified. Through its software, the *MySpace* site allows users to reorganize the layout of the information in their profiles, and add background images, as well as post text, graphic, audio, and video content. Rhonda's page had a ribboned blue background with black text. On the top left, the "His Messenger" graphic offered the only visual representation of Rhonda on the site. The ghostly image was of an ambiguously empty headscarf. When I asked her about it, she said that she was directed by God to use this distinct image of a "talit" or Jewish prayer shawl because her mother was Jewish. When she attended public events, Rhonda wore her own tallit (Rhonda 2008c). Opposite this image on the profile page, Rhonda posted what she termed a "creed": "WE ARE THE HIDDEN PROPHETS WHO HAVE BEEN KEPT FOR THIS HOUR" (Rhonda 2008b).

Below that, two columns flowed downward with a mixture of content collected from around the Worldwide Web that included texts, graphics, sound, and video. One video on the site appeared to be a homemade devotional clip mixing a song by the pop music artist Moby with quotes from ancient Christian martyrs and images from Mel Gibson's *Passion of the Christ*. Below that, she had a pastel graphic of a man applying the Passover blood to the door of his home. Below the Passover graphic, Rhonda posted the text: "WHOEVER OR WHATEVER ENTERS THIS SITE IS COVERED WITH THE BLOOD OF JESUS CHRIST BY HIS AUTHORITY I FORBID ALL FALSE FROM MANIFESTING—IT IS NOT ALLOWED HERE AGAINST THIS MINISTRY EVER AGAIN" (Rhonda 2008b).

Rhonda valued being able to express herself to others online. In this sense, network media seemed to have encouraged her to express herself. *MySpace* as well as other social network sites offer several means for communicating with others. In addition to listing her email address, Rhonda used Internet-based chat or messaging to exchange information in real time. Further, individuals could "subscribe" to Rhonda's blog so that they were notified immediately when she posted something new. With this level of connectivity, it would seem that Rhonda and those who interacted with her on *MySpace* would be able to engage in a significant amount of ritual deliberation. This, however, did not seem to occur.

Most of Rhonda's blog posts did not receive any comments at all. One reason for this was that she primarily made authoritative claims based on her belief that she had special access to the divine. As she put it, the divine "looks out through MY EYES and He speaks via MY LIPS. He has cleared my memory and mind so that I now have THE MIND OF CHRIST" (Rhonda 2008b). This authority enabled her to speak directly to others in a commanding voice, and she did not limit her intended audience to other believers or even people with whom she had some connection. Her very first *MySpace* blog post began: "One of today's news headlines read, 'Rapper Kanye West Poses as Jesus.'" Rhonda went on to rail against a magazine cover featuring West for over 2,500 words. She asserted that "Our God is so amazing . . . . if you could think and imagine for just one moment, how much crap He puts up with from us." Taking the magazine cover as a negative example, she compelled her audience to "walk a walk that exhibits Christ and honors Him" (Rhonda 2006c).

In the post, she went on to recount how the Holy Spirit whispered the word "poser" in her ear as she thought about the magazine cover. Compelled to look up the word in "a really OLD dictionary," Rhonda felt that God guided her to think about the grievous nature of being a "poser." Realizing the heretical nature of portraying oneself as Christ, God directed her to pray for Kanye West. She did so in her blog post by writing: "I DECREE IT UNTO YOU, KANYE, AS THE LORD HAS GIVEN ME UTTERENCE HERE ON YOUR BEHALF . . .BE IT UNTO YOU AS HE HAS SPOKEN IN JESUS' MATCHLESS NAME!" She then encouraged her audience to also pray for West so that his sin of being a poser might be forgiven (Rhonda 2006c).

More authoritative than most others in the movement, Rhonda used *MySpace* as a means to spread the central message that Christ spoke through her: that humanity is in the final days before the End Times. Despite the potential for interactivity provided by social networking sites, the End Times discourse found in this participatory media most often engages in highly authoritative communication. It seems that the emphasis on individual expression fosters less deliberation than do other kinds of participatory media. This becomes clearer in another form of media that is even more focused on individual expression: the video blog.

Video Blogging with Prophetic Authority

The second least common kind of Web page in the sample was the most authoritative. These pages belonged to the participatory medium generally referred to as video blogs or "vlogs." The pages generally featured talking-head style videos in which users authoritatively asserted their beliefs about the End Times. In most cases, comments sections appeared under each video entry, allowing audience members to comment. However, very little ritual deliberation occurred in these comments sections. Instead, video logs seemed particularly well adapted for the expression of those who perceived themselves to be prophets.

For these individuals, video blogging offered a powerful medium for communicating their prophetic messages because video can capture the powerful emotions they experienced while in a trance. In one example of this behavior, a twenty-eight-year old man in Missouri named "James" performed a blessing over several U.S. states by speaking in the voice of God on video. Both James and his wife, "Linda," used Blogger software offered by the free blog-hosting site *Blogspot.com*. Linda's blog was far more typical of personal blogs and suggested that she was only marginally involved in vernacular fundamentalism. Titled simply "Linda's Link," it showed the most activity after the 2007 birth of their son. Her page included announcements about their pregnancy, the birth, and her return to work as a professional counselor. She often addressed an audience of family and friends directly in her blog entries, and she had many links to the blogs or other pages of these audience members. She did not discuss the End Times on her blog (Linda 2008).

James's page, however, was very different. Titled "Of Rest and Harvest," his blog had 173 entries between December 2006 and February 2008. Almost all of his entries began by saying, "God says . . . ." In these entries, James typically recounted a vision or dream he had had about world events. Using the comments sections of his blog posts, James then forwarded news articles he had found from around the Internet that seemed to support his prophesy (James 2008). In his June 7, 2007 blog entry, for example, James prophesized, "The day is coming when the World Government will arise, and when it does[,] so shall the one world church. But those who know the true church will not be governed." He went on to forward two articles supporting his claim, including one about the possibility that a video camera surveillance system would be installed in New York City. For James, this suggested the growing power of a One World Government that would emerge to tightly control individual behavior as it sought to locate and destroy "true Christians" (James 2007).

Though less numerous than these text-based posts, some of James's most powerful blog entries were his video blessings. In one such video entitled, "The faithful might stumble but I will pick them up says the Spirit," he appeared dressed in a bright red Nebraska Corn Huskers watch cap and football jersey. He spoke with quiet passion, saying:

> God said He looked today upon the regions of Oklahoma, Texas, Missouri, and Arkansas, and He says these regions will consume my spirit of love. [In another voice:] "And I will show them mercy throughout the period of 2008. What I give them will be an awakening so great and unusual that they will say we must hear and listen to the servants of the prophets for they are hearing from the Lord God." (James 2008)

When James's newborn baby could be heard starting to cry in the background, it did not seem to disturb the prophetic trance. Almost a year after he had posted it, this video had still received no feedback. In fact, very few of James's video entries received comments in their comments sections.

Another video blogger engaged more typical prophetic interpretation instead of actually engaging trance. However, he received only marginally more comments than did James, and many of these were hostile. Deploying a style more like Marilyn Agee's divinely led interpretation, "Keith," was a forty-three-year-old video blogger whose sermonic teachings on the End Times elicited mostly hostile feedback and very little deliberation. In this case, the video blog was again well suited to his authoritative attitude. Even though he did not present himself as a prophet, his authoritative communication did not encourage deliberation with the people he found online. Instead, those sympathetic to or involved with vernacular Christian fundamentalism posted short affirmative comments under his videos, while others posted hostile feedback (Keith 2007a).

Keith had videotaped and posted seventeen messages before March 2007. These videos had then been forwarded, linked to, and posted by users to at least seven different video hosting forums. They seemed to have been originally posted on a free video hosting site called *Veoh.com*. Ranging from about six minutes to just over an hour in length, the videos were typically about ten minutes long. In total, they contained over 289 minutes of footage. Their topics included messages for specific religious groups such as Christians, Jews, Muslims, "followers of Satan," and atheists. Others dealt with his interpretations of the Book of Isaiah and the Gospel of John, as well as a literal reading of Genesis. While all the videos touched on Keith's central concern that the

End Times were rapidly approaching, six specifically focused on End Times beliefs (Keith 2008).

One typical video, entitled "End Times: Antichrist and False Prophet," began with Keith seated on what appeared to be a folding aluminum lawn chair. He was facing the camera and spoke directly to it. At his left was what appeared to be the speaker of a home stereo system with an American flag draped over it. On top of that rested Keith's well-worn Bible. Keith began this video post much as he did all his posts: in measured and comforting tones. He stated, "Most of us have heard the term 'End Times' used before. And in truth, we are living in the End Times right now." He went on to assert that anyone who "doesn't have God and His Son in their life will be enslaved or killed during the soon coming times." Keith continued:

> The Bible mentions the Antichrist and the False Prophet, and right now they're working behind the scenes consolidating their power for world rulership. Most of us have heard the terms "New World Order" or "One World Government" and so forth and so on. It's all basically leading to the rulership of the Antichrist and the False Prophet. They're gonna have a time where they're gonna rule the world. And they're gonna be directly ruled by Satan. (Keith 2007b)

After he articulated this belief, Keith reached over and picked up his Bible. Reading from Revelation 13: 11–18, he offered Bible verses as proof of his assertions about the One World Government and Antichrist. For nearly ten minutes, Keith discussed the dangerous reality of the approaching End Times with a quiet intensity. Demonstrating compassion for his network audience, Keith implored them to take the Bible seriously. He stated that many people would not be able to recognize the Antichrist or the Mark of the Beast. However, because the Mark was "the ultimate abomination that any person could do," it condemned those who took it to eternal separation from God. Keith seemed driven to bring this message to as many people as he could so that they could avoid that fate. He warned his audience, saying:

> Do not allow yourself to be deceived. So come to know God and his son. And the best way to come to know Them is through God's word, the Bible. Take care of yourself. Remember what I am saying to you. And see if what I am saying to you is the truth by looking in your Bible. Take care. (Keith 2007b)

Though heavily authoritative, Keith was less authoritative than James or Rhonda because he did not claim that God spoke through him. Instead, more like Agee, he implored his audience to look at the Bible for the sources of his claims. As a result, Keith did get some feedback from his Internet audience in the comments sections below the videos. Keith's video blogs had received a total of forty-one comments at the time I took the sample. Of those, three were unclear or nonsensical. Nine were simply affirmative, like "Amen" or "THANKS FOR SHARING MAY GOD BLESS YOU" (Keith 2007b). Eighteen were overtly hostile, like one comment made in response to Keith's video blog entry entitled "Message for the Jews." This commentator began the short post by writing: "shut ur ass up u damm racesest !!!!!!" (Keith 2007c). This comment is particularly interesting because Keith himself is African American. Another four of the comments were Keith's own responses to this hostile commentary.

Only seven of the posted comments to Keith's seventeen videos actually engaged the ideas he expressed by asking questions, offering counterpoints, or otherwise engaging in ritual deliberation. Among those seven, Keith responded to only one. In this case, a Muslim commented on Keith's entry entitled, "A Message to the Muslims." In the comment, the audience member expressed the hope that "someday soon we'll both be united by one religion." Keith rejoined by saying, "United by one religion? It would be a false religion however, and I would not be interested in it. Jesus came from heaven to earth and was born in the flesh from a virgin mother for our sakes" (Keith 2007d). Despite his deep compassion, Keith clearly was not interested in public deliberation about religion.

Overall, Keith's entries received more comments than did those posted by James or Rhonda. However, none of them engendered a significant amount of deliberation. This demonstrates how the video blog as a medium seems better suited to the authoritative expression of single individuals than to interactive deliberation. As a result, this form of participatory media is popular among those involved in vernacular Christian fundamentalism who have strongly authoritative attitudes.

None of these bloggers seemed to have attained the level of popularity or the understanding of deliberation that Marilyn Agee demonstrated on her site. However, video blogs are not yet the primary participatory medium deployed in the movement. Instead, text-based blogs unaffiliated with social networking sites comprised the majority of the Web pages in the sample.

Blogging with Individual Authority

The *Blogger.com* style individual text-based blog was, by far, the most common form of participatory Web page appearing in the sample set. Because it is easy and typically free to post using this sort of blogging software, the medium elicited individualistic expression and the authoritative communication associated with it. However, those blogs that emphasized the comments sections and similar interactive technologies also exhibited significant deliberative communication. Among these blogs, ritual deliberation emerged more robustly than it did on social networking pages or video blogs.

Brittgillette.com is a good example of a moderately popular individual text-based blog within the sample, that exhibits authoritative communication. Using WordPress, a software package very much like Blogger, the blogger did not deploy the "comments" feature at all. As a result, his audience could not comment or coproduce the content on his blog. The front page of the site had a title in white across a light blue top banner which read: 'BrittGillette.Com A Christian Examination of Bible Prophecy and Emerging Technology . . ." A thirty-one-year-old author of two books, Britt Gillette wrote specifically about technologies that he felt demonstrated that the End Times would occur within his lifetime. Britt wrote, "For centuries, Christians have used anecdotal evidence, such as 'things have never been so bad' or 'look at all the evil in the world,' as a basis for believing their generation was the last generation of this age" (Gillette 2008).

Britt argued that his generation had seen a host of "biblical signs," like Israel "is once again a nation," "travel and knowledge have dramatically increased," and the European Union is the "cultural and geographical heir to the ancient Roman Empire." While these are standard components of the End Times narrative, Britt emphasized the role of technology in blog entries such as "The Technologies of Revelation," "Molecular Manufacturing," or "The Singularity." Britt located a host of technologies in his literal reading of the Bible, including satellite communications, nanotechnologies, and a "home-based desktop 3-D printing capability" that he believed were being developed for use in deployment of the Mark of the Beast. Taken together, these signs suggested to Britt that

> One of the most recognizable signs that our generation is in the last days is that ours is the first generation with, or about to acquire, the technology necessary to fulfill many of the end times prophecies. In fact,

the Book of Revelation describes several key events which will transpire on earth during the tribulation period which require mankind to be in possession of advanced technology. Some of these technologies mankind has already acquired; others will be developed in the very near future. (Gillette 2008)

In 2007, Todd Strandberg of *Rapture Ready* copied one of Britt's blog entries about the Mark of the Beast and pasted it as a featured article on *Rapture Ready* (Gillette 2007a; Gillette 2007b). Reading it at *Rapture Ready*, another blogger named Job copied Britt's article and pasted it into his own blog, *Jesus Christology Earnestly Contending for the Faith Once Delivered to the Saints Jude 1:3* (Job 2008a). With two pages appearing in the sample set, *Jesus Christology* also represents another moderately well-known blog. Unlike Britt's blog, however, Job used the commenting feature of his Word-Press software. With this participatory feature enabled, some stronger ritual deliberation was able to emerge.

A thirty-five-year-old man living in Georgia, *Jesus Christology*'s Job was drawn to the ideology of vernacular Christian fundamentalism through what he considered a "spiritual warfare" experience. A lifetime sufferer from severe asthma, Job relied on an inhaler. As he described it: "Because of the longtime overuse of the asthma medicine, I reached the point where it did me virtually no good anymore." When he discovered that his son might also suffer from asthma, he began a regime of fasting in an effort to bring the power of the divine to bear on his health problem. His religious meditation and fasting gave him "revelations of things concerning prophecy, discernment, and spiritual warfare" (Job 2008b).

Job described his belief that "Satan knew that my moment of truth was coming and thought that filling me with doubt, fear, failure, and desperation would cause me to crumble when it came." However, Job did not crumble. Instead, in an inspired moment, he simply threw his inhaler into the trash. Witnessing the event, Job's wife threw her eyeglasses in the trash, and their toddler threw his favorite toy in the trash. "And so we all ran around the house praising God, all three of us!" Job was inspired by this experience to create his own amateur ministry in the form of the *Jesus Christology* blog (Job 2008b).

Specifically rejecting formal churches, Job hoped his ministry would help individuals avoid what he saw as the failure of such institutions. Job believed that during the Tribulation period he would witness God "pouring out his wrath upon and scattering the church." Job wrote:

God is about to judge the church, and when that judgment comes it will be better to be outside the church than to be a sinner in it! [. . .] I pray that I will allow God to use me in this ministry and all those who have similar ministries, such that all who receive this and similar teachings will be spared God's wrath, be part of God's remnant, and do his will. In the name of Jesus Christ, Amen. (Job 2008c)

Believing that Satan and his demons were leading both Christians and non-Christians astray, Job combated this evil influence through spiritual warfare. As he described it, "spiritual warfare is fighting against and overcoming demons, or former angels that have been cast out of God's Kingdom and now follow Satan, with the power and Name of Jesus Christ." As is common among those involved in spiritual warfare, those associated with non-Christian traditions also become targets. According to Job, spiritual warfare must target humans "who (whether knowingly or not) work for Satan with the assistance of demons: witches, satanists, devil worshippers, idolators, etc." (Job 2008d).

While many of Job's posts were largely devoted to linking and forwarding articles like those of Britt above, others cued audience engagement. Because Job had the comments feature of his blog activated, his cues resulted in his blog becoming a location for public ritual deliberation. One example is in a blog entry posted on January 26, 2008. At that time, Barack Obama was embroiled in his campaign for the U.S. presidency. Entitling the entry "Does Anyone Know the Number of Barack HUSSEIN Obama's Name?" Job wrote:

It would seem that one would have to somehow translate Barack HUS-SEIN Obama to either Arabic, Aramaic, Hebrew, Latin, or Greek first and then just add up the position of the letters in the alphabet. [. . .] Don't get me wrong, I really do not think that Obama is the anti-Christ. It is just that we have to keep our eye on all these unifying charismatic figures. (Job 2008e)

This post was openly deliberative because its title was a question, and it actively sought the participation of others who might be able to translate Obama's name and "add up" the letters. The entry elicited nine comments from five individuals in Job's audience. Two people posted requests to engage in a private discussion of the matter. One person attempted to discuss Ronald

Wilson Regan's name, and another user posted the following more directly topical comment:

> Barack Hussein Obama=666, here's why:
> Barack=6?
> Hussein=7
> ?Obama=5
> (all possible combination)?
> 567?576?657?675?756?765?—-?3996(total)/6=666 (Job 2008e)

While these attempts to locate 666 in Obama's name subsided on the blog, the concern about Obama did not. As Obama's victory was all but assured in February of that year, Job's concern grew. On February 14, 2008, he posted another Obama entry entitled: "NO WE CAN'T! BARACK HUSSEIN OBAMA IS A FALSE CHRIST!" In this post, Job asserted that Obama was part of the new Satan-inspired threat he termed "the religious left." He attacked Obama's Protestant denomination, the United Church of Christ, as "one of the most liberal." He stated that Obama's specific church in Chicago was "pastured" by a "racist." Job identified himself as an African American. He then went on to cite the "revival-like" atmosphere surrounding Obama's political campaign. Claiming to have predicted "a 'faux revival'" earlier that year, Job implored his audience, saying: "I am challenging you today to decide who YOU are going to follow, B. Hussein Obama, the most recent false messiah, or Jesus Christ, the true Messiah!!!" (Job 2008f)

This post resulted in the largest number of responses on any blog in the sample set. With twenty-one comments, the entry functioned as a location for ritual deliberation. However, it also drew the attention of outsiders who hampered that deliberation. In this case, Job's blog entry demonstrates both how comments sections can foster ritual deliberation and the need for strong moderation to control the expression of dissent from outsiders in such deliberations.

Six of the twenty-one comments to this post were curt and hostile. The very first comment set the tone, writing simply, "You're about five kinds of @#$%^&$." A short barrage of similar statements followed. Then "Independent Conservative," a longtime commentor on the site, addressed Job directly, referencing a well-known Republican running for president that year: "Job, it looks like the Obama fans are worse than the Romney fans. Proving Obama is a false christ, that many see as their hope."

Job replied:

Oh, most of these fellows are being sent here by this anti-Christian blog that linked to my site [. . .]. They are having real fun with my spiritual warfare content in particular as you might guess. Ah well, at least they are being exposed to the gospel of Jesus Christ. (Job 2008f)

The "anti-Christian blog" Job referred to was another amateur blog entitled *Alicublog*. The blogger running that site posted text copied-and-pasted from Job's entry on Obama (Edroso 2008a). Then (in the comments section of *Alicublog*), the audience members colluded to disrupt Job's blog, saying: "I say we make this Job person's life a waking nightmare" (Edroso 2008b). In quick succession, these users posted six hostile responses on Job's site. Once the disruption dissipated, however, fourteen more posts continued to explore the possibility that Obama was a "false christ" (Job 2008f).

Somewhat ironically, the outsiders who attacked Job's blog never seemed to realize that the copied-and-pasted text about Obama they found so offensive was not actually written by Job. Instead, it was yet another copied-and-pasted piece of content written by a professional minister named Bill Keller who ran a well-known Christian site called *Liveprayer.com* (Keller 2008). In addition to demonstrating how a lack of moderation opens the deliberators to the hostility of outsiders, Job's blog shows how members of the virtual ekklesia aggregate disparate content to foster ritual deliberation.

With a total of twenty pages found by the search engines, a blog entitled *666 Mark of the Beast 666* returned the largest number of pages of any blog in the sample set. This fact suggests that the blog was quite well-known. It exemplifies the most common deployment of individual text-based blog software by individuals involved in the movement. Like Job, this blogger enabled the comments feature of his blogging software. Instead of encouraging audience comments, however, this blog primarily functioned to offer the blogger's aggregation of current events. Between August 2006 and February 2008, there were a total of ten audience comments spread among the 220 blog entries. The entries themselves were primarily news stories gathered from institutional news outlets. Emphasizing information aggregation and individual expression, the ritual deliberation on this blog was very sparse.

Like the Rapture Index, this blog functioned primarily to aggregate and reframe current world events reported on the Internet in terms of the End Times. In this case, the blogger explicitly stated that his purpose was "to bring fellow believers the latest news, stories, events and signs" (Joshua

2008). For the believers reading the blog, the various news stories served to support their shared beliefs about the rapidly approaching End Times. In this way, the technology primarily elicited individual expression. However, this blogger's aggregations contributed to the ekklesia insofar as they functioned as a means by which believers could imagine themselves sharing the ideology of vernacular Christian fundamentalism.

Run by an individual calling himself "Joshua," *666 Mark of the Beast 666* was a heavily modified WordPress blog. Set on a black background, the text of the blog was blood red. Using no graphic or video content, it featured its title across the top followed by a "Welcome!" statement. Along the left side, the site deployed the software to organize blog entries based on six topics: "News," "Prophecy," "Mark of the Beast," "Antichrist," "Satanism," and "Catholic Times" (Joshua 2008). Below that, the audience could browse the entries by date going back two years.

The reverse-dated entries themselves were in the central pane of the site, and were comprised primarily of links to news stories suggestive of End Times predictions or other writings about the End Times collected from around the Web. In his welcome statement, Joshua clearly located his blog in vernacular Christian fundamentalism. He described it as

> A "Website [. . .] dedicated to the study of the End Times, the Rapture, the Tribulation, and the Prophecies in Revelation. We believe that Bible prophecy is to be understood in a literal way and the expressed view of this site is of a pre-millennial return of Christ and pre-tribulational Rapture of the Church. Therefore, this Website is dedicated to bring fellow believers the latest news, stories, events and signs that brings us closer to the End Times. (Joshua 2008)

Heavily viewed by individuals involved in the movement, this blog enacted links between like-minded blogs and forums. In a December 3, 2007 entry, for example, Joshua posted a link to *Elijah the Prophet* without comment (Joshua 2007). Users following his link to *Elijah the Prophet* would find a blog that described itself as "Blogging for the Two Witnesses until They Arrive!" (Glenda 2008a).

With two pages appearing in the sample set, *Elijah the Prophet* was another moderately well-known blog. Built on the WordPress software platform, the blog represents the most technologically complex example of participatory media deployment in the sample. While built with WordPress, "Glenda," its builder, incorporated a host of macros and other smaller software applications designed to work with WordPress. These included "Live traffic feed" (a macro that displays the geographic location and specific pages being accessed by each visitor), an analog clock graphic, a display of local weather in Boston (Glenda's home), a calendar, statistics of the most popular pages, and several macros that located and displayed links to blogs with similar content (Glenda 2008a).

Added in June 2007, *Elijah the Prophet* was actually only one component of Glenda's sprawling Web site called *Heartdaughter*.com. Using phpBB Web site software, her overall site was dominated by an interactive Web-based forum entitled "The Two Witnesses of Revelation ELIJAH and the Daughter of ZION." With twenty-eight topically defined groups ranging from "General Chit Chat" to "End Times Discussions," to "Anti-Christ Kingdom," she presented a complex case of an individual who was highly motivated to host ritual deliberation and had a strong command of the technologies that should encourage it. However, Glenda's attitude was so authoritative that it actually limited the amount of deliberation that occurred on her site. As of February 2008, 103 individuals had signed up to be "members" of her forum, and several posters posted more than twenty entries, making them regular users of the site (Glenda 2008b). Of the 2,470 total posts at that time, however, 2,202 (or nearly 90 percent) were posted by Glenda herself.

A forty-nine-year-old woman living in the Northeastern United States, Glenda had a spiritual rebirth experience in 1979. Starting in about 1992, she "studied all the eschatological (last days stuff) books that I could find." Then God gave her "permission" to study "many extra-biblical books." Glenda came to believe that the Holy Spirit was teaching her to practice "discernment": the ability to tell the difference between true and false doctrines. Then, using Usenet newsgroups in the 1990s, Glenda became involved with "new-agers and lightworkers" (Glenda 2007a).

At that time, she hosted discussions on a 1995 Web site entitled *SearchNet Homepage*. A form of email list technology, *SearchNet* was intended to "provide 'safe areas,'" because "there are many subtle, and not so subtle ways, in message areas, in which people and their different ideas are made to feel, not welcome." In 1996, Glenda dismantled the site due to a lack of financial support (Glenda 1996). However, many of its posted messages were still available in 2008, including those of her collaborators who channeled extraterrestrial beings called "MetaTron" and "Kortron" (Glenda 2008c).

In 2002, Glenda reported having a "breakthrough" instigated by "the Holy Spirit." That year, she posted a "good-bye message" to her New Age friends, with "a few verses admonishing them to stick with Jesus Christ as the only

Christ." For the next four years she worked with "the Lord" to discover "the presence of another 'mind' within me." In 2006, she began to term this entity the "Carnal Mind." Since then, her primary goal has been to overcome this "Carnal Mind" in herself as well as help others overcome their own "Carnal Minds" (Glenda 2007a).

Glenda's posts on the Web site reflected this interest. News items, articles, and even reposts of her own comments on other sites dominated them. In these posts she gave very clear cues of her authoritative attitude. A good example comes from a post where she was articulating her belief that the "Jews" or Israelites described in the Bible were typologically meant to refer to Christians in the End Times:

> The major reason I am writing these things to you today, is to assist you in developing your understanding of God's government. [. . .] All these truths are HARD HARD HARD! I know that. I can not ignore what I have been shown by the Lord since 1979 and more specifically to these matters, since 2002. (Glenda 2007c)

She asserted her authority by acknowledging that her claims were "HARD" to accept, but that they had been "shown by the Lord since 1979." Specifically since 2002, she had felt that God had given her special access to divine truth.

As a result of this heavily authoritative communication, her huge forums remained largely unused by anyone but her and there was less ritual deliberation than the technology she deployed might suggest. However, her use of forum software reflects a desire to host deliberative communication. In the page on rules for posting to her forum she made this clear by writing: "I am not interested in banning any users. I wish the forum to be as open as possible. DO NOT BE AFRAID to share your ideas" (Glenda 2007b). This attitude may have stemmed from Glenda being no stranger to being "banned" herself. In fact, Glenda reported being banned from at least three Christian-oriented forums. This was at least partially the result of her authoritative claims of access to the divine.

As a longtime user and experimenter with Internet media, Glenda's frenetic Web site represents a fantastically complex attempt to create a location for ritual deliberation. Even though she failed to mediate between her personal authority and the power of interactive technologies as effectively as some others in the movement, her rich deployment of network technology suggests a solution to the tension between audience participation and individual control. As it turns out, this solution is the same as that suggested by Marilyn's *Bible Prophecy Corner*. Glenda specifically discussed how she wanted to share ideas with "a group of like-minded people" in what she called "safe areas" made possible by network communication technologies (Glenda 1996).

With the emergence of easy-to-use software for participatory media, it became easier for people to create and use such "safe areas." In the web of communication surrounding vernacular Christian fundamentalism, these areas are typically located on Christian-oriented sites that provide moderated forums in which the like-minded can exchange their ideas. These forums elicited the most deliberative communication of the four common forms appearing in the sample because they did not focus on the aggregation and individual expression of information. At the same time, believers could carefully moderate the communication, thereby reducing the potential of hostile posts from outsiders. In these "safe areas," ritual deliberation flourishes more robustly than in any previous Internet technology. An example of the sort of forum that hosts this ritual deliberation can be found on a familiar site: *Rapture Ready*, home of the Rapture Index.

Coproducing the Virtual Ekklesia

While text-based blogs were by far the most numerous form of participatory media in terms of individual pages in the sample, the forum was the participatory medium that seemed able to host the greatest volume of ritual deliberation. Since 2001, many amateur missionary, individual, and institutional Web sites have added forums as the software has become less technically demanding to use. These forum sites provide locations where different people can engage in deliberation about specific topics. In this way, they function much as did Usenet newsgroups. However, the individuals in these public forums risk facing the hostile comments of others who are not part of the movement. As a result, strong moderators typically keep nonbelievers from participating by editing or removing member-posted content and often requiring each user to register before they can post.

Evidence of the value of moderation on these forums is readily available on Todd Strandberg's *Rapture Ready*. In 2000, Todd deployed an early form of forum software. In 2004, he upgraded to the powerful vBulletin software and the popularity of his forum exploded. By March 2008, it had over 6,000 registered members and nearly half a million posts spread among twenty-eight different topic-specific groups ranging from "Last Days Events" and "One World Government" to "Anything Goes" and "Modern Cults & Religions" (Strandberg 2008c). The forum's ongoing popularity, however, has not been trouble free.

In February 2008, Todd's administrator—who calls himself "Buzzard-Hut"—announced that he and Todd had decided to ban fourteen individuals "for inappropriate conduct and a very poor Christian witness and attitude." As BuzzardHut made clear: "Discussions are from a conservative Christian world view." Todd and BuzzardHut exerted control over the board by threatening that those who diverged too far from its norms of ritual deliberation "[would] be banned" (BuzzardHut 2008).

For participants who demonstrate adequate competence in End Times deliberation, however, the *Rapture Ready* forum functions as one of several very popular End Times-oriented forum sites. Many believers move among these different sites. For example, when a user calling himself "Frisian" joined the large discussion forum site *BibleFourms.org*, he introduced himself by noting his member name on *Rapture Ready*. Locating himself in a cross-forum web of believers interested in ritual deliberation about the End Times, he credited a fellow believer whom he met there with suggesting he join *BibleForums.org*: "I am new. I also post at Rapture Ready. There I am known as frisian1970. Ciscokid had told me of this board" (Frisian 2004).

Using the same software as *Rapture Ready*, *BibleForums.org* contained some forty topical groups ranging from "Symbology of the Bible" and "Apologetics and Evangelism" to "Poetry" and "Testimonies." In 2008, *BibleForums.org* had over 20,000 members and over 1.3 million posts. On a forum site of this size, specific topical groups take on their own characters with regular users and often their own moderators. On *BibleForums.org*, the "End Times Chat" group allows individuals to engage in ritual deliberation about every conceivable issue associated with the End Times. Posts included "The Twelve Horns of the Beasts," "Is the Great Whore of Rev 17 upon the earth today?" and "Where is the U.S. in Bible prophesy?" Overall, "End Times Chat" holds over 4,000 posts at any given time. Together, believers use this forum to engage in a relentless flow of ritual deliberation (*BibleForums.org* 2008b).

In large moderated forums like those associated with *Rapture Ready* and *BibleForums.org*, deliberation emerges more easily because only registered members can post to the forum. When an individual applies to become a member of *BibleForums.org*, for example, she or he is asked: "Have you made the decision to follow Christ?" With a radio button, the potential registrant has three options: "Yes, I am a Christian," "No, I am not a Christian," or "No, I am not, but I am seeking Christ" (*BibleForums.org* 2008a). Through a link, the site administrators describe what a "yes" answer would mean:

Christians believe Jesus to be the only Son of God, who lived a sinless life. He is eternal, uncreated God, and has always been and will always be God [. . .]. Christians further believe that Jesus alone offers salvation, and that it is only possible through and by Him. Apart from Jesus Christ, there is no salvation. (*BibleForums*.org 2006)

Once an individual has a membership, anywhere their username appears (including with each post they place on the forum) a line just below their name reads: "Are you a Christian? Yes, I am a Christian." Reviewing the site, I could not find a single "No, I am not a Christian" member profile.

Like the newsgroups of the mid-1990s, the best medium for ritual deliberation in 2008 proved to be the posting forum. Less like the newsgroups and more like Marilyn's "Pro and Con Index," however, the forum software of participatory media allowed moderators to easily exclude particular individuals and specific content. In the user agreement that each registrant had to read to join *BibleForums.com*, the site administrators were blunt about it: "This board is for an exploration of the Christian Protestant faith, and not the faith of other religions" (*BibleForums.org* 2008b).

Other forum sites appearing in the sample set attracted a range of audience sizes. However, they all targeted Christians. *Christianity.com* exemplifies a huge Web site of this type. Over 3,000 strong, its members were able to read and post to over fifty forums covering different topics. One popular subforum was entitled: "Prophecy & End Times" (*Christianity.com* 2008). This forum alone had thousands of posts archived a year in the past. Another very similar site was much smaller, with only 188 users (*BibleForums.com* 2008a). Yet another forum site that appeared in the sample set, *Just Think Aloud—Didache*, was a highly collaborative "wiki." Functioning much like the well-known *Wikipedia.com*, this forum allowed members to post articles on a particular topic. Once an article was posted, other members could collaboratively write and rewrite the texts. In this case, the wiki software was deployed to invoke what the site builders imagined as a "Didache": "an early Christian writing known as the Teaching of the Twelve Apostles" (Pheugo 2007). In still another example, *MyChurch.org* functioned as a Christian-only version of the major social networking sites like *MySpace* and *Facebook* (*MyChurch.org* 2008).

All these sites implicitly limited their users to Protestant Christians who accepted the End Times as a legitimate basis of deliberation. An individual using *BibleForums.org* claimed that *Rapture Ready*'s forum was known to even more severely "censor folks" by banning those who did not accept a pre-Tribulational Rapture in their End Times scenario. Whether this was true or not was unclear; however, this poster demonstrated *BibleForums.org*'s ability to host ritual deliberation about the End Times when he went on to initiate a debate about exactly when the Rapture would occur—instead of posting on *Rapture Ready* (MattHenry 2006). Another forum, *Fellowship Place*, made it clear that at least sometimes a belief in the End Times was explicitly required to engage in deliberation. In their "About Us" statement, the site administrators wrote:

> We are a body of Born Again Christian believers in Christ Jesus. Our presences here are to Fellowship together and bring glory to God. Discussing Bible prophecy, news and world events and how they fit into the end time message as spoken in 30% of Scripture—In both Old and New Testaments. [. . .] Please feel welcome to join us in Fellowship. As we wait for the rapture of the church, and the second coming of our Lord Jesus Christ. (*Fellowship Place Ministry* 2008)

As the ekklesia based on this ideology has emerged in participatory media, those locations that clearly defined themselves as part of the ekklesia host more ritual deliberation. As for the blogs themselves—the most common form of participatory media—the medium encouraged individual authoritative communication. However, if the blogger chose to display deliberative communication and offered interactive comments sections or a forum, then ritual deliberation did occur.

One text-based blog demonstrates how a savvy moderator can manage the blog technology to maximize ritual deliberation. A well-known figure in the movement since the creation of his *RaptureAlert.com* Web site in 2003, Michael Mickey added a blog to his site in 2008 (Mickey 2008b). This blog hosted more comments than any other individual blog appearing in the sample. Here, the balance between the individually produced blog entries and the carefully managed comments sections demonstrates how blogging software can be used to elicit robust ritual deliberation. Mickey did this by balancing the ability of outsiders to contribute content with the ability of the individual blogger to control that content.

RaptureAlert.com

A forty-four-year-old retired police officer in the Southeastern United States, Michael G. Mickey built *RaptureAlert.com* and is the central authority on its associated blog (Mickey 2008a). Posting almost daily, the volume of comments Michael's blog hosts in response to his posts is evidence of its popularity and success in the ekklesia. A typical exchange occurring on the blog is from February 15, 2008, entitled "A Rumbling in the Middle East." This post generated sixteen comments. In this entry, Michael first referred to his post from the previous day, saying, "In light of yesterday's commentary and the potential implications of recent events in the Middle East, I have to admit I got chills when I read of a magnitude 5 earthquake rattling Lebanon and neighboring countries today" (Mickey 2008c).

In the post from the day before, he had used the subject line, "The Middle East: Back to the Brink." There, he recounted the recent killing of the leader of Hezbollah's "second in command" in Damascus. As a result of the attack, Hezbollah issued a statement "declaring 'open war' on Israel." Michael asked, "A prelude to Gog-Magog?" Citing Mathew 26: 6, he placed this attack in the End Times narrative and finished his 963-word analysis by writing, "The end times drama continues . . ." (Mickey 2008d).

When the earthquake in Lebanon occurred the day after his first post, Michael wrote in the second: "Just another earthquake here in the last days or a harbinger of things to come? Only the Lord knows but I'll bet the air in and around Israel could practically be cut with a knife right now." This post is deliberative because it posited a question. As a result, it functioned as an invitation to ritual deliberation. Further, the question it posited was about a typical End Times world news item—an earthquake—and it was a news item relating to the geographic area most important to the End Times narrative—the Middle East. Although the invitation was from a blogger who individually initiated and controlled the discussions on his site, it was addressed to an audience comprised of individuals who shared the basic ideology of vernacular Christian fundamentalism. Many of these individuals responded immediately by expressing support. Posting in the comments section of this entry, a user identified as "jo anna" wrote:

WOW! I hadn't heard about this one yet. I heard about the 2 in Greece yesterday, but not this one. I've also been reading how lake Mead is drying up and then with the problems Georgia and Florida are having and the HUGE push about global warming! And of course all that's going on war wise in the middle east. My heart is racing at how close we could be to going home! I am so ready to be with Jesus and done with this place! Oh how I pray people accept Christ quickly before it's too late! (Mickey 2008d)

With the ritual deliberation started, Michael responded by writing: "Amen, Jo Anna! A lot is going on and on a variety of fronts. Broadening the spectrum a bit, do you realize we have had FOUR campus shootings in the United States in one short week?" Then, ten different people in fourteen more posts considered nine different world events reported by various news organizations as other indicators that the beginning of the End Time wars were near at hand. These events included the Russian prime minister Vladimir Putin "making threats against western Europe," "FOUR campus shootings in the United States in one short week," and Lake Mead, a popular resort area in the Western United States, "drying up." The deliberation climaxed as one commenter wrote in capital letters: "I AM SO LOOKING FORWARD TO A FRONT ROW SEAT TO THE MAJOR BUTT KICKING SATAN IS GOING TO GET SOON!" (Mickey 2008d)

After this crowning expression of shared belief, a commentor suggested that they pray for those dead and injured in the Lebanese earthquake. That plan then developed into an agreement to pray for one of the commentor's relative's infant son who was having a biopsy the next day (Mickey 2008d). As this example makes clear, the blog associated with *RaptureAlert.com* is a good place for individuals involved in this movement to engage in its characteristic behavior.

The suitability of this location for ritual deliberation is no accident. A regular commentor on a variety of forums, Michael is a very savvy Internet user who is careful to use deliberative communication. Before even creating a blog, he chose to ask his audience about the choice. He recounted the story in a February 6, 2008 post entitled "To blog!":

> As most of you are aware, I have been trying to assess the desire of my readers to have an opportunity to leave comments in relation to the content of the site as once was the case. Based on over 1,500 visits to the page I set up for polling, it seems that some 70% of those polled either want an option to blog or don't care if there is one. Approximately 30% of the site's readers would prefer not to have a blog option. (Mickey 2008e).

In addition to polling his audience about his idea of starting a blog, Michael asked if the blog should be "open for anyone to post their thoughts." Apparently, many in his audience suggested that he use a "Christian forum on the web" like *BibleForums.org* or *MyChurch.org*. However, because Michael did not want to make people register before commenting, he decided to use the common Blogger software to carefully manage the discourse himself. In his post describing the decision, he expressed concern that if outsiders were allowed to post to the new blog, his audience of believers would have "to contend for the faith vigorously in some instances." Instead, Michael decided it was best for

Anyone to be able to comment (even anonymously) and for those comments to be moderated by me prior to posting. That will result in some
delays, periodically, in posted comments appearing on the blog but it
seems the only safe way for the blog to go forward without a good portion
of the site's bloggers being uncomfortable. We'll take things as they come
and see how it goes. (Mickey 2008e).

In this way, Michael created a discursive space where it was safe for people
to engage in deliberation without the threat of divergent ideas or hostile outsiders. Using participatory media software instead of simple HTML, Michael
did the same thing as Marilyn Agee. He created a forum well suited to deliberation about the End Times by limiting the voices heard in the discussion
to those that supported the ideology. Like Marilyn's, his site was particularly
popular in the movement. Individuals both read and participated actively in
the aggregation of information and the ritual deliberation that aggregation
made possible on the site. Even more directly than Marilyn's, Michael's audience coproduced the content on his Web site.

Using the technologies of participatory media, Michael created a location where the self-regulated enclave of vernacular Christian fundamentalism could manifest itself. Fulfilling the need to express itself online, the virtual ekklesia was enacted on *RaptureAlert.com* as one important node in the
vernacular web of communication emerging around vernacular Christian
fundamentalism.

RaptureAlert.com demonstrates how moderated forums and blogs with a
specific focus on the End Times emerged as the best online media for the
movement to engage in the ritual deliberation necessary to enact its virtual
ekklesia. Other participatory media like social networking profile pages
and video blogs could host deliberation in some instances, but these media
proved to be better suited to individual personal expression. As a result, they
tended to exhibit more authoritative communication. The ability to moderate the comments on a topically specific Web page, on the other hand, created communication enclaves in which like-minded individuals could locate
and engage each other in deliberation about the End Times without being
confronted with either hostile outsiders or ideas that strayed too far from the
core beliefs of vernacular Christian fundamentalism.

While these sorts of moderated blogs and forums proved to be good for
vernacular fundamentalism, this kind of online communication may have a
negative impact on those who use them heavily. Unlike new religious movements that use more conventional modes of social control such as strongly

authoritative leaders or clustering members into real-world communities, the members of this movement are empowered to access a huge diversity of ideas from whatever geographic location they happen to inhabit. At the same time, however, they are empowered to use topical community formation to create enclaves of like-minded communication, which can limit their ability to engage in the larger deliberations taking place in the society around them.

When people filter their understanding of history, theology, public events, and other shared experiences through an ideologically specific enclave, they may become used to holding values that the larger society around them rejects or simply cannot understand. This is commonly seen in some well-studied new religious movements like the Heaven's Gate group or the People's Temple. In the virtual ekklesia, however, individuals are geographically dispersed. As a result, they must physically inhabit locations governed by institutions that hold to radically different values than they do. If they are limited in their ability to speak and be heard in these publics, they may become marginalized from the real-world communities in which they live.

6

Toward a Truer Charity

Tolerance in an Age of Network Media

Aggregating a Digital Jesus

On a *RaptureAlert.com* page entitled "Recommended Links," Michael, the Web site's builder, had fifty links to other sites involved in ritual deliberation about the End Times. The second link from the top of his list was to the familiar *Rapture Ready* site built and maintained by Todd Strandberg. Michael described Todd's site as "one of the best prophecy Web sites on the Internet" (Mickey 2008b).

On Todd's site, there were thirty-five links to sites involved in the movement. Among these, many are familiar, including Cheryl and Ernie's site, *Acts 17:11 Bible Studies,* and Marilyn Agee's *Bible Prophecy Corner* (Strandberg 2008a). Todd even referenced Agee's site in blog posts he wrote in 1999, 2005, and 2006. In the 2005 post, he reminded his readers of the many failed predictions Marilyn had made over the years, noting that she "ha[d] been called 'The Queen of Date Setters'" (Strandberg 2005). While it seems that Michael liked Todd's site more than Todd liked Marilyn Agee's, all three of them were connected through a vernacular web of online communication about the End Times.

As we have seen, this web has expanded and adapted with the opportunities made available by new forms of Internet media. Even though communication technologies have been rapidly changing around them, many of the actors in this virtual ekklesia have remained. In 1999, Todd put up a page of seventy-nine links he termed "A Reciprocation of Homogenous Internavigational Referrals." These linked "referrals" included *Lambert Dolphin's Resource Files,* later to be known as *Lambert's Library.* In 2009, Todd's thirty-five remaining links still included one to Lambert's page about the End Times (Dolphin 1999b; Strandberg 1999b). For over ten years, Todd's well-known End Times site linked to Lambert's page on the fringe of this vernacular web. Over those years, untold thousands of individual believers who followed Todd's links from *Rapture Ready* to the *Bible Prophecy Corner* or to *Lambert's Library* and beyond had reenacted the web into existence.

In the continual trickle of Internet traffic, the volition of thousands merges. In aggregate, their choices have etched the ideological paths that serve as the primary authority in vernacular Christian fundamentalism. Here, participants give electronic substance to a movement that is diffuse, wildly diverse, and yet staunchly intolerant of any who stray from its four definitive beliefs. Though Marilyn, Lambert, Todd, and Michael may disagree on the details, their online expressions are part of this virtual ekklesia because those expressions support their shared beliefs.

In order to maintain its dispersed authority for these beliefs, the movement must enforce a minimal level of observable coherence. Without this coherence, the lack of any geographic or institutional ground would give the virtual ekklesia no means with which to enact the ritual deliberation that is its source of being. To guard against this danger, the powerful vernacular authority of aggregate volition evolved with these technologies to create network places to enact ritual deliberation safe from hostile outsiders or too great a diversity of belief. Now, moderated blogs and forums provide the robust virtual spaces in which the movement thrives. However, creating controlled global communication enclaves brings with it a significant danger: that of isolation from local real-world communities.

The potential for such isolation first began to appear in my research when I discovered individuals openly expressing disturbingly intolerant views. As I described in the first chapter, such views are historically latent in some of the dualistic ideas associated with Christian apocalypticism, and they provide the basis from which prejudices can emerge in this virtual ekklesia. When a group of believers can express intolerance without facing resistance, prejudices can persist. If radical certainty fuels those views with a self-sealing ideology, people may cling to them even when doing so does them harm. They risk being harmed if they retain these beliefs at the cost of alienating themselves from the values that support mainstream discourse.

The virtual ekklesia has made it possible for people to create enclaves based on highly idiosyncratic interests like that of the End Times because the Internet allows them to locate each other without reference to geographic location. As a result, digital communication technologies enable them to create virtual communities that foster beliefs that more diverse communities would reject. When that occurs, their ability to be heard on issues in which they may have a very real stake may become compromised because they reject the basic values, ideals, and norms that allow more mainstream discourse to proceed.

Despite this danger, digital communication technologies also suggest another possibility. As individuals have more and more choices about how and where they enact discourse, a new generation of technology-savvy Internet users may demand tolerance in their Internet media experiences. Evidence for this possibility emerges in forum posts on a youth-oriented evangelical Christian Web site. When the progressive Christians who dominate the forum encountered people interested in the fundamentalist ideology, a hostile exchange occurred. Though this hostility was significant, the participants expressed a real desire for open and tolerant communication.

Radical Certainty and a History of Persecution

Among the wide variety of individuals enacting this virtual ekklesia, the vast majority of them place the highest value on compassion for their fellow humans. However, because they subscribe to a self-sealing ideology that is driven by an intense sense of certainty, we have seen them sometimes be dogmatic and insensitive. While those behaviors might make for some occasional hurt feelings, they are not the most intolerant kinds of communication I have documented in this movement. As I explored above, Tim, the optometrist, astronomy buff, and builder of the *Spirit Shower* Web site, believed that the seven-year Tribulation period just before Christ's return will be characterized by the systematic persecution of Christians. During our interview, he described how a secret government was in fact already persecuting him. In his description of this persecution, he expressed surprisingly strong anti-Semitic views.

From reading conspiracy theory both online or in popular publications, Tim had become convinced that a shadowy background force controlled world politics. He stated: "I think the United States . . . or the world is being controlled by the One World Order." This "control" was the result of a long historical process, but in 1999 he felt it "really went into effect a year ago." Tim believed this because

> We had that solar eclipse that I think started the 1,335 days [before a mid-Tribulation Rapture in] February of 1998. Because Clinton, even then in his inaugural address, he talked about how we were following the United Nations' mandates on all of these kinda things with Iraq and the Kosovo thing. These are all things that are One World Order. (Tim 1999c)

I pressed him a little bit on the nearness of the Second Coming suggested by this belief. He asserted that he was not a "dogmatist" about it. He claimed, with great vehemence, that he did not know "for sure" if the predictive dates suggested by his calendar system were correct:

> I am predicting the Fall of 2001. Everything points to that to me—as the Second Coming. But within, let's say, six months of that date, if none of the trumpets or those things . . . events . . . have happened, then obviously I'll say: "Hmmm." Start thinking, "There's gotta be a few things that happen before Jesus comes." (Tim 1999c)

To further shore up his claim that he was not a dogmatist, he went on to describe a case when he changed his thinking.

For a long time, Tim had assumed that the persecution of Christians during the Tribulation would occur in the United States much as it had happened in Russia, as he understood it, before the fall of the Soviet Union. This persecution would be so overwhelming that it would function as a certain indication the Second Coming was near. However, he "had to revamp" his thinking because his astronomical calculations were indicating that the persecution should have already begun. As a result, he came to believe that the U.S. government was, in fact, already persecuting Christians:

> The Christians in America are not politically correct. It's the gay movement that is politically correct. And ya know—that's going on right now too. Pagans are more politically correct. (Tim 1999c)

Here, he was confronted by what appeared to be a failed prediction. According to Tim, the first half of the Tribulation was already under way because his astronomical calculations predicted that the Rapture would occur three days after the "Feast of the Trumpets" in the year 2001. If the Rapture were to occur "mid-Tribulation," as Tim asserted it would, that would locate the start date of the Tribulation three and a half years before September 19, 2001: sometime in 1998. This meant that, in 1999, the Tribulation had already begun. In Tim's mind, the persecution of the Christians must also have already begun because it is a central feature of the Tribulation period in a literal reading of Revelation.

Instead of reassessing his dating predictions based on the fact that he was not being overtly persecuted as he had expected, Tim asserted that, in fact, he *was* being persecuted. To render that reasonable, he recast his understanding of persecution in terms of "political correctness." In so doing, he both maintained his astronomical dating system and accounted for what he perceived as significant evils in the world: the Clinton government, homosexuals, and pagans. Here, Tim's radical certainty can be seen to have led to intolerance based on his dualistic view of the world.

For people like Tim, however, it would be an unfair reduction to suggest that they do not engage in a wide variety of discourses and many different communities both on and offline. From these communities, Tim encountered new ideas which must have, in at least some cases, demanded that he adapt his understanding of the world. During our interview, Tim specifically discussed a particular rabbi he had sought out to ask questions about astronomy. Tim told me that he contacted this rabbi because he felt that Jewish people are generally more intelligent than non-Jewish people. According to Tim, Jewish people have "higher IQs" because they were once "God's chosen people." Now, however, he said that Jewish people were no longer in favor with God, and as a result Tim believed them to be a problem.

Tim felt that "the Jews" were largely responsible for the systematic persecution of Christians he perceived as already under way. He blamed Jewish people because he believed they were running the "One World Order." Very few individuals I talked to in this movement were overtly anti-Semitic. In fact, some ethnically Jewish converts to Christianity are deeply engaged in End Times belief. However, Tim's association between conspiracy theory, anti-Semitism, and the End Times was neither new nor idiosyncratic (Barkun 2003).

Paul Boyer, a well-known historian of prophecy beliefs, has located the link between anti-Semitism and Christian prophecy as far back as the Crusades that sought to conquer and hold Jerusalem for the Europeans. Thought to be a way to hurry Christ's return, these invasions were justified in some texts by portraying both Arabs and Jews as agents of Antichrist (Boyer 1992, 51). Since that time, however, there have been significant shifts and differences in the perception of Jewish people among conservative Christians.

Historian David A. Rausch has documented many examples of pro-Zionism from conservative evangelical theological publications (1979). Other scholars, however, have found anti-Semitism deeply embedded in conservative Christian discourse (Boyer 1992, 217–24; Barkun 1994). In fact, the basic assertion that Tim made about Jewish people in 1999 has been well known among those interested in the End Times since at least the 1970s. Tim claimed that Jewish people fell out of favor with God because they rejected Jesus during His ministry as described in the New Testament. This idea was perhaps most famously articulated in the 1977 text by Dwight Wilson, *Armageddon Now! The Premillenarian Response to Russia and Israel since 1917*.

Tim's claim that Jewish people run a secret government that controls the world's wealth is also widespread and well known. The influential 1991 conspiracy theory text by William Cooper, *Behold a Pale Horse*, republished in total the fraudulent nineteenth-century anti-Semitic text called "The Protocols of the Elders of Zion." "The Protocols" is probably the single best-known text used as evidence of a Jewish world conspiracy. Cooper's 1991 redux and interpretation of the text links the document's claims to the Cold War fears of the late twentieth century (Barkun 2003, 143–47).

This long history of anti-Semitism in conservative Christian thought is, however, complicated by recurring pro-Israel movements. Because the return of the nation-state of Israel and the rebuilding of the Jewish temple in Jerusalem are predicted in Revelation as precursors to the End Times, many people in the movement see modern Israel as an ally. Indeed, the final great wars of Armageddon are thought to focus on a struggle for control of Jerusalem as a holy city. In many scenarios, the modern state of Israel is unfairly attacked by a Russian-Arab alliance.

As a result, the role of the modern state of Israel is often a focus of ritual deliberation. Whenever Christians like Tim have made a connection between supposed powerful secret societies, Jewish people, and the forces of Antichrist, they have faced a fundamental interpretive problem. Because the original writers and audiences of the prophetic texts of the Christian Bible were largely Jewish, Jewish people are typically depicted in both the Old and New Testaments as the beneficiaries of Christ's triumphant return. As a result, it seems hard to imagine they would actually be in league with Satan. So these interpretations are forced to rely on some significant adjustment to become reasonable.

For Tim, the biblical references to Israel, Jerusalem, and the temple were strictly "spiritual" ideas that God uses, in combination with the stars, to communicate to humans. In fact, Tim angrily told me that the many well-known Christian conservatives who saw the establishment of the modern state of Israel and the ultimate reconstruction of its temple as events that must precede the final apocalypse were deeply misled. Some evangelical figures have, in fact, allied themselves with radical Israelis hoping to reclaim the temple site in Jerusalem for Israel so that the End Times might be hastened. For Tim, these sorts of Christians were making a grave error.

As Tim described it, the result of rejecting God when he came to earth as Jesus the first time was that Jewish people were now fundamentally evil. So when Israel was mentioned in a prophetic text, Tim argued that the reference was to all "saved" Christians. He explained: "I am the Bride of Christ. Not some Jewish nation that totally rejects Christ! In fact, if anything they are Satan's people!" He went on to describe a fairly complicated scenario to account both for the fundamental evil he saw in Judaism as well as its involvement with the One World Government:

> When they [the Jewish people] were taken into Babylonian captivity back in the Old Testament, they accepted all the customs of the pagan system that the Babylonians had. That is why ever since they came back from the Babylonian captivity the Jewish nation [has] basically been a lost cause. They set up their whole system . . . if you study the Talmudic writings you find out how demonic they are and how unbelievably . . . *obscene* it is. Have you ever looked at that stuff? [I shake my head no.] (Tim 1999c)

Despite his repeated assertions that Jewish people are "demonic," Tim wanted to make it clear that he, from his own perspective, was not an anti-Semite. It was not that he disliked Jewish people, he said, but simply that the Jewish people have, through the powerful forces of God in history, become the agents of Satan. As such, Tim felt that they controlled Babylon, and that Babylon is the prophetic symbol for the United States and its allies:

> I am not against Jews! Ya know. But . . . they definitely control the banking systems. They definitely control the One World stuff. We know that they have a higher IQ than any other people. Ya know. We've studied all this, so we know that they were, at one time, a blessed people. They were God's people. But no longer. Because they have . . . once they went into the Babylonian captivity they came out with all this pagan stuff. When Jesus was here on earth, he called them "oh generation of vipers." And that's what they were by then. (Tim 1999c)

It is clear from this last quotation, if it was not already, that Tim's belief system was in fact intolerant.

While Tim's case was extreme, many others in the movement expressed a similar intolerance. In addition to Jewish people, this intolerance was sometimes directed toward other ethnic minorities. It also included those with alternate lifestyles such as gay and lesbian people. It most often focused, however, on individuals who harbored spiritual or religious beliefs that were thought to contradict those of Christianity. The intolerance for these people was particularly strong because, like Marilyn and others featured throughout this research expressed it, beliefs that contradict those of vernacular fundamentalism are discredited through the seal-sealing argument that they are errors actively cultivated by Satan and his demons.

For many people in this movement, as I documented above, demons are believed to be very real actors in today's world. However, these evil spirits have limited power unless they are actively encouraged. As a result, it is believed that they routinely try to trick people by impersonating spiritual beings such as spirits, ghosts, or divine entities in other religions. Jane and John made this assertion about space aliens, as did Marilyn Agee about apparitions of the Virgin Mary. This idea feeds intolerance specifically for those whose religious beliefs differ from those of vernacular Christian fundamentalism because it is thought that people who believe or interact with such beings are, knowingly or not, doing the work of Satan.

Dean and Susan from *AlphathroughOmega.com*, for example, described facing demonic attacks as a result of just cursory contact with other religious beliefs. They reported suffering many direct physical attacks while living in a particular apartment when they were first married. After the attacks suddenly stopped, they learned from the landowner that their upstairs neighbor had been evicted. According to their landowner, the neighbor had been discovered enacting "occult" rituals. The proximity of the apartments, Dean contended, allowed the demons his neighbor was contacting to enter into their apartment as well (Dean and Susan 1999).

As Dean and Susan described it, what they called "cults" are the product of demons attempting to gain influence among humans. Speaking of the Church of Latter Day Saints as a "cult," he told me a long story of how even the most indirect contact caused Susan to be brutally attacked by demonic forces.

As Dean recounted it:

God said: "I want you to write about this!" The new [Web] page I just posted up there is called "Demon Domains and Christian Fortresses." That was something God wanted me to put up as fast as possible because . . . well, maybe he had somebody he wanted to see that. Because [there are] a lot of things about demonic domains and such-like that people really don't understand. Prime example: It was a little while ago . . . a couple months ago I think it was. Just down the street [from their home] we have a Mormon Church, and Susan was on her way to go get something from the store and she realized she had forgotten something at home. So she swung into this

Mormon church and swung around the parking lot and came back home. As soon as she walked in the door she became violently sick. And just for it to come on that suddenly? I had a feeling . . . I asked God, "Is Satan behind it?" As soon as I mentioned it, she turned around and saw the church. I said, "That's it!" So what we did was I took and bound and got rid of the demons that were causing the sickness. As soon as I did it she stopped being sick. And what God told us was that even unwittingly she had invaded their territory, which gave them [the Mormon demons] the right to attack her! And I was really worried about that . . . I says, "God! My daughter has to pass by the church every day when she goes on her way to school." What he told us was: "Their authority ends at the street. As long as you don't go on their parking lot, they can't touch you." (Dean and Susan 1999)

Dean and Susan are honest, stable, and compassionate people who deeply care about the welfare of others. However, it is clear that these strong beliefs in demons and the linkage of those beliefs to people they consider non-Christians led them toward intolerance. While Dean and Susan's site was, as I described above, not well known in the movement, another site that focused on these same beliefs was. This site encouraged fellow members of the ekklesia to take action against specific kinds of people.

Battle Ax Brigade described a technique for combating demons at some length on a page entitled "Spiritual Mapping for Effective Spiritual Warfare." The self-identifying mother and homemaker who built the site defined "spiritual mapping" as the first in a series of actions necessary to combat demonic influences on other people:

Spiritual mapping is the process of collating and putting spiritual information concerning a region or people on a map. The accumulated data is used in spiritual warfare to seize that region or group [of people] from the enemy. Spiritual mapping is like having a bright light focused on an otherwise dimly lit area. It allows us to see how the enemy is strategizing and exposes Satan's hidden agenda for that particular region or people group. ("Spiritual Mapping for Effective Spiritual Warfare" 2001)

In support of her mapping strategy, she cited the Gospel of Mark without further explication: "For there is nothing hid, which shall not be manifested; neither was any thing kept secret, but that it should come abroad (Mark 4: 22)." She then went on to describe her mapping in more specific terms:

A study of the history of the land and its peoples is crucial in spiritual mapping. We must be able to understand the mind set, habits, and customs of the "original" people. When studying the history of our county, the team recognized that its earliest people were a particular tribe of Indians. Later, a certain ethnic group predominated [in] the area. So we concentrated our study on finding out the unrighteous practices and beliefs of these people. Generally, you will be dealing with whatever strongholds the original residents opened the door to through their sin. Another mapping team discovered in their area that the original Indians of their community were fascinated with tattooing their whole bodies, and considered it to be their clothing. Today public nudity is a real problem in that community. Also, there are unusually large numbers of tattoo parlors there. These facts better equip them to target their warfare. ("Spiritual Mapping for Effective Spiritual Warfare" 2001)

In this passage, the Web site builder specifically located the contemporary "sins" of public nudity and tattooing as being correlated with the historical presence of American Indians in a certain geographic location. From her perspective, the traditions of American Indians were born of Satanic and demonic influence. She knew this because she felt that American Indian traditions do not preach Christianity. Because she was radically certain of her beliefs, the American Indians were wrong in theirs. All such "errors" about spirituality were, from her perspective, born from the original error Satan and his followers made when they revolted against God and were thrown out of heaven. The fact that American Indians once lived in a specific location led this woman to assume that their influence was at the root of current practices she considered sinful.

In these examples, it is clear that ideas or people who contradict the basic beliefs of vernacular fundamentalism are at least sometimes perceived as dangerous, to be feared, and even to be targeted. Characteristic of self-sealing worldviews, this perception turns the existence of contradictory ideas into evidence of their beliefs. In this last example, the fact that some people have alternate ideas about what is appropriate in this person's town is evidence that American Indians spread the influence of Satan because those ideas about what is appropriate contradict her certain knowledge of the Bible.

While these prejudices have long histories and spiritual rebirth can powerfully activate them, they must not be imagined as mere holdovers. Instead, the enclaves made possible by digital communication technologies have facilitated them, as is powerfully evident in the technologies that have proven best suited for ritual deliberation.

The Dangers of Enclave Communication

Since I began this research in the early 1990s, it appears that American religious belief has become increasingly personalized and fluid. As this occurs, the institutions of the past seem to be losing power in the face of growing opportunities to individually consume and produce vernacular religious ideas. In recent surveys, individuals expressed a sense that they were less affiliated with their religious institutions. They felt less inclined to continue to attend the churches or stay in the denominations in which they were raised. Increasingly, they turned to nondenominational and often Internet-based forms of religious community (Pew 2008). Today's media offer individuals more opportunities to construct personalized systems of belief than ever before in history, and more people than ever are taking these opportunities.

An example of this individual belief construction, vernacular Christian fundamentalism aggregates online communication without reference to any set of institutional documents or leaders. There is no central authority to rein in the diversity of individually expressed interpretations other than the everyday users and creators of these media themselves in the form of their aggregate vernacular authority. To be sure, a diversity of individual interpretations has always existed in Christian belief and practice. During transformative periods in history, in particular, this individual expression has increased even to the point of outright rebellion and fracture.

For those who are involved in vernacular Christian fundamentalism, communication technologies are increasingly making the multiplicity of voices associated with individual expression the norm. In this religious movement, however, individual expression does not result in rebellion or fracture. Instead, social control bubbles upward from the aggregate volition of a myriad individual choices to communicate. For them, the authority to limit diversity emerges in the dynamic expression of participants in this vernacular web.

With the increase in opportunities for involvement associated with participatory media, a feedback loop has emerged between individual expression and individual consumption of media content. At the same time that network communication technologies have made near-unfettered individual expression possible, they have also given those same individuals near-unfettered access to the growing mass of individual expression they are all continually creating. As a result, individuals are enabled not only to voice their own beliefs but also to aggregate a specific mass of voices into idiosyncratic worldviews. While this is empowering for individual believers, it also presents a danger.

Since the advent of mass media, individuals have had access to content that was aggregated for them by what media scholars term "general interest intermediaries" (Sunstein 2007, 8). Traditional kinds of media like newspapers, broadcast radio, and network television function as general interest intermediaries because they seek to collect and present content in ways that appeal to as broad an audience as possible. These media need such support to garner the resources required by the production of the content they offer. Typically, these resources have been generated through government funding, philanthropy, advertising revenues, and media sales.

Beholden to these sources of funding, general interest intermediaries cannot afford to aggregate information in ways that alienate significant groups of people. If they did, they would not be able to find a broad enough audience to support the costs of their production. Because these media enable many individuals to access the same content, they create large publics who share the same media influences. In these large publics, the social mores that reject intolerance for significant participants in the community become normative.

Because those publics are comprised of a wide diversity of individuals, the content, perspectives, and claims they do foster tend to rely on the most broadly shared values. Most often, this has encouraged relatively neutral presentations of issues and narratives that have general social relevance. As a by-product of this effort, mainstream media has increasingly rejected the overt expression of intolerance. Over time, these general interest intermediaries have created the most inclusive fields of public deliberation in history.

Unlike general interest intermediaries, however, much vernacular Internet communication requires very few resources. As a result, this communication can afford to have much smaller audiences (Howard 2005d). Particularly with the rise of participatory media like blogs and forums, individuals need no financial investment or technical expertise beyond Internet access itself to post their ideas. This situation fuels the feedback loop between individual expression and individual consumption.

While individuals caught up in this feedback loop may isolate themselves ideologically, that does not mean they are isolated from general interest intermediaries. This research has found many examples in which they consume content produced by institutional news media Web sites, major newspapers, and network television broadcasts. In these cases, individuals can be seen aggregating that general interest content into the framework supported and articulated by their ideological enclave. From the 9/11 attacks to natural disasters, the research presented in this book has documented the reframing of information in the terms of a specific ideology. The individuals involved in this movement locate, aggregate, and reexpress the information that coincides with their ideology in their own highly individualized participatory media expressions.

With its enclave aggregation, vernacular Christian fundamentalism demonstrates how the new opportunities created by network media can foster beliefs that the larger society rejects. One danger of this phenomenon is that individuals will construct virtual communities where it is acceptable to maintain intolerant beliefs to which a larger audience would offer resistance.

When individuals can construct a community that renders their experiences with the divine meaningful based on a worldview that harbors historical prejudices, communication enclaves powerfully foster the persistence of that intolerance. Vernacular Christian fundamentalism's enclave communication clearly presents a potential danger for those against whom such intolerance is directed. However, it is also presents a danger for the individuals caught up in its powerful feedback loop.

When the participants in vernacular Christian fundamentalism limit their framework of understanding to those facts and ideas that can be assimilated into the End Times narrative, their worldview is authorized by claims that are far more specific than those accepted by the broader publics that govern powerful social formations. Geographic and structural proximity, however, renders individuals in the ideological enclave just as reliant on these social formations as everyone else. They cannot escape the influence of geographically based churches, schools, governments, or the global social structures created by media and trade.

While their shared beliefs allow these individuals to enact a virtual ekklesia, they simultaneously undercut their ability to have influence in these broader social formations because the most potent authorizing claims they accept are seen as totally unrealistic and even absurd by the majority. It appears that some otherwise compassionate and deeply religious people are paying the heavy price of ideological isolation for their increased ability to consume and produce media content.

In the future, it seems that individuals' capacity to use network technologies to construct highly individualized forms of religious belief is likely to keep increasing. In these individually constructed systems of belief, people like those documented here are choosing to create self-filtering enclaves. Facilitating enclave communication, however, is not the only potential outcome of the increased power over religious expression individuals garner from digital communication.

The course that communication technologies are charting for us is not preordained. In the 1990s, the Internet seemed like an emerging egalitarian utopia of tolerant communication. In 2001, that early optimism seemed unfounded. Since 2002, the sudden emergence of participatory media reconstituted and revitalized the possibilities of network technologies. These surprises should serve as strong reminders that the future communication technologies offer us remains uncertain.

Individuals today have access to a far richer and more complex media environment than at any moment before in human history. While some may limit themselves to self-selecting enclaves, many do not. One example is of a technologically savvy group of online evangelical Christians who engaged in forum-based deliberation with more conservative "fundies." In this exchange, the possibility emerges that individuals may increasingly be choosing diversity over enclave communication.

The many different opportunities for individual belief and communication offered to media-savvy Internet users today may be instilling a deep value for tolerant dialogue. These users seem increasingly aware that acknowledging the other is a prerequisite for their own ability to participate in any virtual ekklesia. Without tolerance, dialogue comes under threat. If dialogue fails, so too does any ekklesia built only on the slender webs of digital communication.

Tolerance at RelevantMagazine.com

Young, media-savvy Christians are using all kinds of new technologies to create their own individualistic media worlds. Often, they seem more connected to these media-based communities than they are to those formed around local churches or specific Christian denominations (Smith 2005, 5–6). Coming of age with digital media integrated into their spiritual and religious lives, whole genres, many of them heavily participatory, are being created by and for them. With access to dynamically changing opportunities for connecting with others online, these individuals are exposed to a huge diversity of options for creating their webs of vernacular communication.

While some may strive to reify those webs into closed ideological enclaves, others seek to enact an ekklesia that joins people who value the ability to freely exchange their own individualized systems of belief. Creating online locations for this free exchange of ideas, they transcend specific geography, ideology, and denominational affiliations. However, in order for individuals to participate in such open virtual ekklesia, they must maintain tolerance for the diversity that their individualism fosters. The following examples show that while a desire for tolerance may be shared by many different sorts of people, the tolerance that this diversity requires is not always easy to maintain.

A popular example of evangelical participatory media that strives to provide locations for open dialogue is the self-described "user-driven counterpart" to the subscription-based periodical *Relevant Magazine* entitled *RelevantMagazine.com* (Relevant Media Group 2008f). The son of evangelical media CEO Steven Strang, Cameron Strange started *Relevant Magazine* and its companion Web site *RelevantMagazine.com* in 2003. Only twenty-seven years old at the time, his goal with the new media outlet was to serve "twentysomething Christians" who "want to break stereotypes, challenge status-quo and enact change through the media" (Relevant Media Group 2008f). After its debut, *Publishers Weekly* described Strang's Web site as "the first wave of what Christianity is going to be like in a post-denominational age" (Gannett Company Incorporated 2004).

The site contains extensive archives of articles on topics ranging from the newest college-oriented pop music to a book about the trials and tribulations of spending "12 months following the rules of the Old Testament" (Jacobs 2008). It describes itself as a "faith-based, for-profit multimedia company" that has "no affiliation with any denominations, organizations or other companies" (Relevant Media Group 2008c). It generates revenue by selling advertising space for products ranging from fair-trade coffee to Christian-oriented "hoodies" and T-shirts.

In addition to the institutional content, the site also hosts discussion forums that generate a significant amount of coproduced content. With its participatory media, the site seeks to connect people to "daily life" by creating an online location for everyday Christians to engage in fellowship. The site advocates for a nondenominational ekklesia that is the social aggregate emergent from shared expression: "The Church is not a religious institution or denomination. Rather, the Church universal is made up of those who have become genuine followers of Jesus" (Relevant Media Group 2008e).

To help bring this universal church online, *RelevantMagazine.com* seeks to foster diverse and tolerant deliberative communication. In the words of one of the site's introductory pages:

> We want to engage people in a conversation about faith. We want to challenge worldviews and cause people to see God outside the box they've put Him in. [. . .] We don't believe in legalism and bigotry. We believe in dialogue—about Truth, about faith, about freedom in Christ. (Relevant Media Group 2008e)

This "dialogue" plays out in conversational "threads," initiated by single users' posts and sustained by responses to these posts from other users. These exchanges take place in the six broadly construed topical forums on *RelevantMagazine.com*: "Life," "Culture," "Open," "Podcast Fodder," "Talk to Relevant," and "God." The "God" forum engages topics of religion most directly (Relevant Media Group 2008a and 2008d).

In this forum, the posts range from subjects like "Generation X Christianity" to "Free Will vs. Predestination" (Relevant Media Group 2008b). In one specific exchange, more conservative individuals tried to initiate ritual deliberation based on the End Times narrative. However, the progressive users who dominate the site shut the discussion down. In so doing, they frustrated the open dialogue the site hopes to foster.

In many ways, this behavior was not so different from that documented in the 1990s when liberal Christians using Usenet drove those interested in fundamentalism out of the newsgroups and onto private email lists. From this perspective, it is disappointing that the progressive Christians on this site are still driving more conservative Christians to engage in enclave communication. On the other hand, the users of *RelevantMagazine.com* can be observed doing something that was not common among Christians using Usenet newsgroups before 1999. Today, they can be seen actively struggling to maintain a shared ideal of tolerance by engaging even vernacular Christian fundamentalists in reflective discussions about what exactly constitutes open dialogue and tolerance in their online forum.

Among 274 threads emerging on the "God" forum in May 2008, one entitled "The rapture" was initiated by a recently registered user named "murshac5." Referencing the Rapture, Murshac raised one of the most common issues of ritual deliberation in vernacular Christian fundamentalism. As is typical in attempts to initiate deliberation among those involved in the movement, he used cues that would encourage an engaged response from his audience by assuming that "the Rapture" referenced an important narrative element in the End Times. His post began:

> I'm just wondering what your view on Dispensationalism is? to be honest I haven't studied it deeply enough to form a solid opinion, I just grew up being taught that there would be a Rapture [. . .] what's everybody's take on this? and why? (murshac5 2008)

This cue to ritual deliberation was met with rejection as the progressives that dominate the site tried to shut down any engaged exchange about the topic. Six consecutive posters rejected the possibility of the Rapture. A user identified as "Owenboen" noted: "Just to prepare you [. . .] most of us don't think there is a rapture" (owenboen 2008b). After this barrage of negative feedback, however, Murshac tried again. This time he displayed a greater openness to alternate ideas by recognizing that "there are a ton of opposing" views. In so doing, he shifted away from cueing ritual deliberation about the End Times and toward cueing open dialogue about the meaning of biblical prophecy in general:

> So if there is no rapture of the saints, what do you suppose will happen . . . is there going to be a[n] antichrist appearing at some point? [. . .] I know there are a ton of opposing views on all of this but I'm just curious since I hear The Rapture of the saints being preached and pretty much have believed it my whole life. (murshac5 2008)

In response to Murshac's attempt to initiate more substantive deliberation, a longtime forum user identified as "FNR" took a surprisingly aggressive tone:

> The story of the beginning of the Rapture Doctrine goes like this . . . John Darby was out for a morning prayer walk and stepped in a pile of dog crap. He stooped over, grabbed a stick, and began to scrape it off of his shoe. He then suddenly became ill and vomited. When the dog crap and vomit mixed, he had a sudden vision of people vanishing. He was in the middle of a study of 1 Thessalonians around the same time period. This is the real story. (FNR 2008)

While FNR's belittling of the idea of the Rapture seems intended to shut down the dialogue, several longtime users posted after him trying to reengage Murshac. In fact, the next eighteen posts constituted a largely even-toned and nondenominational discussion. However, this deliberation was not the ritual deliberation of vernacular Christian fundamentalism, because it did not assume that the Rapture was a part of a divinely ordained prophetic narrative. Instead, it engaged in a range of possible meanings for the Book of Revelation and what they might entail. In so doing (and despite FNR's hostility), the forum functioned to create an online discursive space for Christians to exchange diverse ideas.

In the midst of this open dialogue, however, a newer user identified as "jimmy777" joined, whose entrance threatened to derail the exchange. After expressing a strong belief in Rapture, Jimmy engaged in a typical self-sealing argument: "In the last days people will hold on to a flawed system of beliefs that would deny the rapture. It is another signal that Jesus is coming back. Plus many in the last days will depart from the truth (this magazine for one)." Overtly hostile in his attack on *Relevant Magazine* itself, Jimmy then raised the possibility that the users of the forum might label him a "fundy": "If I choose to believe in 'the rapture' does that make me a fundy?" (jimmy777 2008a). On this forum, "fundy," "fundee," or "fundie" has become a slang term for "fundamentalist."

Responding to Jimmy, a regular user identified as "poppalogio" described fundamentalists not on the basis of their beliefs but as individuals who displayed an intolerant attitude: "They absolutely refuse to listen to anyone else's POV [Point of View]" (poppalogio 2008). To bolster his claim, Poppalogio cited a different thread on the God forum entitled, "What Is a Fundamentalist to You?" In this thread, it was clear that the regular users of the forum had a shared understanding of what it meant to be a "fundie." For them, being a fundie was not a good thing.

A self-identifying fundamentalist using the name "daveme7" started the "What Is a Fundamentalist to You?" thread by asking: "I, a fundamentalist, often see people speak negatively of 'fundamentalists.' [. . .] What is your image of a fundamentalist or what is it that they teach that is so wrong?" (daveme7 2008). In the dialogue that followed, a couple of participants expressed their belief in the fundamentalist ideology. However, most respectfully offered reasons for rejecting it. These reasons included its association with politically conservative values and the belief that its biblical interpretations were too simplistic.

When the tone in this exchange began to shift from a discussion of the beliefs associated with fundamentalism to attacks on "fundies," including the inflammatory suggestion that they were members of "cults," the longtime user identified as "Krempel" reminded participants, "It's important to maintain the distinction between 'fundamentalism' which is a belief system, which you may or may not subscribe to, but has adherents who are good people and those who we may affectionately refer to as 'fundies'" (Krempel 2008f).

Prefiguring Poppalogio's claim that "fundies" were defined by their intolerance in the later thread, Krempel here went on to note how the negative connotations of the term referred not to any specific beliefs but to intolerant behavior. Ironically, this same Krempel's sarcastic joking later precipitated an exchange so hostile that it drew the attention of the forum moderators who ultimately shut down "the Rapture" thread.

Many of the participants in "the Rapture" thread—including Krempel, Daveme7, FNR, murshac5, Owenboen, a user identifying as "Robbie Crawford," and the forum administrator identified as "amy kathleen"—were also part of the "What Is a Fundamentalist to You?" thread. Most were very progressive, and all seemed to agree with *Relevant.com's* goal of fostering tolerant dialogue. However, when Jimmy condemned *Relevant Magazine* for contributing to the "many [people] in the last days [who would] depart from the truth," the users of the forum could be seen struggling to maintain their tolerance for his contribution to the discussion. At first, Krempel refuted Jimmy's accusation in a noninflammatory way: "This isn't fair. That's a gross oversimplification." However, Krempel could not help adding a playfully obscene remark stating that nonfundies sometimes "smoke pot, worship the devil, and jerk off to gay porn too" (Krempel 2008a).

Jimmy was offended by the joke, and soon the whole dialogue devolved into hostility. Referencing Krempel's responsibility to evangelize as a lay minister, he attacked Krempel for using language inappropriate for a "minister of God." Responding with more sarcasm, Krempel wrote curtly: "I am the minister of sodomizing" (Krempel 2008b). The hostility rapidly escalating, Jimmy demanded to know if Krempel was referring to "boys." Referencing the geographic location noted for Krempel in his profile, Jimmy threatened: "If I knew what church you were in I would call the police. I will have people look in maryland to see if they know you" (jimmy777 2008b).

For the next sixteen posts, a flurry of insults cascaded down on Jimmy. Owenboen took the opportunity to drive home a point from the "What Is a Fundamentalist to You?" thread about fundies being intolerant: "This is case and point regarding what I said about most fundamentalists in that other thread" (owenboen 2008a). Then, at the height of the verbal melee, Jimmy claimed he had actually called the Maryland police and accused Krempel of being an online child predator seeking to "sodomize" children. Later Krempel pointed out he had only referenced "plain old sodomy" and did not even jokingly admit to child predation (Krempel 2008e). But the damage had been done, and the forum administrator made her first appearance in the discussion. She called for calm, writing:

> For you newbies, you have to remember that sometimes people say things
> in jest (and sometimes in poor taste), but please, if you have a concern ask
> for clarification publicly or privately, just please don't go postal on them
> before you realize that they were joking! (amy kathleen 2008a).

Here the term "newbies" refers to those who are new users of the forum. In this case, the newbies were the two more conservative forum users.

After the administrator's post, relative calm ensued and for the next thirteen posts the two fundie-leaning newbies, Jimmy and Murschac, were not to be found. However, with tempers still running high, Krempel brought up another fundamentalist-leaning user using the name "Robbie Crawford" whom he had encountered during the "What Is a Fundamentalist to You?" discussion. Krempel wrote: "It's just that I called what could be considered a 'truce' with Robbie about three months ago after I lit into him. and then this guy [jimmy777] comes along playing the douche card, and I just . . .. had to play with him" (Krempel 2008c). During this moment of calm in the dialogue, Krempel reflected on the kind of behavior that created hostile exchanges. However, he did not seem ready to take full responsibility for his own participation in that intolerance.

Specifically, Krempel could not resist justifying his actions by reminding his fellow progressive participants that he was able to "call a truce" with another fundie on a previous occasion. Indicating that this previous tolerance sanctioned his "playing" with Jimmy, Krempel described being tempted to goad fellow Christians he deemed intolerant. Making this claim on the thread, Krempel simultaneously demonstrated a shared valuation for tolerant dialogue and the difficulty people sometimes face in maintaining their own tolerance.

When Robbie got wind of Krempel's claim about him, he too posted a response on the new thread. Focusing on Krempel's claim that he "lit into him" before he "called a truce," Robbie used the example to engage the issue of whether the "God" forum successfully fostered tolerant dialogue. Robbie posted: "You lit into me? Christian message board claimer tough guys have got to be the gayest thing since George Michael, 'I lit into him' . . . haha . . . what a pathetic clown . . ." (Robbie Crawford 2008a).

Despite his homophobic comment, this post offers a very interesting insight. Robbie specifically accused Krempel of a behavior typically called "trolling" that he felt occurred regularly and functioned to curtail open dialogue on the forum. Robbie claimed that Krempel and other regular users goaded their fellow Christians to "stumble" by making them angry. Arguing it was unchristian behavior, Robbie suggested that these regular users habitually "band together" and conspire to verbally attack fundamentalist-leaning Christians by "pushing their buttons" until they "react in the flesh." As Robbie described it:

You all sit and stroke each others ego while you feel like feared pedantic ones because you caused a christian to stumble on a message board. Can you even see clear enough to realize how absolutely ****** lame that is? Do you understand what level that puts [you] people on? (Robbie Crawford 2008b)

Responding to Robbie, Krempel denied that the progressive users of the forum were at fault for shutting down dialogue, writing: "I think you overestimate the degree to which regulars on the board conspire together." Then he went on to argue that Jimmy deserved the harsh treatment he had received because he came "running through here like a bull in a china shop." According to Krempel, Jimmy did not "present himself as open to other POV's or even cordial in conversation." Suggesting that a tolerant tone in Jimmy's remarks would have had a more tolerant reception on the forum, Krempel concluded: "See, Robbie. People are accepted here. Even those with differing POV's. But it all hinges on one thing: approach" (Krempel 2008d).

Not quite able to leave it at that, however, Krempel finished his post by justifying his own belligerence as a response to Jimmy's intolerance: "Seems to me that Jimmy was escalating this thing with his inflammatory rhetoric. and frankly, i think what I said was ****ing hilarious" (Krempel 2008d). But Robbie was unconvinced: "Don't kid yourself . . . you banded together and you pushed his buttons . . . just like I've seen you guys do to more people than I can count over the past couple years" (Robbie Crawford 2008b).

Then Jimmy suddenly returned. This time he brought evidence in support of Robbie's claim that the progressives "gang up on" the conservatives. He posted two private messages he had received through the *RelevantMagazine.com* forum. The first was from Krempel. In it, Krempel attempted to justify his "joke." The second message was from the forum administrator Amy Kathleen. In that message, Amy Kathleen wrote to Jimmy:

Krempel was joking and if you would have asked him in sincerity, he would have told you that. If you have that kind of concern about someone [being a child predator], you need to PM them and/or us moderators before threatening them with calling the police based on a silly comment that was meant to ruffle your feathers and nothing more. Does that make sense? I need you to work this out in a civil manner with Krempel. I am sure he had NO idea how badly you would take the comment. Please respond asap. (Jimmy 2008c)

Jimmy did not respond privately. Instead, he posted the two messages publicly and demanded civility: "How am i supposed to work this out when Krempel refuses to apoligize [. . .] ?" (Jimmy 2008c) At that point, Amy Kathleen gave up hope that civility would return and "locked" the thread so that no one could post to it. In the final post as she shut it down, she remarked: "We're done here. Take a step back and go before God. If you need to apologize, do it. If you need to let go, then do it" (amy kathleen 2008b).

From the examination of these exchanges, it is clear that it was difficult or impossible to engage in ritual deliberation about the End Times on this forum. However, they also suggest that both conservatives and progressives share the magazine's stated value for open and tolerant online dialogue.

If that is true, it may be that media-savvy evangelicals are increasingly aware that their own hostility could impede online discourse. Between *RelevantMagazine.com*'s blunt statement that they "believe in dialog," Murshac's acknowledgment that "there are a tone of opposing views" about the Rapture, Krempel's "truce" with Robbie, and his claim that open dialogue "all hinges on one thing: approach," it is clear that they all valued an environment where tolerance frees individuals to express themselves. Even if this value was not always translated into reality, these moments in the exchange are reason enough to suspect that participatory media are having a positive effect on these individuals' ability to engage with diversity.

Among the new generation of Christians growing up with network communication technologies fully integrated into their daily lives, there seems to be a greater awareness of the diverse beliefs of others. While this diversity prevents the vernacular web of Christian fundamentalism from drawing *RelevantMagazine.com* into its ekklesia, the site's users are forming their own vernacular webs of discourse. For many of these users, the webs they create are central to their daily religious and spiritual lives. Valuing those webs more than ever before, this newest generation of users is in a better position to recognize that in order for any virtual ekklesia to persist it must always be engaging in discourse and that the expression of intolerance silences participants and thus threatens any group's ability to generate that necessary discourse.

With a native understanding of this dynamic, it seems very possible that more and more people will insist on acknowledging the validity of alternate voices because they recognize that such acknowledgment is central to encouraging discourse—while this shared value of tolerance is not foreign to any of them because it lies at the heart of the Christian message itself.

Toward a Truer Charity

At least since the writings of the ancient church leader Augustine of Hippo, the central assertion in the Christian message places "charity" or (in Augustine's Latin) *caritas* above all other human values. In the Greek of the New Testament, "caritas" is *agape* and is typically rendered in contemporary English as "brotherly love." Augustine defined his theological concept of "charity" by writing: "I call 'charity' [*caritas*] the motion of the soul toward the enjoyment of God for His own sake, and the enjoyment of one's self and of one's neighbor for the sake of God" (1958, 88). Charity is the love of others that is derived from the love of God. For Augustine, this charity is the definitive Christian principle and it is only on the basis of this principle that individuals can live rightly:

> "Thou shalt love," He said, "the Lord thy God with thy whole heart, and with thy whole soul, and with thy whole mind," and "Thou shalt love thy neighbor as thyself. On these two commandments dependeth the whole law and the prophets." "Now the end of the commandment is charity," and this is twofold: a love of God and a love of thy neighbor. [Mathew 22: 39–40; Timothy 1: 5]. (1958, 22–23)

Today, the message to "love thy neighbor" can still be clearly heard in many Christian contexts. On *Relevant.com*, for example, after accusing the participants of "banding together" and goading others till they "react in the flesh," Robbie Crawford sarcastically asked: "you feel like good christians now?" (2008b). This statement allies itself with Augustine in its view of Christian charity. It suggests that the choice to give up one's own position as a speaker and attend to others as they speak is a compassionate risk because that attention acknowledges the possibility that the speaker may know something the listener does not. In this acknowledgment, the hearer gives up a moment of comfort by taking the risk that she or he may be wrong.

On the other hand, there are few risks in engaging in discourse with the like-minded. In fact, reinforcing shared certainty should increase a speaker's comfort with their understanding of the world. A truer charity, however, would seek to engage individuals with divergent ideas. It would engage them by acknowledging that because they hold their beliefs to be true, those beliefs deserve consideration. In turn, such engaged consideration would hold open the possibility that divergent beliefs may in fact be truer than the beliefs already held by the listener.

This idea is Augustinian because Augustine placed a lack of certainty at the center of his conception of the human experience. For Augustine, the divine transcends the mundane categories of time, purpose, or wisdom but humans cannot. As Augustine put it: "Who can search out the unsearchable depth of [God's] purpose, who can scrutinize the inscrutable wisdom?" (1950, 395). For Augustine, humans must accept God's "unchangeable and eternal design" without the ability to apprehend it fully for themselves. True knowledge, for Augustine, must be accepted "by the faith of piety" (1950, 154).

Augustine argued that, without fully understanding, humans must give up their own will to the divine purpose. For Augustine, the only purpose that humans can attribute to the divine with certainty is the injunction to enact caritas. A Christian enactment of such charity, then, would acknowledge the possibility that others with ideas that diverge from those already held may well be right. To engage others without this compassionate consideration would be an act of hubris—and it would contradict at least one central interpretation of the Christian message.

In vernacular Christian fundamentalism, however, the force of certainty conflicts with this compassionate attention. In many of the examples documented in this research, individuals exhibited what Poppalogio described as an "absolute refusal" to "listen to anyone else's POV" (2008). This refusal to listen is a product of the profound certainty that characterizes the movement. This certainty is partially a result of the adherents' emphasis on the revelatory experience of spiritual rebirth.

Insofar as an individual is radically certain of her or his understanding of the divine, the divine is perceived as less mysterious. Lacking mystery, individuals are more likely to embrace a belief system as self-sealing because the reduction of mystery reduces the impulse to acknowledge the other. The radically certain individual has no need of new or divergent ideas. Such individuals have no motive to engage such ideas because they already possess right knowledge.

As we have seen, vernacular Christian fundamentalism is associated with some historic discourses that harbor significant kinds of prejudice. Among some in the movement, these historic tendencies have merged with a radical sense of certainty that their religious beliefs are the only correct ones, thereby creating a dualistic worldview. In these cases, it has become acceptable to express intolerance for those who are perceived to be under the influence of beliefs that contradict those of vernacular Christian fundamentalism. In the most extreme cases, those in the movement believe that these outsiders present a danger that must be combated.

The way individuals in the movement use participatory media fosters the persistence of these prejudices. Because moderated blogs and forums create enclaves of like-minded communication, individuals can choose to filter their understanding of the world through social formations that allow or even encourage intolerance. While this is bad for those at whom these prejudices are directed, it is also bad for the individuals harboring the intolerance. Because individuals involved in communication enclaves isolate themselves from the publics that are involved in the basic functions of real-world schools, churches, and governments, they compromise their ability to represent their interests in those publics.

However, this deployment of digital communication technologies is not the only one possible. As we saw on *Relevant.com*, some media-savvy Christians are demanding more tolerance in their online religious communities. The implications of these findings are significant because they demonstrate the multiple possibilities the increasing personalization of both religious belief and media consumption may take in the future.

7

Conclusion

Attending to Vernacular Theology

In this research, I have documented the new religious movement of vernacular Christian fundamentalism. The movement is new because its emphasis on the particular prophetic narrative of the End Times renders it distinct from other forms of Christianity. Not only is it new, but it is also a new sort of movement because it has emerged without any central leadership, institutional structures, or geographic location. Instead, its members enact what they term a "virtual ekklesia" through their everyday online communication. Though informal, this communication evolved into a distinct form as it moved from early Internet email lists, through the era of largely static Web pages, and into its most robust manifestation in participatory media.

The movement can be recognized when individuals express its four definitive beliefs: first, a belief in biblical literalism, second, a belief in the experience of spiritual rebirth, third, a belief in the need to evangelize, and fourth, the most distinctive, a belief in the End Times interpretation of biblical prophecy. This cluster of beliefs can be considered a form of fundamentalism because their association reaches back to the historical Christian fundamentalism of the early twentieth century. In that movement, the four basic beliefs were clustered together and then popularized by a series of evangelical figures. Because these four beliefs presented a simple and nondenominational theology, they garnered wide audiences in the new forms of mass media emerging at that time.

The movement is distinct from historical Christian fundamentalism, however, because it has emerged alongside but apart from institutional religion. At first, these four beliefs were broadly associated with conservative Protestant leaders in the late nineteenth and early twentieth centuries. Later, when those leaders lost their struggle for the control of American Protestant institutions, the cluster of beliefs continued to be spread by nondenominational evangelical Christian media. As a result, the beliefs are an example of lived religion because they have come to animate the religious lives of everyday people. The new religious movement based on sharing these beliefs is vernacular because its only authority emerges from the aggregated volition of its members communicating online.

Both everyday religious expression and new religious movements have existed as long as humans have imagined the sacred. This movement, however, uses network communication technologies to create a community based on aggregate vernacular authority alone. This community is a "church" in the early Christian sense of the word "ekklesia." An ekklesia was an assembly of people who shared their belief in the teachings of Christ. This new sort of ekklesia, however, is strictly "virtual." It has no geographic location. Instead, it is virtual in the original sense of the word. It is only manifested in its effect, and that effect is the linking of a group of dispersed individuals who imagine themselves part of an Internet-based religious community.

To create this effect, the individuals in the movement engage in koinonia or "fellowship." Also associated with the early Christian church, this fellowship occurs when individuals share personal expressions of their Christian belief. This practice is common in evangelical Protestantism as "witnessing" or "giving testimony" about one's personal experiences with the divine. With this movement's central theological focus on the End Times, fellowship about topics relevant to the prophetic narrative emerged as a distinctive form of communication specific to the movement.

This communication took the form of ritual deliberation because members of the movement embrace a certainty so profound that they have no real issues or problems about which they need to come to any agreement. Engaging in communication about these beliefs, however, requires individuals to both express themselves and to pay attention to the expression of others. In the movement, ritual deliberation can proceed despite this tension because one thing of which its members are certain is that no human can know exactly when Christ will return. Even when some of its members are tempted to predict dates, they recognize that their predictions may well turn out to be wrong and thus hold open the door for deliberation.

With the mundane goals of typical deliberation beyond reach, this ritual deliberation elevates the ordinary activity of exchanging ideas with a heightened attention to detail that can proceed infinitely precisely because it can never attain anything more than its ongoing performance. In this sense, ritual deliberation functions as do more conventional forms of ritual by serving the purpose of generating a discursive space where its virtual ekklesia can exist. Because the space constructed by online ritual deliberation is only virtual, however, it constitutes a fragile kind of church. If that church is to exist at all, individuals must keep imagining it as a community in which they have a stake. To do that, they must keep up periodic engagements with others online. Ritual deliberation fulfills this need by creating opportunities for engagement.

When the movement shifted the primary location for this ritual deliberation from email lists to the new technologies of the Worldwide Web, an abiding tension between personal authority and deliberation was exacerbated. Without the interactive features that later Web-based technologies would make available, individuals experimented with a variety of ways to express their own sense of authority while still imagining themselves as interacting with others in the movement. As the participatory media technologies often termed "Web 2.0" became widely available, some of these media proved to be poor venues for ritual deliberation. Soon, however, heavily moderated forums and the comment areas in blogs emerged as the technologies most suited to fostering ritual deliberation online. These forms of participatory media make it easy for Web site builders to create interactive spaces on their Web pages. Features embedded in these technologies also enable them to tightly control the communication. Mitigating the impact of hostile outsiders or ideas that contradict their ideology, moderators can simply remove the offending content and ban repeat offenders.

Creating these communication enclaves, however, aggravates two problems in the movement. First, some discourses associated with the movement are prone to expressions of prejudice against those with different religious beliefs. Communication enclaves where individuals can express such prejudices without facing resistance allows intolerance to persist. While this problem is one that might be of more concern to outsiders to the movement, the second problem is potentially harmful to insiders.

When individuals choose to avoid any ideas that do not support the worldview of vernacular Christian fundamentalism, they create a feedback loop between the expression of highly specific beliefs and the consumption of media content that supports those beliefs. This feedback loop then shapes the mediated life-worlds these individuals inhabit. This is potentially harmful because the larger social entities in which they have a very real stake are governed by more broadly inclusive discourse. Because that discourse assumes certain basic shared values that would reject the beliefs of vernacular Christian fundamentalism, these individuals isolate themselves from the real-world communities in which they must physically live.

This problem is most obvious in these newer forms of participatory media because they elicit more individual expression than any previous digital medium, while simultaneously giving people greater access to the expression of others than ever before. Thus the powerful feedback loop emerges as a huge volume of everyday expression is generated, and then immediately becomes available for the same individuals to consume and incorporate into their next communications. However, this feedback loop is not merely a mechanism of the communication technologies. Instead, the individual and cultural forces made available through the Internet and beyond shape each person's choice to engage in online ritual deliberation. People act out of their own volition when they aggregate the online expression now available to them. As a result, these aggregations are not just reflections of external forces. They are also the assertive inflections of the information each individual is incorporating into her or his understanding of the world she or he inhabits. The examples in this book demonstrate that the radical certainty individuals in the movement value encourages them to migrate into self-regulated enclaves of like-minded believers.

This finding has significant implications.

Digital communication technologies have empowered individuals by giving them access to a greater diversity of ideas than ever before. At the same time, it has freed them of the need to adhere to any religious institutions or leaders. Still, they are choosing to engage in communication that isolates them from the discourses that shape the powerful social institutions with which they must live. This isolation is not the result of being the disempowered victims of a dominating leadership. Instead, the choice to participate in communication enclaves places the responsibility for the ideas expressed there squarely on the shoulders of the everyday participants.

The case of vernacular Christian fundamentalism suggests that researchers and scholars seeking to understand how individuals are impacted by their religious ideologies must recognize that the final responsibility for the forms religiosity takes lies with the individual believers. This is not to say that charismatic leaders never take advantage of people or that reified institutions cannot limit the ability of individuals to act. However, it is to recognize that even given privileged access to some of the most powerful technologies of our information age, some people seize the chance to embrace a self-sealing ideology. Without leaders or institutions, these people are not victims.

This movement is a case that shows how everyday agents are the ultimate sources of the aggregate volition that constitutes vernacular authority. As a result, researchers seeking to understand religious authority must reinvigorate their commitment to detailed analyses of the daily communication of everyday believers. As the twenty-first century goes on, the religious behaviors of individuals with Internet access may well come to look more like this virtual ekklesia than they do like the institutional and community oriented religiosity of the last millennium. As new communication technologies emerge, surge to popularity, and are then replaced, religion will undoubtedly continue to change. However, it seems unlikely that it will become more institutional and less vernacular anytime soon. As a result, researchers of religion must reexamine their concepts and methods to best adapt to this ongoing state of change.

Vernacular Christian fundamentalism has brought to our attention individuals who choose certainty for themselves out of the vast digital sea of possibilities. While the reasons for this choice are no doubt as variable as the individuals who choose them, it seems reasonable to assume that they choose this way of being in the world because it offers them something they perceive as a significant benefit. One possibility is that they find that their communication enclave reduces their sense of risk. By reducing the diversity of ideas they confront, they reduce the risk of having to confront challenges to the certainty their movement affords them.

From an Augustinian perspective, engaging alternate voices and divergent ideas serves the valuable purpose of reminding the believer that, in the end, it is "by the faith of piety" and not certainty that God enacts His will on earth. In today's communication media, Augustine might regard sacrificing individual certainty to attend to the other as a kind of caritas. But this sort of Augustinianism does not seem to characterize vernacular Christian fundamentalism. Still, the always-changing technologies of the Internet are connecting more people in more diverse ways all the time. Research on religious belief and expression influenced by digital communication technologies must continue, and, with those efforts, we might come to better understand how these technologies are shaping the religious lives of the twenty-first century.

At the very outset of the research presented in this book, I was confronted with two fundamentally different conceptions of the Protestant divine. First, there was Marilyn Agee's certainty that she could find a single, literal, and knowable truth in the Bible. God called her to publish her interpretations of prophecy by presenting the divinely lit passage: "Publish and conceal not." Armed with this certainty, Marilyn located that truth and communicated it to others. Now, I have demonstrated how the form her simple Web pages took foresaw the primary way individuals in this movement would come to use participatory media. For over a decade, Marilyn has remained at the center of this movement's virtual ekklesia.

However, another figure has continued to linger on the fringes. Following a series of links from her *Bible Prophecy Corner* in 1999 or in 2010, one could find Lambert Dolphin's Web pages. Confronted with an undeniable experience of spiritual rebirth, Lambert sought out other individuals who had this experience. Discovering the possibility of engaging in fellowship online, he began to understand his experience in the terms offered by evangelical Christianity. Instead of gaining radical certainty about any particular set of beliefs from his contact with the divine, however, Lambert's spiritual rebirth led him to focus on acting compassionately by seeking to share his profound sense of calm with others. That goal is well served by his online communication because he accepts a fundamental mystery at the heart of his beliefs. He can engage the widest array of Christian ideas on his Web site because he does not exclude the possibility that other ways of knowing might give different individuals access to the same certainty he has attained in spiritual rebirth.

As Lambert put it, "In fact, it's probably perfectly acceptable to have equivalent models and use the one that you feel most comfortable with—or the one that fits best to your circumstances" (Dolphin 1999f). Lambert refuses to make even this overtly stated pluralism a certainty. He told me it is "probably" acceptable to have different understandings of the divine. In this moment Lambert did not just profess an acceptance of God's mystery; he enacted it.

Discovering just how different Marilyn and Lambert's views of the divine were has fueled this research. How could two very different thinkers be so closely connected online? Now, it is clear. The reason is that, at root, Lambert refuses to reject the possibility that the radical certainty of vernacular Christian fundamentalism is incorrect. As a result, he has placed a carefully created and fully articulated description of the End Times prophetic narrative on his Web site. With these ideas publicly posted, other participants in the movement still make and follow links to his page even into the second decade of this millennium. As individuals weave this vernacular web of communication around his End Times page, the vernacular authority of vernacular Christian fundamentalism assimilates his communicative action into its dynamic social aggregate.

In this assimilation, there is a powerful lesson. Maintaining uncertainty is uncommon because it demands that individuals always entertain the possibility that others might know more rightly. It always imagines that others might be closer to God's truth—even when those others are outsiders who hold beliefs so profoundly foreign that they seem absurd. Lambert's acceptance of mystery is not merely the toleration of alternate ideas. It attributes value to resistance by seeking out deliberative discursive engagement with diverse others even when those others are radically certain.

At this nexus of pluralism and compassion, a truer charity emerges. However, to use the Classical Greek term, its *telos* or "ultimate purpose" requires a move so selfless that it recedes into the realm of the impossible. The truest charity would grant the possibility of certainty to others by withholding it for oneself in every case. In communicative practice, such charity slips out of human grasp and into the realm of the divine. Continually reaching out across the Internet for that telos nonetheless, Lambert's Web pages suggest that there is still much to learn from the vernacular theologies of everyday believers.

Notes

CHAPTER 1

1. When working with online communities, it is often unnecessarily intrusive to request the full names of all respondents. In many cases, I have used only the individuals' online names. To maintain consistency, I generally use only first names in this research. In the case of published authors or where a respondent specifically requested her or his full name be used, I have included first and last names in at least the first instance of the name. In some particularly sensitive cases or where the respondent requested it, I use pseudonyms. To indicate a pseudonym, I have placed the first instance of the name in quotation marks.

CHAPTER 2

1. All citations of online content are represented as closely as possible to their originals. In many cases, this results in nontypical grammar, spelling, and other idiosyncratic language usage.

CHAPTER 4

1. I use the digital storage measurement of megabytes to describe the amount of content on these Web pages. A megabyte can store about 500,000 words or one compressed digital photo taken at a resolution of 3 megapixels. During this period, most sites only used words and simple graphics with far less resolution than a digital photo.

References

Abbate, Janet. 1999. *Inventing the Internet*. Cambridge: MIT Press.

Agee, Marilyn J. 1991. *Exit 2007: The Secret of Secrets Revealed*. Yorba Linda, Calif.: Archer Press.

———. 1995. *Heaven Found: "A Butter and Honey Star."* Riverside, Calif.: Archer Press.

———. 1997. *Revelations 2000*. New York: Avon Books.

———. 1999a. Bible Prophecy Corner. *Bible Prophecy Corner*. Http://www.kiwi. net/~mjagee/index.html (accessed April 1, 1999).

———. 1999b. "My Testimony." *Bible Prophecy Corner*. Http://www.kiwi.net/~mjagee / picture.html (accessed April 1, 1999).

———. 1999c. Personal communication, April 1.

———. 1999d. Pro and Con 223. *Bible Prophecy Corner*. Http://www.kiwi.net/~mjagee/pro-con223.html (accessed April 1).

———. 2001a. Pro and con 802. *Bible Prophecy Corner*. Http://www.geocities.com/Athens/ Cyprus/5341/procon802.html (accessed September 9).

———. 2001b. Pro and con 803. *Bible Prophecy Corner*. Http://www.geocities.com/Athens/ Cyprus/5341/procon803.html (accessed September 12).

———. 2001c. Pro and Con 807. *Bible Prophecy Corner*. Http://www.kiwi.net/~mjagee/pro-con807.html (accessed April 1).

———. 2001d. Pro and con 810. *Bible Prophecy Corner*. Http://www.geocities.com/Athens/ Cyprus/5341/procon810.html (accessed September 15).

———. 2002a. Links. *Prophecy Corner*. Http://www.prophecycorner.com/links/index.htm 2002 (accessed February 1).

———. 2002b. Prophecy Corner. *Prophecy Corner*. Http://www.prophecycorner.com (accessed February 1, 2008).

———, and Edgar. 1999. Personal interview. September 4.

Althusser, Louis. 1984 [1976]. *Essays on Ideology*. London: Verso Press.

Ammerman, Nancy T. 1997. Organized Religion in a Voluntaristic Society. *Sociology of Religion* 58: 203–215.

amy kathleen. 2008a. RE: The rapture. *RelevantMagazine.com*. Http://www.relevantmagazine .com/forums/viewtopic.php?f=4&t=391&st=0&sk=t&sd=a&start=60 (accessed August 1).

———. 2008b. RE: The rapture. *Relevantmagazine.com*. Http://www.relevantmagazine. com/forums/viewtopic.php?f=4&t=391&st=0&sk=t&sd=a&start=110 (accessed August 1).

Anderson, Benedict. 1991. *Imagined Communities: Reflections on the Origin and Spread of Nationalism*. New York: Verso.

Apolito, Paolo. 2005. *The Internet and the Madonna: Religious Visionary Experience on the Web*. Chicago: University of Chicago Press.

Armstrong, Karen. 2000. *The Battle for God*. New York: Alfred A. Knopf.

Asteroff, Roberta. 2001. Searching for the Library: University Home Page Design and Missing Links. *Information Technology and Libraries* 20 (2): 93–99.

Augustine. 1950. *The City of God*. Trans. Marcus Dods. New York: Random House.

———. 1958. *On Christian Doctrine [De doctrina christiana]*. Trans. D. W. Robertson, Jr. New York: Macmillan.

Balkin, Jack. 2004. Digital Speech and Democratic Culture: A Theory of Freedom of Expression for the Information Society. *New York University Law Review* 79 (April): 1–55.

Balmer, Randall, and Lauren F. Winner. 2002. *Protestantism in America*. New York: Columbia University Press.

Barkun, Michael. 1994. *Religion and the Racist Right: The Origins of the Christian Identity Movement*. Chapel Hill: University of North Carolina Press.

———. 2003. *A Culture of Conspiracy: Apocalyptic Visions in Contemporary America*. Berkeley: University of California Press.

Barr, James. 1966. *Old and New in Interpretation: A Study of the Two Testaments*. London: SCM Press.

———. 1978. *Fundamentalism*. Philadelphia: Westminster Press.

Bear, D. M., and P. Fedio. 1977. Quantitative Analysis of Interictal Behavior in Temporal Lobe Epilepsy. *Archives of Neurology* 34: 454–67.

Bell, Catherine. 1997. *Ritual: Perspectives and Dimensions*. New York: Oxford University Press.

Benkler, Yochai. 2008. *The Wealth of Networks: How Social Production Transforms Markets and Freedom*. New Haven: Yale University Press. Http://yupnet.org/benkler/archives/8 (accessed September 1).

Berger, Peter L. 1990 [1967]. *The Sacred Canopy: Elements of a Sociological Theory of Religion*. New York: Anchor Books.

Berlet, Chip, and Matthew N. Lyons. 2000. *Right-Wing Populism in America: Too Close for Comfort*. New York: Guilford Press.

BibleForums.com. 2008. Members List. BibleForums: Judeo Christian Discussion Forums. Http://bibleforums.com/memberlist.php? (accessed February 1).

BibleForums.org. 2006. Definition of "Are you a Christian?" in profile. BibleForums Christian Message Board and Forums. Http://bibleforums.org/forum/showthread. php?t=61168 (accessed August 15).

———. 2008a. Register. *BibleForums Christian Message Board and Forums*. Http://bibleforums.org/forum/register.php?do=checkdate (accessed February 1).

———. 2008b. Welcome to the BibleForums Christian Message Board and Forums. *BibleForums Christian Message Board and Forums*. Http://bibleforums.org/forum/ (accessed February 1).

Blood, Rebecca. 2000. Weblogs: A History and Perspective. *Rebeccablood.com*. Http://www.rebeccablood.net/essays/weblog_history.html (accessed October 1, 2006).

———. 2004. How Blogging Software Reshapes the Online Community. *Communications of the Association for Computer Machinery* 47 (12): 53–55.

Boyer, Paul S. 1992. *When Time Shall Be No More: Prophecy Belief in Modern America*. Cambridge: Harvard University Press.

Bradley, Keith. 1987. On the Roman Slave Supply and Slave Breeding. *Classical Slavery*, Moses Finley, ed. London: Cass Publishers. 42–64.

Brasher, Brenda. 2001a. The Civic Challenge of Virtual Eschatology: Heaven's Gate and Millennial Fever in Cyberspace. *Religion and Social Policy*, Paula D. Nesbitt, ed. Walnut Creek, Calif.: AltaMira Press. 196–209.

———. 2001b. *Give Me That Online Religion*. San Francisco: Jossey-Bass.

Bruce, Dickson D. 1974. *And They All Sang Hallelujah: Plain-Folk Camp-Meeting Religion, 1800–1845*. Knoxville: University of Tennessee Press.

Bryan, Caroline E. [ceb@dbrus.unify.com]. 1994. On-line Posting. April 30, 1994. Re: End Times. <news: bit.listserv.christia>.

Burke, Kenneth. 1973 [1941]. *The Philosophy of Literary Form*. Berkeley: University of California Press.

BuzzardHut. 2008. Members Barred from Christian Citizens Central. *Rapture Ready—Powered by VBulletin*. Http://www.rr-bb.com/showthread.php?t=33970 (accessed February 28).

Byron-Brown, Louis [yronb_l@cs.uwa.oz.au]. 1994. On-line Posting. April 25, 1994 End Times. <news: soc.religion.christian>.

Campbell, Heidi. 2003. Congregation of the Disembodied: A Look at Religious Community Online. *Virtual Morality*. New York: Peter Lang , 179–200.

———. 2005. *Exploring Religious Community Online: We Are One in the Network*. New York: Peter Lang.

Careaga, Andrew. 1999. *E-vangelism. Sharing the Gospel in Cyberspace*. Lafayette, La.: Huntington House.

———. 2001. *eMinistry: Connecting with the Net Generation*. Grand Rapids, Mich.: Kregel Publications.

Carey, James W. 1989. *Communication as Culture: Essays on Media and Society*. New York: Routledge.

Carter, Stephen L. 1991. *The Culture of Disbelief*. New York: Anchor.

Castells, Manuel. 1985. *High Technology, Space and Society London*. Beverley Hills, Calif.: Sage Publishing.

———. 1997. *The Rise of Network Society*. Oxford: Blackwell.

———. 2001. *The Internet Galaxy: Reflections on the Internet, Business, and Society*. Oxford: Oxford University Press.

CERN: The European Organization for Nuclear Research. 2000. A CERN Invention You Are Familiar With: The World-Wide-Web. Http://public.web.cern.ch/Public/ACHIEVEMENTS/web.html (accessed December 1).

Ceruzzi, Paul E. 2003. *A History of Modern Computing*. Cambridge: MIT Press.

Chama, Joshua Cooper Rama. 1996. Finding God on the Web. *Time* 149 (1): 52–59.

Cheryl and Ernie. 1999a. The End of an Age. *Acts 17.11*. Http://www.acts17-11.com/end.html (accessed April 1).

———. 1999b. RE: Basic Questions. July 21, 1999. E-mail to Robert Howard.

———. 1999c. Personal Interview. August 28.

Christianity.com. 2008. Prophecy & End Times. Http://fcnforums.christianity.com/forumid_53/tt.htm (accessed February 1, 2008).

Christian Research Institute ~ Home of the Bible Answer Man, Hank Hanegraaff. 1999. *eQuip.com.* Http://eQuip.com (accessed April 1).

Christian Research Ministries—The Open Scroll—Links. 1999. *TheOpenScroll.com.* Htpp//:home.cwnet.com/crm/sitemap.htm (accessed April 1).

Cialdini, Robert. 1993. *Influence: The Psychology of Persuasion.* New York: Morrow.

Cicero. 1971. *Brutus and Orator,* trans. G. L. Hendrickson. Cambridge: Harvard University Press.

Cimino, Richard, and Don Lattin. 1998. *Shopping for Faith: American Religion in the New Millennium.* New York: John Wiley.

Ciolek, T. Mathew. 2004. Online Religion: The Internet and Religion. *The Internet Encyclopedia Volume Two,* Hossein Bidgoli, ed. New York: John Wiley, 798–811.

Clark, Brian E. [brian@telerama.lm.com]. 1994. On-line Posting. Re: End Times. April 29. <news: bit.listserv.christia>.

Clark, Lynn Schofield. 2003. *From Angels to Aliens: Teenagers, the Media, and the Supernatural.* Oxford: Oxford University Press.

Coombs, J. V. 1904. *Religious Delusions: Studies of the False Faiths of To-day.* Cincinnati: Standard Publishers.

Cowan, Douglas E. 2005. *Cyberhenge: Modern Pagans on the Internet.* New York: Routledge.

daveme7. 2008. What Is a Fundamentalist to You? *Relevantmagazine.com.* Http://www.relevantmagazine.com/forums/viewtopic.php?f=4&t=383&st=0&sk=t&sd=a (accessed August 1).

Davis, Winston. 2000. Heaven's Gate: A Study of Religious Obedience. *Nova Religio: The Journal of Alternative and Emergent Religions* 3: 241–67.

Dawson, Lorne. 2000. Researching Religion in Cyberspace: Issues and Strategies. *Religion on the Internet: Research Prospects and Promises.* New York: JAI Press. 25–54.

———. and Douglas Cowan, eds. 2004. *Religion Online: Finding Faith on the Internet.* New York: Routledge.

Dean. 1999a. Alpha Thru Omega. *Alphathruomega.com.* Htpp://alphathruomega.com (accessed April 1).

———. 1999b. End Times Bible Study Part IV. *Alphathruomega.com.* Http://alphathruomega.com/endtimes/part4.html (accessed April 1).

———. 1999c. Hedges. *Alphathruomega.com.* Htpp://alphathruomega.com/warefare/hedges.html (accessed April 1).

———. 1999d. Spiritual Warfare Topic List (more to come). *Alphathruomega.com.* <> (accessed April 1).

———. 1999e. "Welcome to My Personal Page! :)." April 1, 1999. *Alphathruomega.com.* Htpp://alphathruomega.com/personal/mystory.html (accessed April 1).

———, and Susan. 1999. October 5. Personal interview.

Dillon, Andrew, and Barbara A. Gushrowski. 2000. Genres and the Web: Is the Personal Home Page the First Uniquely Digital Genre? *Journal of the American Society for Information Science and Technology* 51 (2): 202–5.

DLEIBOLD@yorkvm1.bitnet. 1992. On-line Posting. April 19 1992. Jesus returns in 1996? <news: soc.religion.christian>.

Dolphin, Lambert. 1999a. A Very Brief Resume. *Lambert's Library.* Http://ldolphin.org/Ltdres.html (accessed April 1).

————. 1999b . Lambert Dolphin's Library. *Lambert's Library.* Http://ldolphin.org/assbib. shtml (accessed April 1).

————. 1999c. Lambert Dolphin's Resource Files. *Lambert's Library.* Http://Ldolphin.org (accessed April 1).

————. 1999d. Lambert's Eschatological Charts. *Lambert's Library.* Http://Ldolphin.org / eschat.html (accessed April 1).

————. 1999e. The Names of God. *Lambert's Library.* Http://www.ldolphin.org/Names.html (accessed April 1).

————. 1999f. Personal interview. September 7.

Downey, John, and Natalie Fenton. 2003. New Media, Counter Publicity, and the Public Sphere. *New Media and Society* 5 (2): 185–202.

Durkheim, Emile. 1915. *The Elementary Forms of the Religious Life.* Joseph Ward Swain, trans. New York: Free Press.

Eagleton, Terry. 1991. *Ideology: An Introduction.* London: Verso Press.

Eck, Diana L. 2001. *A New Religious America: How a "Christian Country" Has Now Become the World's Most Religiously Diverse Nation.* San Francisco: Harper Collins.

Ediger, Bruce [bediger@teal.csn.org]. 1994. Re: Apocalypse and Years of the Beast! October 31. E-mail to Robert Howard.

Editor <tribtalk@tribnews.net>. 1999. [tribtalk] List going offline. September 24. E-mail List Posting. <tribtalk@tribnews.net>.

Edroso, Roy. 2008a. Speaking in Tongues. *Alicublog.* Http://alicublog.blogspot. com/2008/02/speaking-in-tongues.html (accessed February 12).

————. 2008b. Comments. *Alicublog.* Http://www.haloscan.com/comments/ edroso/213531270659411955/ (accessed February 15).

Eichler, Margrit. 1971. "Charismatic and Ideological Leadership in Secular and Religious Millenarian Movements: A Sociological Study." Ph.D. dissertation, Duke University.

Eisenstein, Elizabeth L. 1979. *The Printing Press as an Agent of Change: Communications and Cultural Transformations in Early-Modern Europe.* Cambridge: Cambridge University Press.

Eliade, Mircea. 1959 [1957]. *The Sacred and the Profane: The Nature of Religion,* Willard R. Trask, trans. New York: Harcourt Brace.

Ellis, Bill. 2000. *Raising the Devil: Satanism, New Religions, and the Media.* Lexington: University Press of Kentucky.

Ellwood, Robert S. 1988. Contemporary Religion as Folk Religion. *The History and Future of Faith: Religion Past, Present, and to Come.* New York: Crossroads, 118–30.

Erickson, Hal. 1992. *Religious Radio and Television in the United States, 1921–1991: The Programs and Personalities.* Jefferson, N.C.: McFarland.

The Eyedoctor's Site—Links. 1999. *The Eyedoctor's Site.* Http://www.se.mediaone. net/~hereiam/ (accessed April 1).

Fellowship Place Ministry. 2008. About. *FellowshipPlaceMinistry.com.* Http://fellowshippla-ceministry.com/blog/about (accessed February 1).

Fenster, Mark. 2008 [1999]. *Conspiracy Theories: Secrecy and Power in American Culture.* Minneapolis: University of Minnesota Press.

Fernback, Jan. 2002. Internet Ritual: A Case of the Construction of Computer-Mediated Neopagan Religious Meaning. *Practicing Religion in the Age of Media,* Stewart Hoover and Lynn Scofield Clark, eds. New York: Columbia University Press, 254–75.

Finney, Charles G. 1968. *Lectures on Revivals of Religion*. New York: Fleming H. Revell Company.

Fischer, Claude S. 1992. *America Calling: A Social History of the Telephone to 1940*. Berkeley: University of California Press.

Fisher, Walter. 1985. The Narrative Paradigm: In the Beginning. *Journal of Communication* 35 (4): 73–89.

FNR. 2008. RE: The rapture. *Relevantmagazine.com*. Http://www.relevantmagazine.com/forums/viewtopic.php?f=4&t=391&st=0&sk=t&sd=a&start=10 (accessed August 1).

Frisian. 2004. Hello I love you, I will tell you my name. *BibleForums Christian Message Board and Forums*. Http://bibleforums.org/forum/showthread.php?t=23546 (accessed October 9).

Frykholm, Amy Johnson. 2004. *Rapture Culture: Left Behind in Evangelical America*. Oxford: Oxford University Press.

Gannett Company Incorporated. 2004. A New Generation Spreads the Word. *USA Today*. Http://www.usatoday.com/life/lifestyle/2004-06-23-christian-mag_x.htm (accessed August 1, 2008).

Garfinkle, Harold. 1967. *Studies in Ethnomethodology*. Englewood Cliffs, N.J.: Prentice-Hall.

Geertz, Clifford. 1973. *The Interpretation of Cultures: Selected Essays*. New York: Basic Books.

———. 1983. *Local Knowledge: Further Essays in Interpretive Anthropology*. New York: Basic Books.

Gillette, Britt. 2007a. 666: The Mystery of Revelation. *Rapture Ready*. Http://www.raptureready.com/featured/gillette/666.html (accessed November 8).

———. 2007b. 666: The Mystery of Revelation. *Brittgillette.com*. Http://brittgillette.com/WordPress/?p=41 (accessed July 8).

———. 2008. The Holy Spirit. *Brittgillette.com*. Http://brittgillette.com/WordPress/ (accessed February 4).

Glenda. 1996. About SearchNet. *Door to SearchNet*. Http://world.std.com/~snet/snet.htm (February 24).

———. 2007a. Admin Background and Intent *Elijah the Prophet Blogging for the Two Witnesses until They Arrive!* Http://heartdaughter.com/overcomers/index.php?topic=4.0;wap2 (accessed February 7).

———. 2007b. RULES for the OverComers' Message Forum! *The Two Witnesses Of Revelation ELIJAH and The Daughter of ZION*. Http://heartdaughter.com/overcomers/index.php?topic=3.0> (accessed February 12).

———. 2007c. Where Will You Put YOUR FAITH ??? *Elijah the Prophet Blogging for the Two Witnesses until They Arrive!* Http://heartdaughter.com/overcomers/index.php/topic,49.0.html (accessed February 7).

———. 2008a. Elijah The Prophet. *Elijah the Prophet Blogging for the Two Witnesses until They Arrive!* Http://heartdaughter.com/blogs/elijah/ (accessed February 1).

———. 2008b. The Two Witnesses—Statistics Center. *Elijah the Prophet Blogging for the Two Witnesses until They Arrive!* Http://heartdaughter.com/overcomers/index.php?action=stats (accessed February 1).

———. 2008c. SearchNet Home Page. *SearchNet*. Http://world.std.com/~snet/index.htm (accessed February 1).

Goodman, Felicitas D. 1972. *Speaking in Tongues: A Cross-Cultural Study of Glossolalia*. Chicago: University of Chicago Press.

Gospel Communications International. 1999. CrossSearch Site: Alpha thru Omega Site. *CrossSearch.com*. Http://www.crosssearch.com/Science_and_Social_Science/Theology_and_Issues/Prophecy/40600.php (accessed April 1).

Graham, Billy. 1977. *How to Be Born Again*. Waco, Tex.: Word Books.

———. 1983. *Approaching Hoofbeats: The Four Horsemen of the Apocalypse*. Waco, Tex.: Word Books.

GVU. 2001a. GVU's Third WWW User Survey Programming Years Graphs. *GVU WWW User Surveys*. The Graphics, Visualization & Usability Center at Georgia Tech (GVU). Http://www.cc.gatech.edu/gvu/user_surveys/survey-04-1995/graphs/info/prog_years.html (accessed April 1).

———. 2001b. GVU's Tenth WWW User Survey Graphs. *GVU WWW User Surveys*. The Graphics, Visualization & Usability Center at Georgia Tech (GVU). Http://www.cc.gatech.edu/gvu/user_surveys/survey-1998-10/graphs/graphs.html (accessed April 1).

———. 2001c. GVU's Tenth WWW User Survey Graphs: Graphs and Tables of the Results. *GVU WWW User Surveys*. The Graphics, Visualization & Usability Center at Georgia Tech (GVU). Http://www.cc.gatech.edu/gvu/user_surveys/survey-1998-10/graphs/graphs.html (accessed April 1).

———. 2001d. WWW User Survey—HTML Results Graphs. *GVU WWW User Surveys*. The Graphics, Visualization & Usability Center at Georgia Tech (GVU). Http://www.gvu.gatech.edu/user_surveys/survey-01-1994/graphs/results-html.html (accessed April 1).

Habermas, Jürgen. 1974. The Public Sphere. *New German Critique* 1: 49–55.

Hadden, Jeffery. K. 1987. Desacralizing Secularization Theory. *Social Forces* 65 (3): 587–611.

———. 1989. Is There Such a Thing as Global Fundamentalism? *Secularization and Fundamentalism Reconsidered*. J. K. Hadden and A. Shupe, eds. New York: Paragon House, 109–22.

———, and Douglas E. Cowan, eds. 2000. *Religion on the Internet: Research Prospects and Promises*. New York: JAI Press.

———, and Anson Shupe. 1988. *Televangelism: Power and Politics on God's Frontier*. New York: Henry Holt.

Hakken, David. 1999. *Cyborgs@cyberspace? An Ethnographer Looks at the Future*. New York: Routledge.

Hall, David D., ed. 1997. *Lived Religion in America: Toward a History of Practice*. Princeton: Princeton University Press.

Hamilton, John Kohnen [jkohnen@comix.cs.uoregon.edu]. 1992. re: Jesus returns in 1996? April 15. <news: soc.religion.christian>.

Harris, Harriet A. 1998. *Fundamentalism and Evangelicals*. Oxford: Clarendon Press.

Hatch, Nathan. 1989. *The Democratization of American Christianity*. New Haven: Yale University Press.

Hauben, Michael. 1996. Chapter Five: The Vision of Interactive Computing and the Future. *Netizen: An Anthology*. Columbia University. Http://www.columbia.edu/~rh120/ch106.x05 (accessed June 6).

———, and Ronda Hauben. 1997. *Netizens: On the History and Impact of Usenet and the Internet*. Los Alamitos, Calif.: IEEE Computer Society Press.

Hauben, Ronda. 2001. The Evolution of Usenet: The Poor Man's Arpanet. *Netizens: An Anthology.* Http://www.columbia.edu/~rh120/ch106.x02#full%20cite (accessed April 1, 2001).

Have You Heard of the Four Spiritual Laws? 2001. *Jesus Who? Home Page.* Http://www. greatcom.org/laws/ (accessed April 1).

Haythornthwaite, Caroline. 2000. Online Personal Networks: Size, Composition and Media Use among Distance Learners. *New Media and Society* 2 (2): 195–226.

Hendershot, Heather. 2004. *Shaking the World for Jesus: Media and Conservative Evangelical Culture.* Chicago: University of Chicago Press.

Henning, Jeffery. 2003. The Blogging Iceberg. *Perseus.com.* Http://www.perseus.com/blog-survey/thebloggingiceberg.html (accessed January 4, 2006).

Herring, Susan. C., Lois Ann Scheidt, Sabrina Bonus, and Elijah Wright. 2004. Bridging the Gap: A Genre Analysis of Weblogs. *Proceedings of the 37th Hawai'i International Conference on System Sciences (HICSS-37).* Http://www.blogninja.com/DDGDD04.doc (accessed October 1, 2006).

Hofstadter, Richard. 1967. *The Paranoid Style in American Politics and Other Essays.* New York: Knopf.

Højsgaard, Morten T., and Margit Warburg. 2005. *Religion and Cyberspace.* New York: Routledge.

Hoover, Stewart M. 1988. *Mass Media Religion: The Social Sources of the Electronic Church.* Newbury Park, Calif.: Sage Publications.

———, and Lynn Scofield Clark, eds. 2002. *Practicing Religion in the Age of Media.* New York: Columbia University Press.

———, Lynn Scofield Clark, and Lee Rainie. 2004 . Faith Online: 64% of Wired Americans Have Used the Internet for Spiritual or Religious Information. *Pew Internet and American Life Project.* Http://www.pewInternet.org/reports/toc.asp?Report=119 (Accessed April 1, 2005).

How to Be Born Again. 2001. *Born Again Christian Info.* Http://www.born-again-christian. info/how.to.be.born.again.htm (accessed April 1, 2001).

Howard, Philip N. 2002. Network Ethnography and Hypermedia organization: New Organizations, New Media, New Myths. *New Media & Society* 4 (4): 550–74.

———, and Steve Jones. 2004. *Society Online: The Internet in Context.* Thousand Oaks, Calif.: Sage Publications.

Howard, Robert Glenn. [IZZY9MR@mvs.oac.ucla.edu]. 1994. On-line Posting. YEARS of the BEAST. October 30, 1994. <news: bit.listserv.christia>.

———. 1997. Apocalypse in Your In-Box: End Times Communication on the Internet. *Western Folklore* 56: 295–315.

———. 1998. Toward a Folk Rhetorical Approach to Emerging Myth: The Case of Apocalyptic Techno-Gaianism on the World-Wide-Web. *Folklore Forum* 29: 53–73.

———. 2000. On-Line Ethnography of Dispensationalist Discourse: Revealed versus Negotiated Truth. *Religion on the Internet*, Douglas Cowan and Jeffery K. Hadden, eds. New York: Elsevier Press, 225–46.

———. 2005a. A Theory of Vernacular Rhetoric: The Case of the 'Sinner's Prayer' Online. *Folklore* 116 (3): 175–91.

———. 2005b. The Double Bind of the Protestant Reformation: The Birth of Fundamentalism and the Necessity of Pluralism. *Journal of Church and State* 47 (1): 101–18.

———. 2005c. Sustainability and Radical Rhetorical Closure: The Case of the 1996 "Heaven's Gate" Newsgroup Campaign. *Journal of Communication and Religion* 28 (1): 99–130.

———. 2005d. Toward a Theory of the Worldwide Web Vernacular: The Case for Pet Cloning. *Journal of Folklore Research* 42: 323–60.

———. 2006a. Fundamentalism. *Encyclopedia of Religion, Communication, and Media.* Daniel Stout, ed. New York: Berkshire Publishing, 155–60.

———. 2006b. Rhetoric of the Rejected Body at Heaven's Gate. *Gender and Apocalyptic Desire*, Lee Quinby and Brenda Brasher, eds. London: Equinox Press, 145–65.

———. 2006c. Sustainability and Narrative Plasticity in Online Apocalyptic Discourse after September 11, 2001. *Journal of Media and Religion* 5.1 (March): 25–47.

———. 2008a. Electronic Hybridity: The Persistent Processes of the Vernacular Web. *Journal of American Folklore* 121 (Spring): 192–218.

———. 2008b. The Vernacular Web of Participatory Media. *Critical Studies in Media Communication* 25 (December): 490–512.

———. 2009a. Crusading on the Vernacular Web: The Folk Beliefs and Practices of Online Spiritual Warfare. *Folklore and the Internet: Vernacular Expression in a Digital World*, Trevor J. Blank, ed. Logan, Utah: Utah State University Press, 126–41.

———. 2009b. An End Times Virtual "Ekklesia": Ritual Deliberation in Participatory Media. *The End All Around Us: Apocalyptic Texts and Popular Culture*, John Walliss and Kenneth G. C. Newport, eds. London: Equinox Press, 212–32.

———. 2009c. The Vernacular Ideology of Christian Fundamentalism on the World Wide Web. *Fundamentalisms and the Media*, Stewart M. Hoover and Nadia Kaneva, eds. London: Continuum, 126–41.

———. 2009d. Vernacular Media, Vernacular Belief: Locating Christian Fundamentalism in the Vernacular Web. *Western Folklore.* 403–429.

———. 2010a. Enacting a Virtual "Ekklesia": Online Christian Fundamentalism as Vernacular Religion. *New Media and Society.* 12 (2010) 729–744.

———. 2010b. The Vernacular Mode: Locating the Non-Institutional in the Practice of Citizenship. *Public Modalities*, Rob Asen and Daniel Brower, eds. Tuscaloosa: University of Alabama Press. 240–61.

Hutchinson, William R. 2003. *Religious Pluralism in America: The Contentious History of a Founding Idea.* New Haven: Yale University Press.

Jack Van Impe Presents. 1994. Weekly broadcast from Troy, Michigan: Jack Van Impe Ministries, October and November.

———. 1997. May 1. Weekly broadcast from Troy, Michigan: Jack Van Impe Ministries.

Jacobs, Al. 2008. My Biblical Year. *Relevantmagazine.com.* Http://www.relevantmagazine.com/god_article.php?id=7536 (accessed August 1, 2008).

James, William. 1958. *The Varieties of Religious Experience: A Study in Human Nature being the Gifford Lectures on Natural Religion Delivered at Edinburgh 1901–1902.* Ontario, Canada: Penguin Books.

James. 2007. One World Government in the End Times Age. *Blogspot.com.* Http://jcudell.blogspot.com/2007/06/one-world-government-in-end-times-age.html (accessed June 27).

———. 2008. Of Rest and Harvest. *Blogspot.com.* Http://jcudell.blogspot.com/ (February 1).

Jane and John. 1999. October 17. Personal interview.

Jenkins, Henry. 1992. *Textual Poachers: Television Fans and Participatory Culture*. New York: Routledge.

———. 1995. *Science Fiction Audiences: Watching Doctor Who and Star Trek*. New York: Routledge.

———, Katherine Clinton, Ravi Purushotma, Alice J. Robison, and Margaret Weigel. 2006a. Confronting the Challenges of Participatory Culture: Media Education for the 21st Century. *Digitallearning.com*. Http://www.digitallearning.macfound.org/site/c. enJLKQNlFiG/b.2108773/apps/nl/content2.asp?content_id=%7BCD911571-0240-4714-A93B-1D0C07C7B6C1%7D&notoc=1 (accessed January 19, 2007).

———. 2006b. *Convergence Culture: Where Old and New Media Collide*. New York: NYU Press.

Jerz, Dennis G. 2003. On the Trail of the Memex: Vannevar Bush, Weblogs, and the Google Galaxy. *Dichtung Digital*. Http://www.dichtung-digital.org/2003/issue/1/jerz/index.htm (accessed October 1, 2006).

jimmy777. 2008a. Re: The rapture. *Relevantmagazine.com*. Http://www.relevantmagazine.com/forums/viewtopic.php?f=4&t=391&st=0&sk=t&sd=a&start=20 (August 1).

———. 2008b. Re: The rapture. *Relevantmagazine.com*. Http://www.relevantmagazine.com/forums/viewtopic.php?f=4&t=391&st=0&sk=t&sd=a&start=50 (accessed August 1).

———. 2008c. Re: The rapture. *Relevantmagazine.com*. Http://www.relevantmagazine.com/forums/viewtopic.php?f=4&t=391&st=0&sk=t&sd=a&start=110 (accessed August 1).

Job. 2008a. A Brief List of Reasons Why Christians Should Not Support Barack HUSSEIN Obama. *Jesus Christology Earnestly Contending for the Faith Once Delivered to the Saints Jude 1:3*. Http://healtheland.wordpress.com/category/anti-christ/ (accessed February 14).

———. 2008b. Testimony Time. *Heal the Land Ministries*. Http://www.healtheland.brave-host.com/Archives/Devos/TestimonyTime.htm (accessed February 1).

———. 2008c. Purpose. *Heal the Land Ministries*. Http://www.healtheland.bravehost.com/General_Docs/Purpose.htm (accessed February 1).

———. 2008d. Spiritual Warfare. *Heal the Land Ministries*. Http://www.healtheland.brave-host.com/General_Docs/Subdirec/SpiritualWarfare.htm (accessed February 1).

———. 2008e. Does Anyone Know the Number of Barack HUSSEIN Obama's Name? Http://healtheland.wordpress.com/2008/01/26/does-anyone-know-the-number-of-barack-hussein-obamas-name/#comments (accessed January 26).

———. 2008f. NO WE CAN'T! BARACK HUSSEIN OBAMA IS A FALSE CHRIST! *Heal the Land Ministries*. Http://healtheland.wordpress.com/2008/02/14/no-we-cant-barack-hussein-obama-is-a-false-christ/ (accessed February 14).

Jones, Steve G., Ed. 1997. *Virtual Culture: Identity and Communication in Cybersociety*. London: Sage Publications.

— Ed., 1999. *Doing Internet Research: Critical Issues and Methods for Examining the Net*. Thousand Oaks, Calif.: Sage Publications.

Joshua. 2006. Internet "Rapture Index" has been garnering major media attention . . . - Raw Story. *666 Mark of the Beast 666*. Http://www.666markofthebeast.com/2006/08/16/internet-rapture-index-has-been-garnering-major-media-attention-raw-story/ (accessed August 16).

———. 2007. Elijah the Prophet—Antichrist. Http://www.666markofthebeast.com/2007/12/03/elijah-the-prophet-antichrist/ (accessed December 3).

———. 2008. Welcome to 666 Mark of the Beast. *666 Mark of the Beast 666*. Http://www.666markofthebeast.com/ (accessed February 1).

Kane, Steven. 1974. Ritual Possession in a Southern Appalachian Religious Sect. *Journal of American Folklore* 87: 293–303.

Keith. 2007a. End Times Deception. *Vsandbox*. Http://www.vsocial.com/video/?d=81704 (accessed April 10).

———. 2007b. End Times: Antichrist and False Prophet. *Veoh*. Http://www.veoh.com/videos/v301990TPdBNhza (accessed February 1, 2008).

———. 2007c. Message to those who practice Judaism. *Veoh*. Http://www.veoh.com/videos/v555062GtxTpsbG (accessed February 1, 2008).

———. 2007d. A message to the Muslims. *Veoh*. Http://www.veoh.com/videos/v468447kBTSyYtd (accessed February 1, 2008).

———. 2008. Excile444's Videos. *Veoh*. Http://www.veoh.com/userVideos.html?username=exile444 (accessed February 1).

Keller, Bill. 2008. Today's Daily Devotional. *Live Prayer: The First Global Prayer Meeting*. Http://www.liveprayer.com/today.cfm (accessed February 1).

Kellstedt, Lyman, and C. Smidt. 1991. Measuring Fundamentalism: An Analysis of Different Operational Strategies. *Journal for the Scientific Study of Religion* 30: 259–78.

Kenneth. 2007. A question for you . . . *MySpace*. Http://blog.myspace.com/index.cfm?fuseaction=blog.view&friendID=164752885&blogID=252794507&Mytoken=44A E7F76-7311-448B-98581E077DC988E719675468 (accessed April 13).

Kleinrock. L. 1961. Information Flow in Large Communication Nets. *RLE Quarterly Progress Report July*. Http://www.lk.cs.ucla.edu/LK/Bib/REPORT/RLEreport-1961.html (accessed April 1, 2006)

———. 1964. *Communication Nets: Stochastic Message Flow and Delay*. New York: Mcgraw-Hill.

Krempel. 2008a. RE: The rapture. *Relevantmagazine.com*. Http://www.relevantmagazine.com/forums/viewtopic.php?f=4&t=391&st=0&sk=t&sd=a&start=40 (accessed August 1).

———. 2008b. RE: The rapture. *Relevantmagazine.com*. Http://www.relevantmagazine.com/forums/viewtopic.php?f=4&t=391&st=0&sk=t&sd=a&start=50 (accessed August 1).

———. 2008c. RE: The rapture. *Relevantmagazine.com*. Http://www.relevantmagazine.com/forums/viewtopic.php?f=4&t=391&st=0&sk=t&sd=a&start=70 (accessed August 1).

———. 2008d. RE: The rapture. *Relevantmagazine.com*. Http://www.relevantmagazine.com/forums/viewtopic.php?f=4&t=391&st=0&sk=t&sd=a&start=100 (accessed August 1).

———. 2008e. RE: The rapture. *Relevantmagazine.com*. Http://www.relevantmagazine.com/forums/viewtopic.php?f=4&t=391&st=0&sk=t&sd=a&start=110 (August 1).

———. 2008f. RE: What Is Fundamentalism to You? *Relevantmagazine.com*. Http://www.relevantmagazine.com/forums/viewtopic.php?f=4&t=383&st=0&sk=t&sd=a (accessed August 1,).

lab@biostat.mc.duke.edu. 1994. Re: Jack Van Impe and Years of the Beast. November, 1 1994. E-mail to Robert Howard.

Lalich, Janja. 2004. *Bounded Choice: True Believers and Charismatic Cults*. Berkeley: University of California Press.

Lantis, Margaret. 1960. Vernacular Culture. *American Anthropologist* 62: 202–216.

Larsen, Elena. 2001. CyberFaith: How Americans Pursue Religion Online. *Pew Internet and American Life Project.* Http://www.pewInternet.org/pdfs/PIP_CyberFaith_Report. pdf (accessed November 1, 2005).

Larson, Edward J. 1997. *Summer for the Gods: The Scopes Trial and America's Continuing Debate over Science and Religion.* Cambridge: Harvard University Press.

Lawless, Elaine J. 1988. *God's Peculiar People: Women's Voices and Folk Tradition in a Pentecostal Church.* Lexington: University of Kentucky Press.

LaHaye, Tim, and Jerry B. Jenkins. 1995. *Left Behind: A Novel of the Earth's Last Days.* Wheaton, Ill.: Tyndale House Publishers.

Leiner, Barry M., Vinton G. Cerf, David D. Clark, Robert E. Kahn, Leonard Kleinrock, Daniel C. Lynch, Jon Postel, Larry G. Roberts, and Stephen Wolff. 2000. A Brief History of the Internet. *Internet Society (ISOC).* Http://www.isoc.org/internet-history/brief. html (accessed July 1).

Lenhart, Amanda, and Mary Madden. 2005. Teen Content Creators and Consumers. *Pew Internet & American Life Project* Http://www.pewinternet.org/pdfs/PIP_Teens_Content_Creation.pdf (accessed January 6, 2006).

Lessig, Lawrence. 2002 [2001]. *The Future of Ideas: The Fate of the Commons in a Connected World.* New York: Vintage Books.

———. 2008. *Remix: Making Art and Commerce Thrive in the Hybrid Economy.* London: Bloomsbury Academic.

Leví-Strauss, Claude. 1981 [1971]. *The Naked Man,* John and Doreen Weightman, trans. New York: Harper & Row.

Lewis, James R. 2001. *Odd Gods: New Religions and the Cult Controversy.* New York: Prometheus Books.

Licklider, J.C.R. 1960. Man-Computer Symbiosis. *IRE Transactions on Human Factors in Electronics* HFE-1: 4–11.

———, and R. W. Taylor. 1968. The Computer as a Communication Device. *Science and Technology* (April): 21–31.

Lifton, Walter J. 1989. *Thought Reform and the Psychology of Totalism: A Study of Brainwashing in China.* Chapel Hill: University of North Carolina Press.

Linda. 2008. Linda's Link. *Blogspot.com.* Http://jludell.blogspot.com/ (accessed February 1).

Linderman, Alf, and Mia Lövheim. 2003. Internet and Religion: The Making of Meaning, Identity and Community through Computer Mediated Communication. *Mediating Religion: Conversations in Media, Culture and Religion,* Sophia Marriage and Jolyon Mitchell, eds. Edinburgh: T & T Clark/Continuum, 229–40.

Lindlof, Thomas R. 2002. Interpretive Community: An Approach to Media and Religion. *Journal of Media and Religion* 1(1): 61–74

Lindsey, Hal. 1994. *Planet Earth—2000 A.D.: Will Mankind Survive?* Palos Verdes, Calif.: Western Front.

———, and C. C. Carlson. 1970. *The Late Great Planet Earth.* New York : Bantam Books.

Lochhead, David. 1997. *Shifting Realities: Information Technology and the Church.* Geneva: WCC Publications.

McGuire, Meredith B. 2008. *Lived Religion: Faith and Practice in Everyday Life.* New York: Oxford University Press.

McKee, John K. [tribtalk@tribnews.net]. 1999. [tribtalk] List going offline. On-line post-ing. September 24. <list:tribtalk@onelist.com>.

McLaren, Peter. 1995. *Rethinking Media Literacy: A Critical Pedagogy of Representation*. New York: Peter Lang .

McLuhan, Marshal. 1964. *Understanding Media: The Extensions of Man*. New York: New American Library.

Mannheim, Karl. 1980 [1922–24]. *Structures of Thinking*. London: Routledge & Kegan Paul.

Manovich, Lev. 2001. *The Language of New Media*. Cambridge: MIT Press.

Markham, Annette N. 1998. *Life Online: Researching Real Experience in Virtual Space*. Walnut Creek, Calif.: AltaMira Press.

Marsden, George. 1980. *Fundamentalism and American Culture: The Shaping of Twentieth Century Evangelicalism, 1870–1925*. New York: Oxford University Press.

Martin, William. 1988. Mass Communications. *Encyclopedia of the American Religious Experience: Studies of Traditions and Movements*, Charles H. Lippy and Peter W. Williams, eds. New York: Scribners.

Marty, Martin. 1986. *Modern American Religion: Under God, Indivisible, 1941–1960*. Chicago: University of Chicago Press.

———, and R. Scott Appleby. 1991. *Fundamentalisms Observed, The Fundamentalism Project, Volume 1*. M. R. Marty and R. S. Appleby, eds. Chicago: University of Chicago Press.

———, and ———. 1993. *Fundamentalisms and Society, The Fundamentalism Project, Volume 2*. M. R. Marty and R. S. Appleby, eds. Chicago: University of Chicago Press.

———, and———. 1993. *Fundamentalisms and the State, The Fundamentalisms Project, Volume 3*. Martin R. Marty and R. Scott Appleby, eds. Chicago: University of Chicago Press.

———, and ———. 1994. *Accounting for Fundamentalisms, The Fundamentalism Project, Volume 4*. Martin R. Marty and R. Scott Appleby, eds. Chicago: University of Chicago Press.

———, and ———. 1995. *Fundamentalisms Comprehended, The Fundamentalism Project, Volume 5*. Martin R. Marty and R. Scott Appleby, eds. Chicago: University of Chicago Press.

MattHenry. 2006. Is There a Thread Missing? *BibleForums Christian Message Board and Forums*. Http://bibleforums.org/forum/showthread.php?t=55306 (accessed Mary 21).

Melton, J. Gordon. 1999. The Rise of the Study of New Religions. *CENSUR: Center for Studies on New Religions*. Http://www.skepsis.nl/onlinetexts.html (accessed April 1, 2006).

Mickey, Michael. 2008a. The Blog. *RaptureAlert.com: The Blog*. Http://rapturealert.blogspot.com/ (accessed February 1).

———. 2008b. RaptureAlert.com: Sounding the Alarm that Jesus Christ Is Coming Soon! *RaptureAlert.com*. Http://rapturealert.blogspot.com/ (accessed February 1).

———. 2008c. A Rumbling in The Middle East. *RaptureAlert.com: The Blog*. Http://www.blogger.com/comment.g?blogID=7527279812767969161&postID=410073931187569533 (accessed February 15).

———. 2008d. The Middle East: Back to the Brink. *RaptureAlert.com: The Blog*. Http://rapturealert.blogspot.com/2008/02/middle-east-back-to-brink.html (accessed February 14).

———. 2008e. To Blog! *RaptureAlert.com: The Blog*. Http://rapturealert.blogspot.com/2008/02/to-blog_06.html (accessed February 14).

Miller, Carolyn, and Dawn Shepard. 2004. Blogging as Social Action: A Genre Analysis of the Weblog. *Into the Blogosphere: Rhetoric, Community, and Culture of Weblogs.* Http://blog.lib.umn.edu/blogosphere/blogging_as_social_action_a_genre_analysis_of_the_weblog.html (accessed January 11, 2006).

Miller, Timothy. 1991. *When Prophets Die: The Postcharismatic Fate of New Religious Movements.* Albany.: SUNY Press.

———, ed. 1995. *America's Alternative Religions.* Albany: SUNY Press.

Moore, R. Laurence. 1994. *Selling God: American Religion in the Marketplace of Culture.* Oxford: Oxford University Press.

Mould, Tom. 2009. Narratives of Personal Revelation Among Latter-day Saints. *Western Folklore.* 68: 431-479.

murshac5. 2008. The Rapture. *Relevantmagazine.com.* Http://www.relevantmagazine.com/forums/viewtopic.php?f=4&t=391&st=0&sk=t&sd=a(accessed August 1).

MyChurch.org. 2008. *MyChurch.org.* Http://www.mychurch.org (accessed February 1).

Nelson, Theodor H. 1974. *Computer Lib: You Can and Must Understand Computers Now/Dream Machines: New Freedoms Through Computer Screens—A Minority Report.* Chicago: Hugo's Book Service.

Nord, David Paul. 1984. The Evangelical Origins of Mass Media in America, 1815–1835. *Journalism Monographs.* 88: 1–30.

O'Leary, Stephen D. 1994. *Arguing the Apocalypse: A Theory of Millennial Rhetoric.* New York: Oxford University Press.

O'Reilly, Tim. 2005. What Is Web 2.0? Design Patterns and Business Models for the Next Generation of Software. O'Reillynet. Http://www.oreillynet.com/lpt/a/6228 (November 10, 2006).

Olasky, Marvin. 1990. Democracy and the secularization of the American Press. *American Evangelicals and the Mass Media*, Quentin J. Schultze, Ed. Grand Rapids, Michigan: Academie Publishing. 47—68.

Oldenberg, Ray. 1989. *The Great Good Places: Cafes, Coffee Shops, Community Centers, Beauty Parlors, General Stores, Bars, Hangouts, and How They Get You Through the Day.* New York: Paragon House.

One Accord Coffee House. 1999. *One Accord Concerts.* Http:// www.oneaccordconcerts.com/ (accessed April 1, 1999).

Ong, Walter J. 1982. *Orality and Literacy: The Technologizing of the Word.* New York: Methuen.

Ono, Kent A., and John M. Sloop. 1995. The Critique of Vernacular Discourse. *Communication Monographs* 62 (March): 19–46.

———, and ———. 2002. *Shifting Borders: Rhetoric, Immigration, and California's Proposition 187.* Philadelphia: Temple University Press.

Orsi, Robert A. 1997. Everyday Miracles: The Study of Lived Religion. *Lived Religion in America: Toward a History of Practice.* David D. Hall, ed. Princeton: Princeton University Press.

———, ed. 1999. *Gods of the City: Religion and the American Urban Landscape.* Bloomington: Indiana University Press.

owenboen. 2008a. RE: The Rapture? *Relevantmagazine.com.* Http://www.relevantmagazine.com/forums/viewtopic.php?f=4&t=391&st=0&sk=t&sd=a&start=60 (accessed August 1).

————. 2008b. RE: What Is a Fundamentalist to You? *Relevantmagazine.com*. Http://www.
relevantmagazine.com/forums/viewtopic.php?f=4&t=383&st=0&sk=t&sd=a&start=20
(accessed August 1).

Packard, William. 1988. *Evangelism in America: From Tents to TV*. New York: Paragon
House.

Papacharissi, Zizi. 2002. The Virtual Sphere: The Internet as a Public Sphere. *New Media
and Society* 4 (1): 9–27.

Partners and Friends. 1999. *One Accord Concerts*. Http:// www.oneaccordconcerts.com/
(accessed April 1).

Paul. 2007. How Are the Recent Sex Scandals in the Church Affecting You? *MySpace*.
Http://blog.myspace.com/index.cfm?fuseaction=blog&friendID=34977504&blogMont-
h=&BlogDay=&blogYear=&Mytoken=D4AAC3D6-4385-4235-A4CC5AF14ECC0
00E153415137 (accessed June 27).

Peck, Janice. 1993. *The Gods of Televangelism: The Crisis of Meaning and the Appeal of Religious Television*. Cresskill, N.J.: Hampton Press.

Peggie. 1999. Peggie's Place. *PeggiesPlace.com*. Http://peggiesplace.gospelcom.net/Bible.
htm (accessed April 1).

Perkin, Harold. 2000. American Fundamentalism and the Selling of God. *Political Quarterly* 79–89.

Persinger, Michael. A. 1993. Complex Partial Epileptic Signs as a Continuum from
Normals to Epileptics: Normative Data and Clinical Populations. *Journal of Clinical
Psychology* 49: 33–45.

————. 2001. The Neuropsychiatry of Paranormal Experiences. *Journal of Neuropsychiatry
and Clinical Neuroscience* 13 (4): 515–24.

————, and K. Makarec. 1992. The Feeling of a Presence and Verbal Meaningfulness in
Context of Temporal Lobe Function: Factor Analytic Verification of the Muses? *Brain
and Cognition* 20: 217–26.

Peter. 1999a. Cults. Http://www.tribnews.net/fweeks/cults.html (accessed April 1).

————. 1999b. Ministries. Http:// (accessed April 1).

————. 1999c. Mormonism: Cult or Christian? Http://www.tribnews.net/fweeks/mormon-
ism.html (accessed April 1).

————. 1999d. August 11, 1999. Personal interview.

Peters, John Durham. 1999. *Speaking into the Air: A History of the Idea of Communication*.
Chicago: University of Chicago Press.

Pew. 2005. January Daily Tracking Survey. *Pew Internet*. Http://www.pewinternet.org/
datasets/Jan%202005%20tracking%20topline.zip (accessed January 6, 2006).

————. 2008. U.S. Religious Landscape Survey. *The Pew Forum on Religion and Public Life*.
Http://religions.pewforum.org/pdf/report-religious-landscape-study-full.pdf (accessed
February 1).

Pheugo. 2007. Just Think Aloud—Didache. *Just Think Aloud—Didache*. Http://justthink-
outloud.com/didache/doku.php (accessed January 21).

poppalogio. 2008. RE: What Is a Fundamentalist to You? *Relevantmagazine.com*. Http://
www.relevantmagazine.com/forums/viewtopic.php?f=4&t=391&st=0&sk=t&sd=a&st
art=30 (accessed August 1).

Primiano, Leonard Norman. 1995. Vernacular Religion and the Search for Method in Religious Folklife. *Western Folklore* 54: 37–56.

———. 2001. What Is Vernacular Catholicism? The "Dignity" Example. *Acta Ethnographica Hungarica* 46: 51–58.

Putnam, Robert D. 2000. *Bowling Alone: The Collapse and Revival of American Community.* New York: Simon & Schuster.

Rausch, David A. 1979. *Zionism within Early American Fundamentalism 1878–1918.* New York: Edwin Mellon Press.

Rawls, John. 1996 [1993]. *Political Liberalism.* New York: Columbia University Press.

Redfield, Robert. 1930. *Tepoztlan, A Mexican Village: A Study of Folk Life.* Chicago:University of Chicago Press.

Reid, Ronald F. 1983. Apocalypticism and Typology: Rhetorical Dimensions of a Symbolic Reality. *Quarterly Journal of Speech* 69.3 (August): 229–48.

Relevant Media Group. 2008a. Board Index: Culture. *Relevantmagazine.com.* Http://www.relevantmagazine.com/forums/viewforum.php?f=5&sid=9bab43932cdf9a73adaa51654 03c2546 (accessed August 1).

———. 2008b. Board Index: God. *Relevantmagazine.com.* Http://www.relevantmagazine.com/forums/viewforum.php?f=4&st=0&sk=t&sd=d (accessed August 1).

———. 2008c. FAQ. *Relevantmagazine.com.* Http://www.relevantmagazine.com/misc_faq.php (accessed August 1).

———. 2008d. Forums. *Relevantmagazine.com.* Http://www.relevantmagazine.com/forums/ (accessed August 1).

———. 2008e. What We Believe. *Relevantmagazine.com.* Http://www.relevantmagazine.com/misc_beliefs.php (accessed August 1).

———. 2008f. Who We Are. *Relevantmagazine.com.* Http://www.relevantmagazine.com/misc_who_we_are.php (accessed August 1).

Rheingold, Howard. 1992. *Virtual Reality.* New York: Touchstone Books.

———. 2000 [1993]. *The Virtual Community: Homesteading on the Electronic Frontier.* Cambridge: MIT Press.

———. 2001. Why Can't We Use Technology to Solve Social Problems? Http://www.edge.org/documents/questions/q2001.2.html#Rheingold (accessed January 1, 2003).

Rhonda. 2005. Prophecy Today. *Rhonda's Place for Jesus.* Http://www.geocities.com/rhondajb/PROPHETIC.htm (accessed February 1, 2008).

———. 2006a. Peach, Persecution, and Positioning. *End Time Prophetic Vision.* Http://www.etpv.org/2006/ppaper.html (accessed March 20).

———. 2006b. In His Unfailing Love Ministries. *Rhonda's Place for Jesus.* Http://www.geocities.com/rhondajb/ (accessed February 1, 2008).

———. 2006c. Passion of the Kanye? *BlogMySpace.* Http://blog.myspace.com/index.cfm?fuseaction=blog.listAll&friendID=54504106&startID=88191732&StartPostedDate=2006-02-15%2015:55:00.0&next=1&page=23&Mytoken=279F8A46-D20E-461C-AD43E34CBB48718E17150783 (accessed January 24).

———. 2007. Lets Talk. *Rhonda's Place for Jesus.* Http://www.geocities.com/rhondajb/LETSTALK120707.htm (accessed December 7).

———. 2008a. Christian Links. *Rhonda's Place for Jesus.* Http://www.geocities.com/rhondajb/LINKS.htm (accessed February 1).

———. 2008b. MySpace.com—His Messenger. *MySpace.* Http://profile.myspace.com/index.cfm?fuseaction=user.viewprofile&friendID=54504106 (accessed February 1).

———. 2008c. RE: ???. Email to Robert Howard (March 9).

Robbie Crawford. 2008a. RE: The Rapture. *Relevantmagazine.com.* Http://www.relevantmagazine.com/forums/viewtopic.php?f=4&t=391&st=0&sk=t&sd=a&start=80 (accessed August 1).

———. 2008b. RE: The Rapture. *Relevantmagazine.com.* Http://www.relevantmagazine.com/forums/viewtopic.php?f=4&t=391&st=0&sk=t&sd=a&start=100 (accessed August 1).

Robbins, Thomas, and Susan J. Palmer, eds. 1997. *Millennium, Messiahs, and Mayhem: Contemporary Apocalyptic Movements.* New York: Routledge.

Robbins, Thomas, and Benjamin Zablocki, eds. 2001. *Misunderstanding Cults: Searching for Objectivity in a Controversial Field.* Toronto: University of Toronto Press.

Robertson, Pat. 1991. *The New World Order.* Dallas, Tex.: Word Publications.

Roof, Wade Clark. 1999. *Spiritual Marketplace: Baby Boomers and the Remaking of American Religion.* Princeton: Princeton University Press.

Russell, Jack M. 1996. *Symbols Unveiled: Revealing the Symbols in the Book of Revelation.* Redding, Calif.: Jack Russell.

———. 1999a. Symbols Unveiled. Http://www.angelfire.com/biz/wcr6/ (accessed April 1).

———. 1999b. Personal interview. August 27.

S. M. [SEANNA@bnr.ca]. 1992. On-line Posting. re: Jesus Returns in 1996? April 16. <news:soc.religion.christian>

Saliba, John A. 1995. *Understanding New Religious Movements.* Grand Rapids, Mich.: William B. Eerdmans.

Schein, Edgar H. 1971. *Coercive Persuasion: A Socio-Psychological Analysis of the "Brainwashing" of American Civilian Prisoners by the Chinese Communists.* New York: W. W. Norton.

Schultze, Quentin. J. 1988. Evangelical Radio and the Rise of the Electronic Church. *Journal of Broadcasting and Electronic Media* 32: 289–306.

———. 1991. *Televangelism and American Culture: The Business of Popular Religion.* Grand Rapids, Mich.: Baker Book House.

———. 2002. *Habits of the High-Tech Heart.* Grand Rapids, Mich.: Baker Academic Press.

———. 2003. *Christianity and the Mass Media in America: Toward a Democratic Accommodation.* East Lansing: Michigan State University Press.

Segaller, Stephen. 1998. *Nerds 2.0.1: A Brief History of the Internet.* New York, New York: TV Books, L.L.C.

Shupe, Anson. 1997. Christian Reconstructionism and the Angry Rhetoric of Neo-Postmillennialism. *Millennium, Messiahs, and Mayhem: Contemporary Apocalyptic Movements,* Thomas Robbins and Susan J. Palmer, eds. New York: Routledge, 195–206.

Simon. 1999. Personal interview. November 29.

Singer, Margaret. 2003 [1995]. *Cults in Our Midst: The Continuing Fight against Their Hidden Menace.* San Francisco: Josey-Bass.

Slack, Roger S., and Robin A. Williams. 2000. The Dialectics of Place and Space: On Community in the "Information Age." New Media & Society 2 (3): 313–34.

Slater, E., and A. W. Beard. 1963. The Schizophrenic-Like Psychosis of Epilepsy. *British Journal of Psychiatry* 109: 95–150.

Slouka, Mark. 1995. *War of the Worlds: Cyberspace and the High-Tech Assault on Reality.* New York: Basic Books.

Smith, Christian. 2005. *Soul Searching: The Religious and Spiritual Lives of American Teenagers.* Oxford: Oxford University Press.

Smith, John. 1989. *The Book of Mormon: Another Testament of Jesus Christ.* Salt Lake City: The Church of Jesus Christ of Latter Day Saints.

Smith, Jonathan Z. 1987. *To Take Place: Toward Theory in Ritual.* Chicago: University of Chicago Press.

Spiritual Mapping for Effective Spiritual Warfare. 2001. *Battle Axe Brigade.* Http://www.battleaxe.org/map.html (accessed April 1).

Stanhope, Steven [stanhope@umcc.umich.edu]. 1994. jack van impe and the apocalypse. November 2, 1994. E-mail to Robert Howard.

Stephen [rlangley@sfasu.edu]. 1994. Jack Van Impe and prophecy. October 25, 1994. E-mail to Robert Howard.

Stout, Daniel A., and Judith M. Buddenbaum. 1996. *Religion and Mass Media: Audiences and Adaptations.* Thousand Oaks, Calif.: Sage Publications.

Strandberg, Todd. 1999a. Rapture Ready. *Rapture Ready.* Http://www.novia.net:~todd/todd/index.html (accessed August 10).

———. 1999b. RAPTURE READY'S LINK PAGE. *Rapture Ready.* Http://www.novia.net:~todd/todd/rapzlink.html (accessed August 10).

———. 2005. My Judgment Day: October 3–4, 2005. *Rapture Ready.* Http://www.raptureready.com/nm/56.html (accessed September 19).

———. 2008a. The Link Page. *Rapture Ready.* Http://www.raptureready.com/zzraplink.html (accessed February 1).

———. 2008b. The Rapture Index. *Rapture Ready.* Http://www.raptureready.com/rap2.html (accessed March 1).

———. 2008c. Rapture Ready. *Rapture Ready – Powered by VBulletin.* Http://www.rr-bb.com/ (accessed March 1).

Strozier, Charles B. 1994. *Apocalypse: On the Psychology of Fundamentalism in America.* Boston: Beacon Press.

———, and Michael Flynn, eds. 1997. *The Year 2000: Essays on the End.* New York: NYU Press.

Sunstein, Cass. 2001. *Republic.com.* Princeton: Princeton University Press.

———. 2007. *Republic.com 2.0.* Princeton: Princeton University Press.

Technorati Data. 2006. About Technorati. *Technorati.com.* Http://www.technorati.com/about/ (accessed January 6).

———. 2008. About Technorati. *Technorati.com.* Http://www.technorati.com/about/ (accessed April 21).

Telcordia—Press Release: Internet Hosts Reach 100 Million Worldwide. 2001. *Telcordia.* Telcordia Technologies. Http://www.telcordia.com/newsroom/pressreleases/01052001.html (accessed April 1).

The Shed.org. FBC Youth Ministries. 1999. *TheShed.org.* Http://www.theshed.org/links.shtml (accessed April 1, 1999).

Tillin, Tricia. 2003. KCP: The Roots of the Revival. *Cross Word.* Http://intotruth.org/kcp/kcp-roots.html (accessed February 1, 2008).

Tim. 1999a. The Temple. Http://www.spiritshower.com/temple.htm (accessed April 1, 1999).

———. 1999b. The Last 70 Weeks. Http://www.spiritshower.com/70weeks.htm (accessed April 1).

———. 1999c. Personal Interview. September 19.

Titon, Jeff Todd. 1988. *Powerhouse for God: Speech, Chant, and Song in an Appalachian Baptist Church*. Austin: University of Texas Press.

TribNews Network. 1999. TribNews. Http://tribnews.net/ (accessed April 1).

TribNews Network. 2008. Statement of Faith. Http://www.tnnonline.net/statementoffaith.html (accessed January 12).

Turkle, Sherry. 1995. *Life on the Screen: Identity in the Age of the Internet*. New York: Simon & Schuster.

Turnbull, Giles. 2002. The State of the Blog Part 2: Blogger Present. *We've Got Blog: How Weblogs Are Changing Our Culture*, Rebbeca Blood, ed. Cambridge, Mass.: Perseus. 81–85.

Turner, Fred. 2006. *From Counterculture to Cyberculture: Stewart Brand, the Whole Earth Network, and the Rise of Digital Utopianism*. Chicago: University of Chicago Press.

Van Impe, Jack. 1990. *New Age Spirits from the Underworld*. Troy, Mich.: Jack Van Impe Ministries.

Victor, Jeffrey S. 1993. *Satanic Panic: The Creation of a Contemporary Legend*. Chicago: Open Court Publishing.

Walzer, Michael. 1985. *Interpretation and Social Criticism*. Cambridge: Harvard University Press.

Warnick, Barbara. 2002. *Critical Literacy in a Digital Era: Technology, Rhetoric, and the Public Interest*. Mahwah, N.J.: Lawrence Erlbaum Associates.

———, Mike Xenos, Danielle Endres, and John Gastil. 2005. Effects of Campaign-to-User and Text-Based Interactivity in Political Candidate Campaign Web Sites. *Journal of Computer-Mediated Communication, 10* (3). Http://jcmc.indiana.edu/vol10/issue3/warnick.html (accessed October 31, 2007).

Watcher. 1999a. Watcher Website Statement of Faith. *Watcher Website*. Http://www.mt.net/~watcher/most.html (accessed April 1).

———. 1999b. Rapture on Pentecost ? Tribulation 98 : Antichrist , Israel , Jerusalem Temple, Rapture. *Watcher Website*. Http://www.mt.net/~watcher/pentacost.html (accessed April 1).

———. 1999c. UFOs, Aliens & Antichrist: The Angelic Conspiracy & End Times Deception. *Watcher Website*. Http://www.mt.net/~watcher/index.html (accessed April 1).

———. 1999d. Salvation, Jesus Christ, End Time Prophecy, Jesus Christ Alone. April 1, 1999. *Watcher Website*. Http://www.mt.net/~watcher/most.html (accessed April 1).

Weber, Max. 1978 [1956]. *Economy and Society: An Outline of Interpretive Sociology*, Guenther Roth and Claus Wittich, eds. Berkeley: University of California Press.

Welch, Wendy Opal. 1998. A Moment Too Quiet to Be Heard: Conversion Experiences of Suburban Christians Examined. *Southern Folklore* 55.3: 253–77.

Welch, Kathleen E. 1999. *Electric Rhetoric: Classical Rhetoric, Oralism, and a New Literacy*. Cambridge: MIT Press.

Wellman, Barry, and Milena Gulia. 1999. Virtual Communities as Communities: Net Surfers Don't Ride Alone. *Communities in Cyberspace*, Marc A. Smith and Peter Kollock, eds. 167–94.

———, and Caroline Haythornthwaite, eds. 2002. *The Internet in Everyday Life*. Oxford: Blackwell.

Wessinger, Catherine. 2000a. *How the Millennium Comes Violently: From Jonestown to Heaven's Gate*. New York: Seven Bridges Press.

———. 2000b. *Millennialism, Persecution, and Violence: Historical Cases*, Catherine Wessinger ed. Syracuse: Syracuse University Press.

Westermann, William L. 1984 [1953]. *The Slave Systems of Greek and Roman Antiquity*. Philadelphia: American Philosophical Society.

Wilson, Dwight. 1977. *Armageddon Now! The Premillennial Response to Russia and Isreal since 1917*. Tyler, Tex.: Institute for Christian Economics.

Winner, Langdon. 1977. *Autonomous Technology: Technics-Out-of-Control as a Theme in Political Thought*. Cambridge: MIT Press.

———. 1986. *The Whale and the Reactor: A Search for Limits in an Age of High Technology*. Chicago: University of Chicago Press.

Wojcik, Daniel. 1997. *The End of the World as We Know It: Faith, Fatalism, and Apocalypse in America*. New York: NYU Press.

———. 2000. Fatalism. *Encyclopedia of Millennialism and Millennial Movements*, Richard Landes ed. London: Routledge, 149–55.

Woodbury, Gregory G. 1994. Net Cultural Assumptions. *Amateur Computerist*. 6.2/3, (Fall/Winter 1994-5). Ftp://wuarchive.wustl.edu/doc/misc/acn/ (accessed March 1, 2000).

Woodberry, Robert D., and Christian S. Smith. 1998. Fundamentalism et al.: Conservative Protestants in America. *Annual Review of Sociology* 24: 25–56.

World Wide Web Consortium. 2000. A Little History of the World-Wide-Web. Http://www.w3.org/History.html (accessed December 1).

Worship Center of Redding California. 1999. *Worship Center*. Http://www.geocities.com/Athens/Oracle/1928/ (April 1).

Ying, Milton J. 1957. *Religion Society and the Individual*. New York: Macmillan.

Yoder, Don. 1974. Toward a Definition of Folk Religion. *Western Folklore*. 33: 2–15.

Zablocki, Benjamin D. 1980. *Alienation and Charisma: A Study of Contemporary American Communes*. New York: Free Press.

Zarefsky, David. 1995. *The Roots of American Community, The Carroll C. Arnold Distinguished Lecture Presented at the Annual Convention of the Speech Communication Association*. Boston: Allyn and Bacon.

Zulick, Margaret D. 1997. Generative Rhetoric and Public Argument: A Classical Approach. *Argumentation and Advocacy* 33 (Winter): 109–19.

Index

evil: dualism, 64; Jews, 151; mainstream society, 15, 64, 150; problem, 15
evolution, 9, 38, 41
extraterrestrial aliens, 104–111, 136–137, 153
Eyedoctor's Site, The, 84, 89, 103

Facebook, 121, 140
failed prediction: acceptable, 24; criticism of, 146; error, 61; Marilyn, 1998-2001, 105–107; Marilyn admits, 31–33; Marilyn discusses, 100–101; mocked, 52
faith healing, 42, 99
false prophet: Maitreya, 66; NASA employee, 51; Obama, Barack, 133; Peter, 97, 99; steals church, 31; Tribulation Period, 64
Famous Five Points, 38
Feast of Trumpets, 29–31, 149
feedback loop: alienation, 15; competency, 55; dangers, 156–159; participatory media, 113, 116–117, 156–158, 173–174; reinforce norms, 56
fellowship, 11–12; aggressive, 97–100; critique, 81, 90, 92–94; managed, 73, 101; online, 73–77, 172; social networking tools, 123–124; valued, 72; Worldwide Web, 76–77
filtering: email lists, 65; enclaves, 158
Finney, Charles, 39
Fisher, Walter, 24
"flaming" (online), 165–167
Flood, Great, 29
FNR, 162–170
folk religion 6, 43–44
folklore: culture, 17; demons, 80; folklorist, 5, 15–16; studies, 5, 15, 36–37; Vanishing Hitchhiker legend, 65–66; vernacular, 5–6
forums, online: administrator, 165–167; growth, 112–113; locking threads, 167; moderated, 138–145; rules, 137; searching for, 54
Four Spiritual Laws, 43
"friend," "friending," 122
Friendster, 121
Frisian, 139
Fuller, Charles E., 42

Fuller Theological Seminary, 42
fundamentalism: analytic term, 8; caricature, 41; cognitive, 4, 8; first coined, 40; Five Points, 38; general definitions, 7–8; historical Christian, 7, 37–41, 43–45, 171; ideological, 8, 41; nondenominational, 39–41; technology, 38; term rejected, 41, 43. *See also* vernacular Christian fundamentalism
Fundamentals, The, 38–39
"fundie," 15870

Garfinkle, Harold, 5
Geertz, Clifford, 20
General Agreement on Tariffs and Trade (GATT), 63
general interest intermediaries, 157
Genesis, Book of: Dean, 79; divided over interpretation, 38–41; Jane and John, 104; Keith, 127
genocide, 95
Geocities, 123
geography: communities, 53–54; overcome, 72, 159, 145, 171–172; not overcome, 158–159; not shared, 11–14; virtual ekklesia without, 147
Gibson, Mel, 124
Gillette, Britt, 130–131
Glenda, 135–138
globalization, 70
Gog-Magog, 142
Gorbachev, Mikhail, 51
government: documents, 63; funding Web sites, 157; influence on limited, 170; persecuting Christians, 149; secret, 148, 151; secular, 4; Web sites, 67–68, 158
Graham, Billy, 9, 42–43
Great Britain, 39–40
Gulf War I, 56–57

Habermas, Jürgen, 16
hackers, 67, 69
Hall, David, 5–6
Heartdaughter.com, 136
Heaven's Gate, 14, 103, 145
Hebrew calendar, 29, 84–85
Hitler, Adolph, 95

prediction: dreams, 86, 99, 126; Mayan calendar, 114; "Rapture Index," 116–117; ritual purpose, 24. *See also* failed prediction

Presbyterianism, 38, 40, 71

Primiano, Leonard, 5–6

"Pro and Con": "223," 103–111; "802," 26; "803," 26–33; "807," 31; "810" 31

"Pro and Con Index," 25–33; forum, 69, 114–115, 140; September, 11, 2001, 102–111

profile pages, 121–124

proof-texting, 9, 47–48, 128

"Protocols of the Elders of Zion, The," 151

public sphere, 16–18, 145, 157–159, 170

Putin, Vladimir, 143

racism, 129, 133

radical certainty: attention, 172; Cheryl and Ernie, 71–72; compassion, 169; Dean and Susan, 81, 101; face-to-face, 33; hope, 44–45; Jack, 92; Jane and John, 104, 108–109; Lambert, 83; Marilyn, 35–37; millennial web, 84, 111–112; persecution, 148–153; prejudice, 147; spiritual rebirth, 9–10; Tim, 84, 87–88, 101; unknowability, 58–59

Rapture, 28–29; fear, 106–107; Jane and John versus Marilyn, 104–111; *Late Great Planet Earth*, 57–58; mid-Tribulation, 104–111, 148–149; missed, 31; multiple interpretations, 28; *Rapture Ready*, 140–141; *Relevant.com*, 160–170; secret, 57; Tim, 149–156; two-phased, 105–107

"Rapture Index," 115–117, 134

Rapture Ready, 114–117; banning, 140; Britt, 131; as forum, 138–139; Marilyn, 146–148; Rapture discussion limited, 141; *Rapture-Alert.com*, 146–147

RaptureAlert.com, 141–148

Rausch, David A., 150

Rauschenbusch, Walter, 38

"read/write culture," 16

Regan, Ronald, 132–133

Relevant.com, 163–170

Relevant Magazine, 160

RelevantMagazine.com, 160–170

religion: dominant, 10; elite, 6. *See also* folk religion; institutional; lived religion; vernacular religion

responsibility, 4, 14, 174–177

Revelation, Book of: Antichrist, 64; asteroids, 26–27; Jack, 92; not predictive, 93; nuclear attack, 61–62; predictive, 27, 55–58, 92–93; technology, 130

revelatory experience: "Ahah!" 85–86; Apolito, Paolo, 18–19; authority, 72; charisma, 18; rejecting, 108. *See also* spiritual rebirth

Rheingold, Howard, 13

rhetoric, 7, 15, 39, 42, 166

rhetoric of conversion, 39, 42–43

Rhonda, 122–125

Riley, William B., 40

ritual, 59–60; American Indian, 71; communication, 21, 42–43; social divine, 19. *See also* ritual deliberation

ritual deliberation, 58–66; blogs, 73, 102, 132–134; ceaseless, 60; certainty, 33, 44–45; competency, 55–58; different, 59; emergence, 43, 49; flexibility, 59, 61–65; forums, 13545; generates virtual ekklesia, 3–4, 61; invitation to, 48; membership, 9–11, 14; moderator, 141–145; modularity, 61–62, 65; *MySpace*, 125; participatory media, 113–117, 12021; ritual, 59–60; September 11, 2001, 24–30, 43–44; shut down, 51, 106; social networking, 121–124; topical community formation, 55, 59; value of, 31, 33; Worldwide Web, 67–73

Robbie Crawford, 165–170

Robertson, Pat, 56

Romney, Mitt, 133

Rosh Hashanah, 29, 32

rumor, 63

Russia, 57–58, 61, 143, 149

Satan is Alive and Well on Planet Earth, 63

Satan: Antichrist (*see* Antichrist); *Battle Ax Brigade*, 154; Dean and Susan, 78–81, 153–156; error, 153; 155; followers of, 127; "getting a butt kicking," 143; incarnation of, 64; Jane and John, 108–109; Jews,

151–153; Job, 131–133; Joshua, 135; Marilyn, 34, 106; Mormons, 95; Peter, 95–97; Tim, 85, 151–153

Saudi Arabia, 57, 123

Schultze, Quentin, 39

Scofield, C. I., 40

Scofield Reference Bible, 40

Scopes, John, 40–41

SearchNet Homepage, 136

Second Coming: 2000, 112; announcement of, 65; encouraging, 122; flexibility, 58; judging the Church, 132; nearness, 10; overemphasis, 76; praying for, 142

Second Life, 12

"secret Rapture," 57

"seer states," 123

self-sealing ideology: certainty, 148; choosing, 174; flourishing, 189; mystery, 169; new religious movements, 146; harmful, 147; vernacular authority, 3

September 11, 2001, 23, 26–33, 99

"Seven Day Warning," 29–30

Seventh Day Adventist, 85

shared ideology: competence, 61; excluding others, 54, 113, 142–144, 173; insulating, 59; marking individuals, 55–56; ritually enacted, 24, 66

signs, 26, 29, 86, 130, 134

Simpsons, The, 108

"Sinner's Prayer": Graham, Billy, 43, Jack, 92; Peter, 95, 98

slavery, 5–7

Smith, Jonathan, 60

Smith, Joseph, 98

social aggregate. *See* aggregation

social control: in new religious movements, 14; participatory media, 144–145; vernacular webs, 18–20

social divine, 19, 147, 176

social justice, 38, 53

social networking tools, 12125

society: beliefs rejected by, 158; knowing itself, 19; less religious, 21. *See also* mainstream society

sociology, 5, 16

sodomy, 164

solstice, 32

Soviet Union, 57, 149

"speaking in tongues," 37, 85

Sphinx, 108

Spirit Shower, 86–89, 148–156

spiritual mapping, 154–155

spiritual rebirth: belief, 8–10; Bible, 33–34; certainty, 33, 37; Cheryl and Ernie, 71; cues, 84; Dean, 80–81, 83; dualism, 35; Glenda, 136; Holy Spirit, 39, 99; intolerance, 155; Jack, 90–92; Jane and John, 104, 108; Keswick, 39; Lambert, 20, 83; Marilyn, 34; Moody, 39–40, 43; Niagara Bible conferences, 39; Peter, 98–99; Protestantism, 37–39; reality, 35–37; sensation of, 34–37, 83, 98; Tim, 85, 91; vernacular Christian fundamentalism, 35, 44–45

spiritual warfare: *Battle Ax Brigade*, 154; Dean and Susan, 79–81, 153–156; Job, 131; mapping, 254; Rhonda, 123–124

Stewart, Lyman, 38–39

Strandberg, Todd: biography, 115–17; Britt, 131; Marilyn is "Queen of Date Setters," 146; moderated forum, 138–139

Strange, Cameron, 160

Strange, Steven, 160

Strange Universe, 103

Strozier, Charles B., 8

Susan, 78–81, 153–156

Symbols Unveiled, 90–94

Talmud, 152

tarrying, 36

Technorati, 121

telepresence, 18

televangelism, 43, 56, 62

television: aggregated, 122; audience, 53; cable, 53; evangelism, 42–43; general interest intermediary, 157; news from, 24; popularized, 42; September 11, 2001, 23

telos, 177

temple, LDS, 15354

terrorism: asteroids, 32; plots feared, 114; shocked by, 44, 70

About the Author

ROBERT GLENN HOWARD is Associate Professor in the Department of Communication Arts at the University of Wisconsin-Madison.
Currently he is director of Digital Studies, associate director of the Folklore
Program at Wisconsin, and editor of the journal *Western Folklore*. For more
information visit: http://rghoward.com.